THE JESUS YEARS

A Chronological Study of the Life of Christ

by

Thomas D. Thurman

Maps: Robert Huffman

Drawings: Romilda Dilley

A Division of Standard Publishing
Cincinnati, Ohio
40061

DEDICATED TO my sister who helped me find my faith, to my wife who helped me develop it, and to my three children whose lives have helped convince me of the wisdom of it.

Photo credits: pages 21, 33, 102, 111, 182—Carter; pages 82, 150—Roberts; page 106—Three Lions; pages 119, 153, 165, 213—Beegle; page 160—Thomas.

Library of Congress Catalog Card Number: 77-80314

ISBN: 0-87239-136-1

CONTENTS

PREFACE

Various methods may be used to study the life of Christ. Perhaps the most popular is a book-by-book study of the four principal records of His life—Matthew, Mark, Luke, and John. There is much that is commendable in such an approach. One obvious advantage is that it allows a rather quick investigation of the essential details of the Gospel story. By studying any one of the accounts, a general overview of Jesus' life may be gained. Some disadvantages, however, depreciate such a system. For example, if one studies Matthew, then Mark, then Luke, there will be much repetition of material since the three cover many of the same events. Called "the synoptics," the three literally "see together" many incidents.

Another method that is frequently used is a topical study. Certain important aspects of Jesus' life are chosen arbitrarily by a writer or teacher, or perhaps by the student himself. Relevant passages from the Gospels are selected, perhaps by the use of a concordance, and studied. Such an approach was used in my book, *Jesus, the Son of God,* published in 1962 by Standard Publishing. A good feature of this approach is that it allows for concentration on those areas of the Lord's life considered to be most significant. On the other hand much valuable and helpful information may be overlooked by the person making the selections.

Perhaps the best method, the one employed in these twenty-six lessons, is a chronological one, that is, a *time-sequence* study. Applied to Jesus, it means an investigation of all we know about His life, event by event, day by day. The chief benefit of this approach is obvious—it gives a comprehensive picture not possible with other methods.

Naturally, certain problems are connected with this approach, as with the others. Before such a study can be made, the four accounts must be harmonized. This is by no means an easy task. Mark, with brevity and a spirit of urgency, ignores altogether Christ's birth and childhood. Matthew and Luke, while both begin with His nativity, give different details concerning the event. John, fortunately, aids us in the dating process. His mention of four Passovers in Jesus' ministry is the clue which enables us to establish the length of His ministry as approximately 3½ years. John also, obviously by design, fills in some of the gaps in Jesus' life created by omissions of the other three writers.

We were aided in our work by the efforts of a number of predecessors. From as early as the second century, when Tatian published his Diatessaron, attempts have been made to harmonize the four Gospels. The particular arrangement of events followed in this text is that of the late R.C. Foster, for many years professor of Greek and New Testament at The Cincinnati Bible Seminary.

The format of these lessons has been designed to help in the teaching/learning process. Especially valuable should be the time line which shows on each page a date for the events being discussed. (The letters used in some of the time lines represent months or days.) Of similar value should be the maps which locate the places referred to in the lessons. The marginal descriptions of the events may prove to be of great help in locating the subjects under discussion. At the conclusion of each lesson are suggestions for projects designed to increase the student's comprehension. These assignments, if taken seriously, will prepare the student for each succeeding lesson.

I trust you will find this to be a profitable study.

BACKGROUNDS

TOPICS AND TEXTS

Luke's Prologue . . . Luke 1:1-4
Christ's Pre-existence and Incarnation . . . John 1:1-18
The Genealogies . . . Matthew 1:1-17; Luke 3:23-38

CONTEXT AND CONTINUITY

The life of Jesus was not an isolated event and it cannot be understood properly if treated as such. Jesus was born and lived in a particular part of this world and at a specific point in time. Without such a background, some of the events in the Gospels are practically meaningless to us today, separated from them as we are, by almost twenty centuries.

A very important part of this background is a knowledge of the Old Testament Scriptures and of the institutions of the Old Testament era. The temple with its priesthood and elaborate sacrificial system, the feast days and the occasions which prompted their establishment, the kingdom concept and the Messianic expectancy are a few examples. A working knowledge of these concepts which began in the Old Testament period and were still very much in evidence among the Jews two thousand years ago will enrich one's study of Jesus' life.

It was "in the days of Herod, the king of Judea," when Caesar Augustus ruled the Roman Empire, that Jesus was born. It was during the governorship of Pilate that Jesus was crucified. Thus some knowledge of these men and the political systems they represented is beneficial in understanding Christ's life and ministry. The political systems of the Roman Empire were quite complex. When it is realized with what accuracy the various offices are described and proper titles used in the New Testament, one's appreciation of the Bible is increased.

Judea, Samaria, and Galilee, the Jordan River and the Sea of Galilee, Jerusalem, Capernaum, and Nazareth are frequently mentioned in the Gospels. Knowing where these places were located, the condition of the weather, the means of livelihood of the people, and similar facts would be beneficial. Several good texts dealing with the geography of the lands of the Bible are on the market. It would be wise to secure and read one or more of these. Perhaps such books are available in your church library.

Some information concerning the Gospel writers, such as their occupations, qualifications for writing, lives before and after writing, etc., would be an asset. Very little is known about the

four, so we must be careful to avoid accepting the legends and traditions about them as though they were facts.

With some background in these areas the student is prepared to embark upon an investigation of the life of Him who claimed to be "the way, the truth, and the life" (John 14:6).

INQUIRIES AND INSIGHTS

Luke's Prologue . . . Luke 1:1-4

1. How many accounts of the life of Christ are there?

Luke refers to "many" as having taken in hand the task of writing about Jesus. We have no way of knowing how many did so. Of the numerous accounts circulating in the early church, four have been preserved in the Bible. These have in common the mark of divine inspiration. Still extant are a number of apocryphal ("hidden," perhaps referring to the authorship) gospels.

2. What eyewitnesses were available when Luke wrote?

The Gospel of Luke was written in or near A. D. 60, approximately thirty years after the resurrection of Jesus. At such an early date there were still living many individuals who had seen and known the Christ. Some, such as the apostles (most of whom were still living), Mary His mother, the other women who journeyed in His group, a number of those on whom He performed miracles, could give excellent eyewitness accounts of many of the events described by Luke and the other Gospel writers. Notice that Luke states that the eyewitnesses were also "ministers of the word." That they were willing to be servants of the One about whom they testified greatly enhances their testimony. Having seen and heard Him, and having been drawn to Him, they devoted their lives to serving Him.

3. How did Luke gain his perfect understanding?

It was gained by contacting the eyewitnesses referred to in 1:2. As a traveling companion of Paul (Acts 16:10, 11), he met many of the great leaders of the early church and no doubt availed himself of the opportunity to question them about Jesus. Perhaps a prior question would be in order: *Why did Luke have to check with eyewitnesses if he were truly inspired of God?* William Barclay has well answered the question: "God's inspiration does not come to the man who sits with folded hands and lazy mind and only waits, but to the mind which thinks and seeks and searches. True inspiration comes when the seeking mind of man meets the revealing Spirit of God."—William Barclay, *The Gospel of Luke*, p. 2.

4. Who was Theophilus?

Luke calls him "most excellent Theophilus," a title normally used for a high Roman government official. Nothing more is known about him than that he was also the recipient of the book of Acts (1:1). Perhaps he was a sincere seeker of truth, and Luke took the responsibility of declaring it to him. The name literally means, "friend of God."

Christ's Pre-existence and Incarnation . . . John 1:1-18

1. What is the meaning of "the Word"?

In both the Jewish and Greek world the term *word (logos),* was widely known and discussed. By employing the word, John attracted the attention of a wide reading audience and helped to explain to the Greek—in a term understood equally well by the Jew—the relationship of Jesus to God. The word can also be translated "reason," although no one English word can express its full meaning. In effect John is saying: "For many years you have discussed the *logos.* Some of your greatest thinkers have devoted much time and thought to an understanding of its meaning. Let me tell you that Jesus of Nazareth is that Word."

2. Was Jesus active in the events of this world before His incarnation?

John declares that He was (1:3), and so does the author of Hebrews (1:2). These passages help to clarify Genesis 1:26. The extent to which Jesus was an active participant in the Old Testament world is a topic for speculation.

3. How were all things made by Him?

As the Word spoken by God, Jesus was the agent through whom all creation came into existence. Genesis relates how at each creative act God said what should come to pass. To a Jew, a word was far more than a mere sound. It almost could be said to have an independent existence and the capacity for doing things. This fact gives new significance to the term, "the Word," and increases its suitability as a name for Jesus.

4. Is the pre-existence of Christ taught elsewhere in the Bible?

This doctrine can be found in the following pas-

WHO WAS THEOPHILUS?

"It seemed good to me also, having had perfect understanding of all things from the very first, to write unto thee in order, most excellent Theophilus" (Luke 1:3).

"The former treatise have I made, O Theophilus, of all that Jesus began both to do and teach" (Acts 1:1).

"All things were made by him; and without him was not any thing made that was made" (John 1:3).

"Hath in these last days spoken unto us by his Son, whom he hath appointed heir of all things, by whom also he made the worlds" (Hebrews 1:2).

7

sages: Micah 5:2; John 8:58; John 17:5, 24; Colossians 1:16, 17; Hebrews 1:1-4; 1 John 1:1, 2; Revelation 22:13.

5. Who were "his own" who did not receive Him?

In a very special way Palestine was God's land (Hosea 9:3; Jeremiah 2:7) and her people God's people (Deuteronomy 7:6; 14:2). It was to this nation rather than to the Greeks, Romans, or others that Jesus was sent. The Jews should have accepted Him gladly, but instead they rejected and crucified Him (Matthew 27:25; Acts 2:22, 23). Even the people of His own hometown refused to accept His claims and would have killed Him had they been able (Luke 4:16-30).

6. How do men become sons of God?

In a sense all men are already the children of God, for as our Creator He is also our Father. By virtue of disobedience, however, this relationship is severed, and men must once again become His sons. This is accomplished through a process of birth which involves both human and divine elements. When man believes, not merely intellectually, but fully, absolutely, God brings about a new birth and produces a new creature. Over this process men have no power. It is not by their will, their vote, their decision, but by God's will that men are born again. (See John 3:1-8.)

7. How did the Word become flesh?

Unlike Matthew and Luke, John does not state how Jesus came into the world.

8. What is the meaning of "we beheld his glory"?

The word translated "beheld" is *theaomai* and can be found more than twenty times in the New Testament where it is always used of physical sight. John makes it clear that it was not a spiritual vision of the Word which men had seen, but a physical one. The Word had actually become flesh, and men had actually seen Him.

The Genealogies ... Matthew 1:1-17; Luke 3:23-38

1. What is the meaning of "the book of the generation of Jesus Christ"?

This phrase was in common usage among the Jews to introduce a record of a man's lineage (see Genesis 5:1; 6:9). It is comparable to saying "the account of the ancestry of Jesus Christ," or, "the genealogical table of Jesus Christ."

2. What are the differences between Matthew's and Luke's accounts?

Matthew traces Jesus' lineage forward from Abraham, whereas Luke begins with Christ and goes backward to Adam and to God who made him. Numerous attempts have been made to reconcile the lists, the most satisfactory being that Matthew presents the genealogy of Joseph and Luke the genealogy of Mary. According to this solution Joseph was in reality the son-in-law of Heli.

3. What special arrangement does Matthew use?

It is a mnemonic presentation. For purposes of memorization, Matthew divided the Hebrew history from Abraham to Christ into three divisions, each containing fourteen generations. This system would equip the believing Jew with a ready defense of the Davidic descent of Christ and at the same time prove that He was indeed a son of Abraham. In order to perfect his system Matthew purposely eliminated several generations. These could be supplied by the Jewish Christians if a question concerning them should arise. It was perfectly proper to refer to a second or third generation descendant as having been begotten by the grandfather or great-grandfather.

4. Could a Jew today establish his relationship to David?

In A. D. 70, when Titus destroyed the temple in Jerusalem, the records of the Jewish people were destroyed. Today it would be impossible for a person to establish his kinship to David. No present-day "Messiah" can prove his claim by appealing to his relationship to David.

WHEN AND WHERE

It was in or near the year 430 B.C. when the prophet Malachi wrote his book and brought to a conclusion the Old Testament canon. During the next four hundred years, both the pen and the voice of the inspired prophet were silent. Since the Bible doesn't tell us about this period we must turn elsewhere for our information. The following sources are helpful:

1. *The Apocrypha.* The Apocrypha is a collection of uninspired writings composed after the close of the Old Testament period. In English versions the Apocrypha contains fifteen separate books which may be grouped in the following categories:

   a. Additions to various Old Testament books—7 books;

   b. Continuation of canonical books—2 books;

MATTHEW'S GENEALOGIES

Abraham
Isaac
Jacob
Judah
Pharez
Hezron
Ram
Amminadab
Nahshon
Salmon
Boaz
Obed
Jesse
David
   Solomon
   Rehoboam
   Abijah
   Asa
   Jehoshaphat
   Jehoram
   Uzziah
   Jotham
   Ahaz
   Hezekiah
   Manasseh
   Amon
   Josiah
   Jeconiah
      Shealtiel
      Zerubbabel
      Abiud
      Eliakim
      Azor
      Zadok
      Achim
      Eliud
      Eleazar
      Matthan
      Jacob
      Joseph
      Jesus

APOCRYPHA

I & II Esdras
Tobit
Judith
Rest of Esther
Wisdom of Solomon
Ecclesiasticus
Baruch with
   Epistle of Jeremy
Prayer of Azariah
Susanna
Bel and the Dragon
Prayer of Manasses
I & II Maccabees

WORKS OF JOSEPHUS

Autobiography
Antiquities of the Jews
The Jewish Wars
Against Apion

PERIODS BETWEEN THE TESTAMENTS

Persian   - 538-332
Macedonian - 332-323
Egyptian   - 323-204
Syrian   - 204-167
Maccabean - 167-63
Roman   - 63 ff

   c. Romances—2 books;
   d. Wisdom books—2 books;
   e. Historical books—2 books.
Although rejected by Protestants as being uninspired, many large pulpit Bibles contain these books because of their historical value.

2. The Works of Josephus. Josephus was a Jewish soldier and historian who was born in A. D. 37. In addition to an autobiography, he wrote *The Antiquities of the Jews* (a history of the world from creation), *The Jewish Wars,* which tells of the struggles of his people from 170 B.C. to his own time, and an apologetical work entitled *Against Apion.* These books were written sometime between A. D. 75—100.

3. Other Jewish, Greek, and Roman authors— such as Philo, Strabo, Polybius, and Livy.

The interval between the Testaments can be divided into the six following periods, each named after the power that dominated Palestine at that particular time:

   1. The Persian Period, 538—332 B. C.
   2. The Macedonian Period, 332-323 B. C.
   3. The Egyptian Period, 323—204 B. C.
   4. The Syrian Period, 204—167 B. C.
   5. The Maccabean Period, 167—63 B. C.
   6. The Roman Period, 63 B. C.—A. D. 70 and later.

For a discussion of these periods see the following:

   An Outline of Bible History by B. S. Dean (Ch. XIII);

   The Life and Times of Jesus the Messiah by Alfred Edersheim (Book I);

   An Introduction to the Life of Christ by R. C. Foster (Ch. VII).

As your map exercise for this lesson, refer to the map of the Mediterranean world and locate these countries: Italy, Greece, Palestine, Egypt, and Persia. Memorize their geographical relationship.

PROJECTS AND PLANS

Make a chart of the genealogical tables of Jesus as presented by Matthew and Luke. Indicate the places where the two merge, and be able to explain why they do, why there are two tables, and why Matthew omits certain names from his list.

In preparation for the next lesson, read one of the following chapters:

   Chapter 1, "Scriptural Sources"—R. C. Foster, *An Introduction to the Life of Christ;*

   Chapter 11, "The Life of Christ"—Merrill C. Tenney, *New Testament Survey.*

THE BIRTH OF JESUS

TOPICS AND TEXTS

Jesus' Birth Announced to Mary . . . Luke 1:26-38
Mary Visits Elisabeth . . . Luke 1:39-56
Jesus' Birth Announced to Joseph . . . Matthew 1:18-25
The Birth of Jesus . . . Matthew 2:1; Luke 2:1-7
The Angels and the Shepherds . . . Luke 2:8-20
Jesus Circumcised and Named . . . Luke 2:21
Jesus Presented in the Temple . . . Luke 2:22-38
The Visit of the Wise-men . . . Matthew 2:1-12
The Flight Into Egypt and the Slaughter of the Innocents . . . Matthew 2:13-18

CONTEXT AND CONTINUITY

Perhaps it was on an early spring day, as Mary went about her chores, that Gabriel appeared to her with his startling announcement. "You," he said, "have found favor with God and are going to have a son named Jesus who will be called the Son of the Highest." Mary was bewildered by this strange message. Out of her bewilderment she asked a most logical question, "How shall this be, seeing I know not a man?" (Luke 1:34). Gabriel then explained the miraculous nature of the conception by saying: "The Holy Ghost shall come upon thee, and the power of the Highest shall overshadow thee: therefore also that holy thing which shall be born of thee shall be called the Son of God" (Luke 1:35).

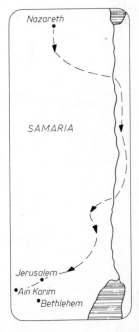

Prior to his departure, Mary's strange visitor further informed her that one of her relatives, Elisabeth, an old woman who had never been able to have children, was pregnant with a son. He indicated that in Elisabeth's case, as in her own, this was a miracle of God. Elisabeth's conception had also merited a visit from Gabriel. Some six months earlier, Gabriel had appeared to Elisabeth's husband, an old priest named Zechariah, by promising him a son who was to be named John.

When Mary learned of Elisabeth's condition, she departed at once to visit her. It was probably to gain comfort and further insight that Mary made this hasty trip into the hill country of Judea. That Mary would so react was known to God and was, no doubt, His purpose for having Gabriel give her this information.

Mary remained with Elisabeth for about three months, and then returned to Nazareth. Since she was now several months pregnant it was necessary that another visit be made by Gabriel, to Joseph her "fiance," to explain what was happening. Joseph had already seen Mary's condition and, knowing full well that he was not the child's father, had determined to sever their relationship.

Out of consideration to Mary, he had decided to do it privately. It was at this time that Gabriel made his third appearance and convinced Joseph that he should take Mary to be his wife.

The simple, heart-touching story of Joseph's and Mary's trip to Bethlehem, the over-crowded conditions, the birth in the stable, and the visit of the shepherds and Wise-men is familiar to us. A word about the chronology of the events, however, is in order. It was on the night of His birth that the angels visited the shepherds and they in turn visited the Christ child. Eight days after this, Jesus was named and circumcised, and forty days after His birth He was presented in the temple. It was some time later that the Magi made their appearance and presented their gifts. When they departed, Joseph was warned of a plot by Herod and, by divine instruction, took the child and His mother into Egypt. There they remained until after the death of Herod. They then returned to Palestine and settled again in their home town, Nazareth, where Jesus lived until He began His ministry.

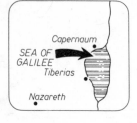

Capernaum

SEA OF GALILEE

Tiberias

Nazareth

INQUIRIES AND INSIGHTS

Jesus' Birth Announced to Mary . . . Luke 1:26-38

1. What do we know about Mary?
Very little is revealed in the Bible about her. If we are correct in assuming that Luke presents her genealogy (3:23-28), then we know her line of descent all the way from Adam. After giving birth to Jesus she had several other children (Matthew 13:55, 56). She became a follower of her Son, remaining with Him until His death. Being entrusted to the care of the apostle John, she is last mentioned in Acts 1:14. There are many traditions that unduly exalt and glorify her.

2. How binding was the tie between Mary and Joseph?
They were betrothed. To the Jew this state was as binding as matrimony itself. Edersheim states: "Their relationship (was) as sacred as if they had already been wedded. Any breach of it would be treated as adultery; nor could the bond be dissolved except, as after marriage, by regular divorce. Yet months might intervene between the betrothal and marriage."—*The Life and Times of Jesus the Messiah,* p. 150.

3. How would Jesus sit upon the throne of David?
This is a figurative expression; there was no actual throne upon which He was to sit. It is a reference

B.C. | A.D.

| | | | | 6 | 5 | 4 | 3 | 2 | 1 | 1 | 2 | 3 | 4 | 5 | 6 | 7 | 8 | | | |

to His messiahship. As a descendant of David He would inherit his kingly title and position. Both His earthly father (Luke 1:27) and His mother (Acts 13:23; Romans 1:3) were descendants of Israel's great king.

Mary Visits Elisabeth . . . Luke 1:39-56

1. What was the purpose of this visit?

Gabriel, in his announcement to Mary, had informed her of Elisabeth's condition. Furthermore, from his words Mary learned that God, in some direct way, was responsible for Elisabeth's pregnancy, even as He was for her own. Under these circumstances it was quite normal for Mary to desire the companionship of one who would lend a sympathetic and understanding ear.

2. How did Elisabeth know the identity of Mary's unborn child?

Such knowledge could have come to her only by divine revelation. The text informs us that she "was filled with the Holy Ghost."

3. How account for Mary's lovely response?

Mary's beautiful, poetic response to Elisabeth's salutation is called the Magnificat (from the Latin word for "magnify"). It is presented by Luke as an impromptu response and, as such, can be explained on no other basis than the inspiration of God. Concerning the poem, Edersheim states: "It was the antiphonal morning psalmody of the Messianic day as it broke, of which the words were still all of the old dispensation, but their music of the new."—Alfred Edersheim, *The Life and Times of Jesus the Messiah*, p. 153.

Jesus' Birth Announced to Joseph . . . Matthew 1:18-25

1. What do we know about Joseph?

We are told that he was of royal descent (Luke 1:27), that he practiced the carpenter's trade (Greek, *tekton*—a worker in wood, a carpenter), that he was poor (the gift of turtledoves or pigeons was technically called "the offering of the poor"), and that he was God-fearing (Matthew 1:24). Beyond this we cannot be certain. He is last mentioned in Luke 2:41-52, a fact which has led many, from the early days of the church, to conclude that he died before Jesus began His ministry. This supposition has produced, in turn, the tradition that Joseph was much older than Mary. One early scholar stated that he was more than eighty at the time of his marriage, and an apocryphal gospel (*History of Joseph*) sets his age at ninety,

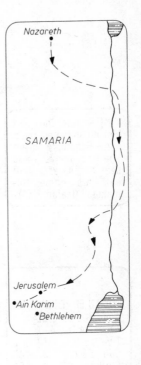

13

B.C. | A.D.

6 5 4 3 2 1 | 1 2 3 4 5 6 7 8

and at one hundred and eleven when he died. However, it should be remembered that these are traditions, not facts.

2. What was the historical occasion for the giving of the prophecy concerning the virgin birth?

Ahaz, king of Judah, feared a confederacy of powers that had formed against his people. To give him comfort, Isaiah went to him with the power to perform a sign from God to convince him that he had nothing to fear from the coalition. Ahaz would not accept Isaiah's word nor call for a sign from God, but God gave the sign nevertheless. Read the full prophecy in Isaiah 7:14-16. Writers differ as to whether there was an immediate historical fulfillment of the prophecy in the birth of a child in Isaiah's day as well as the ultimate fulfillment in the birth of Jesus.

3. What is learned from verse 25?

Matthew declares that Joseph and Mary did not enter into a normal husband-wife relationship *till* she had brought forth her firstborn son. The "till" indicates that after the birth of Jesus, Joseph knew her as a husband. To this union were born several children (Matthew 13:55, 56).

The Birth of Jesus . . . Matthew 2:1; Luke 2:1-7

1. Who was Caesar Augustus?

Gaius Julius Caesar Octavianus (his full name), the first Roman emperor, lived from 63 B.C. to A.D. 14. He ruled in this capacity from 31 B.C. until his death. He was the nephew of the well-known Julius Caesar.

2. Does the text say "taxing"?

The Greek word *apographa* is defined as "an enrollment on the public record of persons, together with their property and income, as the basis of a valuation to determine how much tax should be levied upon each one." The American Standard rendering, "enrollment," is more accurate than the King James' "taxing," although it is conceded that the enrollment was doubtless for the purpose of taxation.

3. When did Cyrenius reign?

Cyrenius (also Quirinius) was twice governor of Syria. If Zumpt is correct in his chronology, he held this position 6-4 B.C. and again A.D. 6-11. It was during his first governorship that a census was concluded which would be the one mentioned by Luke.

"Therefore the Lord himself shall give you a sign; Behold, a virgin shall conceive, and bear a son, and shall call his name Immanuel" (Isaiah 7:14).

ROMAN EMPERORS

Augustus 30 B.C.-A.D. 14

Tiberius	14 - 37
Caligula	37 - 41
Claudius	41 - 54
Nero	54 - 68
Galba	68
Otho	69
Vitellius	69
Vespasian	69 - 79
Titus	79 - 81
Domitian	81 - 96
Nerva	96 - 98
Trajan	98 - 117

The Angels and the Shepherds . . . Luke 2:8-20

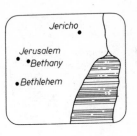

Jericho
Jerusalem
Bethany
Bethlehem

1. Who were the shepherds?
We are told nothing concerning their identity. Some have concluded that they were in charge of the temple flocks. Though a mere speculation, it has its basis in the fact that such flocks were kept near Bethlehem. Barclay states: "It is a lovely thought that the shepherds who looked after the Temple lambs were the first to see the Lamb of God who takes away the sin of the world."—WIlliam Barclay, *The Gospel of Luke,* p. 17.

2. What are swaddling clothes?
Swaddling clothes are bands which closely confine the limbs of a baby. Tenney states: "The child was placed diagonally on a square piece of cloth which was folded over the infant's feet and sides. Around this bundle swaddling bands were wound."—Merrill C. Tenney, *Pictorial Bible Dictionary,* p. 815. Although given as a sign to the shepherds, the use of swaddling clothes was not peculiar to the care of the infant Jesus. The sign to the shepherds was that in spite of being in a manger, the child was receiving the tender care of a mother who loved Him.

Jesus Circumcised and Named . . . Luke 2:21

1. Why wait eight days to circumcise and name Him?
From the time of Abraham, circumcision of all males on the eighth day was required by the Lord (Genesis 17:12; see also Leviticus 12:3). So sacred was this act that it could be performed even on a Sabbath. A custom of the Jews allowed for the naming of a girl anytime within thirty days of her birth, whereas a son was always to be named on the eighth day.

2. What is the meaning of *Jesus?*
Jesus is the Greek form of the Hebrew *Joshua* or *Jehoshua,* and means "Jehovah the Savior." The name was not uncommon among the Jews, often being given to their sons out of love for Jehovah who was their Savior and Sustainer. With the Christ it had special significance. Nor did it come to Him by parental choice, for He was "so named of the angel before he was conceived in the womb" (Luke 2:21).

"JESUS"

Joshua
Jehoshua
Jehovah the Savior

Jesus Presented in the Temple . . . Luke 2:22-38

1. What is the meaning of "present him to the Lord"?
This was the second of three ceremonies normally

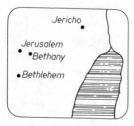

required at the birth of a firstborn son. The first one was that of circumcision, and the last one that of the mother's purification after childbirth. This presentation ceremony, called "the Redemption of the Firstborn," is mentioned in Numbers 18:16. As the firstborn son of the household, Jesus had to be redeemed by the payment to the priests of five shekels of the sanctuary. This presentation took place at least thirty-one days after the child's birth.

2. Who was purified?

Luke speaks of "their purification" (2:22 American Standard Version), which might lead one to the incorrect position that both Jesus and Mary were purified. The "their" refers to the Jews; it was their custom about which Luke spoke. This ceremony is commanded and explained in Leviticus 12.

3. What is known about Simeon?

Nothing more is known about this man than that which is contained within these eleven verses of Luke. From the description given, it is apparent that he was a very godly man.

4. What is known about Anna?

Our source of information is scant—only three verses of Scripture. She is called a prophetess and is declared to be of the tribe of Asher. One of her distinctions was her great age—between 104 and 107 years old.

The Visit of the Wise-men . . . Matthew 2:1-12

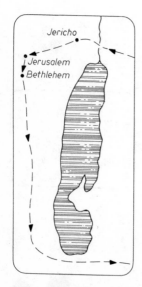

1. Who were the Magi?

Matthew merely identifies them as "wise men from the east." This leaves unanswered many questions concerning them. The oldest tradition traces them to Arabia, but other attempts have been made to connect them with Persia, Babylonia, the northern part of Mesopotamia, and Parthia. Their number, variously estimated at from three to twelve, is not revealed in the Scriptures. Likely they were priest-sages who possessed a knowledge of astrology, and who, through contacts with the Jews, came to know something concerning their anticipated Messiah.

2. When did the Wise-men arrive?

We do not know. The traditional view pictures them as arriving on the same night that Jesus was born, but we know that this is incorrect. Two things must be taken into consideration: (1) When they arrived, Mary, Joseph, and Jesus were no longer in the stable, but in a house (Matthew

2:11). Obviously, after the great crowds had departed from Bethlehem, Joseph secured a home for his wife and her Son. (2) The events mentioned in Luke 2:21-38 had to transpire before the flight into Egypt. That trip evidently began on the same night that the Wise-men departed for their own country (Matthew 2:13, 14). This would mean that they did not arrive until at least forty days after the birth. Some commentaries date their coming as much as two years after His birth, but there is no necessity for such a view.

3. What type person was Herod?

The title, "the Great," did not come to this half-Jew, half-Idumean without some justification. Among other accomplishments, he made a lasting peace with Rome, secured from the Romans the title *king,* kept order within Palestine, and built the third (in point of time) temple in Jerusalem. However, on the deficit side of his character is a long list including the murder of his wife, Mariamne, her mother, Alexandra, and three of his sons (which led Caesar Augustus to remark that it was safer to be his pig than his son). Certainly one with such a warped mind would be capable of ordering the killing of the babies of Bethlehem. (See chart on p. 237.)

The Flight Into Egypt and the Slaughter of the Innocents . . . Matthew 2:13-18

1. When did this journey begin?

Probably it began at night, immediately following the departure of the Magi. All haste would be made to get the child out of the territory of the insanely suspicious and ruthless Herod. Perhaps the costly journey and sojourn were financed with the gifts presented by the Wise-men.

2. Why kill the children up to two years of age?

Herod, being of a suspicious nature, probably felt that the Wise-men had deceived him, and therefore, to be certain that the correct child was destroyed, raised the age to two years. Some writers feel that this does not mean those who had completed their second year of life, but only entered it, i.e., thirteen months and younger.

3. How many children were slain?

All the male children in Bethlehem and in the borders thereof, up to two years of age, were killed. Considering the size of Bethlehem this number would not be large, probably twenty at the most.

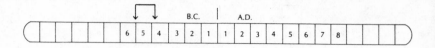

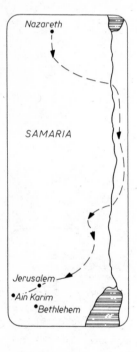

WHEN AND WHERE

The birth of Jesus is dated very accurately according to the system employed in the Roman world two thousand years ago. One must remember that the distinctions *B.C.* and *A.D.* did not exist. We cannot expect to read in the New Testament, "In the month of December in the first year of our Lord." Although a month could have been named, the phrase, "in the year of our Lord," would have meant nothing. It was only at a much later time that the date lines of the world were curved around the manger of Bethlehem.

In order to explain to their first readers the time of Jesus' birth, both Matthew and Luke presented this event in conjunction with other well-known events. It was, they said, in the days of Herod, the king of Judea (Matthew 2:1; Luke 1:5), when Caesar Augustus ruled the Roman Empire (Luke 2:1), and at the time of the first enrollment when Cyrenius was governor of Syria (Luke 2:2).

All factors considered, it appears that His birth occurred in late 749 or early 750 U.C. *(ab urbe condita,* "from the building of Rome"), although 747 and 748 are also possible dates. According to our Christian calendar this would put the birth of Jesus in late 5 or early 4 B.C. This discrepancy is due to an error of four years made in the sixth century by a monk, Dionysius Exiguus. A very thorough discussion of this subject is presented by Samuel J. Andrews in *The Life of Our Lord Upon the Earth,* pp. 1-20.

Several cities and villages (Nazareth, Jerusalem, Bethlehem) and a number of countries (Arabia, Parthia, Mesopotamia, Babylonia, Persia) are mentioned in this lesson. Locate each of these places on the map.

PROJECTS AND PLANS

Write a paper concerning the rite of circumcision. Help can be found in *The International Standard Bible Encyclopedia* in an article by T. Lewis, pp. 656, 657, and in *Pictorial Bible Dictionary* by Merrill C. Tenney, p. 172.

To prepare for the next lesson, read chapter VIII, "The Youth of Jesus," in *Studies in the Life of Christ* by R.C. Foster, and chapter IX, "The Child-Life in Nazareth," in *The Life and Times of Jesus the Messiah* by Alfred Edersheim.

Lesson Three

THE YOUTH OF JESUS

TOPICS AND TEXTS

The Return From Egypt and Settlement at Nazareth . . . Matthew 2:19-23; Luke 2:39
The Youth of Jesus . . . Luke 2:40-52

CONTEXT AND CONTINUITY

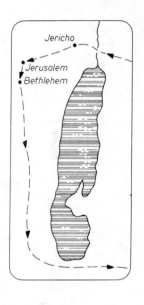

After the departure of the Wise-men, an angel spoke to Joseph warning him about Herod's plot, telling him what he should do. Heeding the warning, Joseph took Mary and the child and fled southward into Egypt. The route they followed, tradition says, passed through Hebron and Gaza, and ended in the Egyptian village of Metariyeh. Various spots along that way are pointed out to modern tourists as having had some connection with the historical journey. Very likely the route shown is the actual one. At least it has in its favor that it was then the closest route between Bethlehem and Egypt. On the other hand, a strong case could be made for Joseph's avoidance of such a direct course for fear of Herod. Such a journey would require about two weeks, or perhaps, traveling with a baby, a little longer.

The length of their sojourn in Egypt has been the cause of much conjecture. The Scriptures are silent on the subject, merely stating: "When Herod was dead, behold, an angel of the Lord appeareth in a dream to Joseph in Egypt, saying, Arise, and take the young child and his mother, and go into the land of Israel" (Matthew 2:19, 20). The time has been variously estimated at from three or four weeks (Caspari) to seven years (Tatian). Realizing that Herod died soon after the birth of Christ, we would assume that the duration of the stay in Egypt was but a few months.

When they had returned to Israel, Joseph learned that Archelaus reigned in the place of his father, Herod, and the implications of this frightened Joseph. Being warned by God in a dream, he took his family into Galilee and settled once again in Nazareth. Here Jesus lived until He began His ministry.

Each generation of Christians has been intrigued by the youth of Jesus. Many of the early Christians, as they speculated on this theme, allowed their imaginations free rein. The results are seen in several of the apocryphal gospels where Jesus is pictured as a young miracle worker or as a wrathful god-in-miniature who would take vengeance on those who displeased Him. At the opposite end of the opinion-pendulum is the view that Jesus was an ordinary child, passing through the stages of mistake-making, question-asking,

19

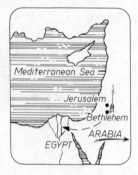

and excuse-offering just as any normal boy does. The former view borders on the ridiculous and is contrary to John's Gospel where the miracle in Cana is called His "beginning of miracles" (John 2:11). The latter view belittles the Son of God, making Him guilty of childhood sins which would disqualify Him as the perfect sacrifice. Such a view is totally out of harmony with the Scriptural presentation of Jesus as the one perfect, sinless individual (John 8:46).

Somewhere between these extremes is the correct position. We can be certain that Jesus was adequate for every situation that presented itself throughout His entire life. As baby, child, youth, and man, Jesus had within Him a perfect blending of the divine and the human. Thus He was able to live above sin, as is essential for deity, while leading the normal life required of a human. More than these general observations becomes speculation.

When we are brought face to face with that which we actually know concerning the youth of Jesus, we must admit that it is very little indeed. The last thirteen verses in Luke 2 contain the total factual information concerning the Lord from His infancy to His baptism. Whatever opinion we may formulate relative to this phase of His life must harmonize with this passage or be discarded as erroneous.

INQUIRIES AND INSIGHTS

The Return From Egypt and Settlement at Nazareth . . . Matthew 2:19-23; Luke 2:39

1. When did Herod die?

Josephus says: "He died the fifth day after he had caused Antipater to be slain, having reigned since he caused Antigonus to be slain, thirty-four years, but since he had been declared king by the Romans, thirty-seven" (*Antiquities*, XVII: 8:1). This latter event occurred in 714 U.C., which means he died in 750 or possibly 751 U.C. (4 or 3 B.C.) Furthermore, Josephus tells us that he executed some insurgents on the night of an eclipse of the moon, and astronomers have fixed this date as the night of the 12th or 13th of March, 4 B.C. We know he was still living at this time, and also that by the 5th of April he was dead, for the Passover fell on the 12th of April in that year, and Josephus states that before this feast Archelaus had observed the seven days of mourning for his dead father. We conclude that he died sometime between the 13th of March and the 4th of April, 4 B.C. when he was seventy years old.

> "He died the fifth day after he had caused Antipater to be slain, having reigned since he caused Antigonus to be slain, thirty-four years, but since he had been declared king by the Romans, thirty-seven" (Antiquities, XVII: 8:1).

			B.C.		A.D.											8th		
	6	5	4	3	2	1	1	2	3	4	5	6	7	8	J	F	M	A

2. How old was Jesus when He was brought back to Israel?

Probably not more than a few months old, although opinions vary greatly. One apocryphal gospel states that He was one year old; another, three. Tatian says He was seven; Epiphanius, two; Athanasius, four; Baronius, eight. Modern scholarship is also much divided. Jesus' age when taken to Egypt, as well as the length of His stay, are indefinites which confuse the issue and make it impossible to be certain.

3. What type person was Archelaus?

In Herod's fourth and final will, Archelaus, one of his sons, was appointed king of certain territories which his father had ruled. Antipas, another son, was appointed tetrarch of Galilee and Perea. Philip, still another son, was named tetrarch of the territory east of the Jordan. With but few changes, the will was approved by Augustus Caesar. One change was that Archelaus should at first wear the title *ethnarch* instead of *king*. He was to rule over Judea, Idumea, and Samaria. He began his reign by endeavoring to "out-Herod" Herod. At least three thousand of the most influential people in the land were put to death to quell a rebellion. Edersheim says of Archelaus: "He began his rule by crushing all resistance by the wholesale slaughter of his opponents. Of the High-Priestly office he disposed after the manner of his father. But he far surpassed him in cruelty, oppression, luxury, the grossest egotism, and the lowest sensuality, and that, without possessing the talent or the energy of Herod."—Alfred Edersheim, *The Life and Times of Jesus the Messiah*, p. 2.

4. What sort of place was Nazareth?

Although called a city in the Gospels, it was apparently a small and relatively unimportant one. This conclusion is based on the fact that there is no mention of Nazareth in either the Old Testament or in the works of Josephus. Furthermore, Nathanael's question, "Can there any good thing come out of Nazareth?" implies that for some unknown reason it was a place with a very poor reputation. The type and frequency of contacts with the outside world by the inhabitants of Nazareth are subjects about which writers differ. It appears that the lower caravan route from Acre to Damascus, the Via Maris, passed through the city. If this is true, and it seems rather certain, then on her streets could be seen world travelers and businessmen whose conversations would range over a wide variety of topics. Also, it appears that

> "He began his rule by crushing all resistance by the wholesale slaughter of his opponents. Of the High-Priestly office he disposed after the manner of his father. But he far surpassed him in cruelty, oppression, luxury, and grossest egotism, and the lowest sensuality, and that, without possessing the talent or energy of Herod."—Edersheim

Modern Nazareth

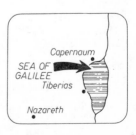

21

Nazareth was a gathering place for priests as they prepared to go up to Jerusalem to serve in the temple. We would like to believe that Jesus was brought up in such an environment, having contact with world travelers and temple priests.

5. Why was Jesus called a Nazarene?

Matthew states that the prophets said He should be called a Nazarene. However, an investigation of the Old Testament reveals that there is no passage that specifically predicted this. Apparently Matthew had Isaiah 11:1 in mind: "And there shall come forth a rod out of the stem of Jesse, and a Branch shall grow out of his roots." The word for branch is *netser,* and it is possible that Nazareth is derived from this same word. Thus Jesus is called the *Nazarene* ("Branch-one") because He came from "Branch City."

The Youth of Jesus . . . Luke 2:40-52

1. What was the Feast of the Passover?

The Passover was an annual feast of the Jews, held on the evening of the 14th of Nisan, and followed by a seven day's festival of unleavened bread to which the name Passover was also applied. (See Leviticus 23:4-8.) It was held in commemoration of the Exodus, the meal reminding the Jews of the last meal which their forefathers had eaten in Egypt (Exodus 12:1-11). The name was derived from the *passing over* of the households of the obedient Jews by the Lord when He visited the Egyptians to slay their firstborn (Exodus 12:12-14).

2. Had Jesus previously attended the Feast?

We do not know, but it is improbable. It was at twelve that He became a son of the law and, as such, subject to the Old Testament ordinances.

3. How account for the parents' inattention to Jesus?

Pilgrims going to and returning from the feasts in Jerusalem usually traveled together in large groups. According to the custom of the day the women and young children traveled in one group and the men in another. Since the men moved faster, the women would leave earlier in the day but would be overtaken by evening. Apparently Joseph thought Jesus was walking with His mother, and she believed Him to be with Joseph. It was not until evening that He was missed. Since it was often true of Eastern travelers that the first day's journey was a short one (the travelers starting late and stopping early), it is possible that Mary and Joseph had not gone more than six or

---

FEAST OF PASSOVER

—to commemorate the deliverance of the Israelites from Egyptian bondage. The name Passover was derived from the fact that God "passed over" (spared) the firstborn of obedient Israelites during the last of the Egyptian plagues; sometimes called feast of Unleavened Bread, due to strict abstinence from leaven during the observance.

eight miles when they discovered Jesus' absence. We must also remember that Jesus was not an ordinary child. He had never been known to disobey either His parents' commands or wishes. Therefore they had no reason to be unduly concerned about His whereabouts for He had never given them cause to worry.

4. How figure the three days?
Likely Jesus was missing only one full day and part of two others. These would be: (1) The day of Mary's and Joseph's departure from Jerusalem, when He was first missed; (2) The day of their return and search; (3) The day when He was found. By this reckoning two nights elapsed before He was found. Where or how He spent these hours is unknown.

5. Who were the doctors?
The reference is to the teachers of the law, the rabbis. Possibly these men were the members of the Sanhedrin, the highest Jewish tribunal.

6. Was Jesus disputing with the teachers?
Probably not, for it was not according to His plan to reveal His identity at this time. He definitely was not striving to display His knowledge or to ridicule the teachers of the law. This would have been out of character for an ordinary boy of twelve who had been reared properly, to say nothing of the Son of God. Jesus was participating in a teaching and learning session, though it must have been apparent to the teachers that He had perfect understanding of everything a twelve-year-old should know.

7. Why were Mary and Joseph amazed?
Although the child's real identity had been revealed to them, no doubt they were frequently amazed by both His actions and His words. In this particular situation His understanding and answers astonished the people and amazed His parents.

8. How were Mary and Joseph to know that Jesus would be about His Father's business?
The angelic announcements and miraculous events surrounding His nativity should have convinced them that He had a higher allegiance than that to earthly parents.

9. In what four ways did Jesus increase?
He developed what may be called a well-rounded personality, although *well-squared* would be

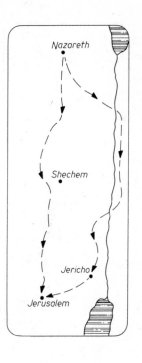

Nazareth

Shechem

Jericho

Jerusalem

23

Jesus grew . . .
. . . intellectually
. . . physically
. . . spiritually
. . . socially

more accurate. He grew mentally, physically, spiritually, and socially. We are not to conclude from the fact that He increased in favor with God that there was once a time when He did not enjoy God's favor. Rather, the text conveys the thought that as Jesus grew in age and ability He increased proportionately in His relationship to God. *In a sense* the aged Christian who has lived a life of consecration is more in the favor of God than the young convert. In a somewhat analogous way, age brought more of God's favor to Jesus.

WHEN AND WHERE

Early in the year 750 U.C. (4 B.C.) the Magi made their visit to Bethlehem and returned to their own country. Soon—probably the very same night—Joseph took his family and fled to Egypt. The length of their sojourn has already been discussed. If we are correct in assuming that they stayed only a few months, then it was perhaps sometime between May and August when they returned and settled in Nazareth.

Jesus reached His twelfth birthday in late 760 or early 761 U.C. (A.D. 7 or 8). This would make the Passover of Luke 2 the one celebrated in A.D. 8. In that year the Passover fell on April 8th.

In this lesson we have been concerned with a considerable amount of traveling—from Bethlehem to Egypt and then back to Nazareth. Trace on the map the steps of Joseph and his family.

PROJECTS AND PLANS

Using the suggested outline concerning the growth of Jesus which is mentioned in question number nine, under the topic, "The Youth of Jesus," prepare a brief talk on the theme, "The Well-Squared Personality of Jesus."

Read chapter III, "The Annunciation of St. John the Baptist," in *The Life and Times of Jesus the Messiah,* by Alfred Edersheim.

Nazareth

Shechem

Jericho

Jerusalem

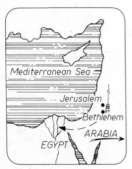

Mediterranean Sea

Jerusalem

Bethlehem

ARABIA

EGYPT

JOHN THE FORERUNNER

TOPICS AND TEXTS

The Birth of John Announced . . . Luke 1:5-25
The Birth and Naming of John . . . Luke 1:57-80
The Beginning of John's Ministry . . . Matthew 3:1-6; Mark 1:1-6; Luke 3:1-6
An Example of John's Preaching . . . Matthew 3:7-12; Mark 1:7, 8; Luke 3:7-18

CONTEXT AND CONTINUITY

Concerning eighteen important years of Jesus' life, from age twelve to thirty, we know practically nothing. Two verses, Luke 2:51, 52, cover the entire period. We are merely told, in general terms, of the relationship Jesus had with His parents (He was subject unto them), and of His normal development (He advanced in wisdom and stature, and in favor with God and man). When He was "about thirty years of age" (Luke 3:23), He left Nazareth and journeyed to the Jordan River to be baptized by John.

At the time of Jesus' baptism, John was experiencing a great deal of popularity. In fact, his fame had spread all across the land, penetrating even the exclusive circles of Pharisees and Sadducees in Jerusalem (Matthew 3:5-7). The priests and Levites had also heard of him and had come from Jerusalem with their questions about his identity (John 1:19).

John is one of the most interesting characters, and, according to Jesus' testimony, one of the greatest personalities in the entire Bible. Unfortunately, there is a scarcity of information concerning this "voice that cried in the wilderness."

In recent years attempts have been made to connect him with the Essenes, a group of zealous, devout, celibate Jews who lived a monastic type of life. While it is true that there are similarities between John and this group, no definite relationship has been established. There is neither a Bible statement nor a known Essene reference that connects John with the sect. It is not likely that such information will be forthcoming.

Since John plays such an important role in the New Testament, we will pause in our study of Jesus' life and devote a lesson to John's birth and early ministry. The first two sections of this lesson are misplaced chronologically. These events preceded the birth of Jesus, but the consideration of them has been reserved until now in order to give more continuity to the consideration of both Jesus' and John's lives.

This lesson will take us from the Holy Place in Jerusalem to Zechariah's home in the hill country of Judea and on to the scene of John's ministry at the Jordan River.

> "Then went out to him Jerusalem, and all Judea, and all the region round about Jordan, and were baptized of him in Jordan, confessing their sins" (Matthew 3:5, 6).

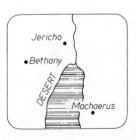

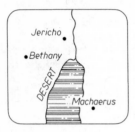

INQUIRIES AND INSIGHTS

The Birth of John Announced . . . Luke 1:5-25

1. What is known about Zechariah and Elisabeth?

Apart from the reference to them in this chapter (Luke 1), there is no other mention of this godly couple in the Bible. Fortunately, Luke tells us a number of facts about them. They were both of priestly families; although they had prayed for children, they had none; they lived in a city of Judah; Zechariah was of the course of Abia. Most important, "they were both righteous before God, walking in all the commandments and ordinances of the Lord blameless."

2. Was Zechariah the high priest?

No, he was not. He is called a *priest,* not *high priest;* he was a member of one of the courses, but high priests were not; he lived in *a city* of Judah, rather than *the city,* Jerusalem, where a high priest would have lived; he was selected by lot to perform his service, whereas the duties of a high priest were specifically outlined.

3. What was the course of Abia?

Because the priests became so numerous, they could not all officiate at the altar. David divided them into twenty-four courses or classes. This act is described in 1 Chronicles 24 which mentions the course of Abia (Abijah in Hebrew) as the eighth one. Josephus says that in his day there were about twenty thousand priests. The Talmud says there were even more. At Passover, Pentecost, and the feast of Tabernacles, all of the priests served, but the rest of the year was divided among the courses. Since there were so many in each course (an average of nearly 850, if Josephus' figure is accurate), the various duties were assigned by the casting of lots. If a man was selected to burn incense, as was Zechariah, he was considered to be rich and was thereafter excluded from the privilege of being selected for this honorable and highly desirable task.

4. Where did the angel stand in the Holy Place?

Matthew says he stood on the right side of the altar of incense. This would be toward the side where the table of shewbread stood. When Zechariah entered he was facing the west, looking directly toward the veil that separated the Holy Place from the Holy of Holies. Immediately in front of this veil was the altar of incense. On his left, or the

COURSES OF PRIESTS

1. Jehoiarib
2. Jedaiah
3. Harim
4. Seorim
5. Malchijah
6. Mijamin
7. Hokkoz
*8. Abijah
9. Jeshuah
10. Shecaniah
11. Eliashib
12. Jakim
13. Huppah
14. Jeshebeab
15. Bilgah
16. Immer
17. Hezir
18. Aphses
19. Pethahiah
20. Jehezekel
21. Jachin
22. Gamul
23. Delaiah
24. Maaziah

south, was the golden candlestick, and on his right, or north, the table of shewbread. Evidently, the angel was facing the east.

5. Why was Zechariah afraid?

Angelic appearances usually produced fear (Luke 1:29, 30; Luke 2:9; Matthew 28:4). Zechariah was no doubt already filled with great awe and wonderment on this solemn occasion. An angel appearing and speaking to him, when nothing comparable had occurred for over four hundred years, was adequate reason for his fear.

6. What prayer of Zechariah and Elisabeth did God hear?

This devout couple had long prayed for a child but seemingly in vain. As the years had come and gone and Elisabeth had passed the age of child-bearing, less pious people would have despaired of praying, but not these godly folks. Perhaps at the very moment that Gabriel appeared, while "the whole multitude of the people were praying without," Zechariah was praying from his heart for a child.

7. Are there other Bible examples of children being born to aged parents?

Yes, there is the famous example of Isaac's birth to the aged Sarah and Abraham (Genesis 18:1-15; 21:1-8). Notice also the miraculous element in the conception of Samson (Judges 13:2, 3) and Samuel (1 Samuel 1:19, 20).

8. What did Gabriel promise to Zechariah?

Gabriel promised that: (1) Zechariah would have a son who would bring him gladness and cause others to rejoice; (2) this son would be great in God's sight; (3) he would drink no strong drink; (4) he would be filled with the Holy Spirit; (5) he would turn the hearts of many in the correct way; (6) he would prepare a people for the Lord.

The Birth and Naming of John . . . Luke 1:57-80

1. How did Elisabeth spend the months prior to John's birth?

Luke 1:24 states that she hid herself for five months. Whether this hiding was in some obscure spot or simply in her house is not known. In the month that followed this period of separation, Gabriel made his visit to Mary, and immediately afterwards she went to visit Elisabeth and remained with her for about three months. Probably Mary departed from Elisabeth's home shortly before John's birth. This would have been done to

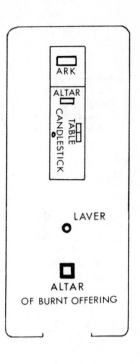

ARK
ALTAR
TABLE
CANDLESTICK

LAVER

ALTAR
OF BURNT OFFERING

John promised to be:
—good and glad
—truly great
—Spirit-filled
—persuasive
—forerunner

27

avoid unnecessary explanations to friends and kinsmen concerning her own condition. No doubt this three-month period was a blessing to both women as they shared their hopes.

2. What is the meaning of John's name?

John is a short form of *Jehohanan*, which means "Jehovah's gift" or "Jehovah is gracious." That he was so named was a shock to relatives who expected the boy to be called *Zechariah*, after his father.

3. Why was Zechariah at this time granted his speech?

Because of his unbelief, Zechariah had been made dumb (evidently deaf also, Luke 1:62), "until the day that these things shall be performed" (Luke 1:20). Later, with his faith made evident, his speech was restored. Edersheim declares: "His last words had been those of unbelief, his first were those of praise; his last words had been a question of doubt, his first were a hymn of assurance."—*The Life and Times of Jesus the Messiah*, p. 158.

4. How account for Zechariah's beautiful prophecy?

Luke 1:67 answers this question. It was by the power of the Holy Spirit that he spoke. His words can be divided into two parts, the first pertaining to Jesus, the second to John, with the transition coming after verse 75.

5. How did John spend his early life?

Luke declares that he was "in the deserts till the day of his shewing unto Israel" (1:80). This implies a life of obscurity. Because of his parentage, John was qualified to be a priest, but never became one. Perhaps he was orphaned at an early age, for there is no further mention of his parents.

The Beginning of John's Ministry . . . Matthew 3:1-6; Mark 1:1-6; Luke 3:1-6

1. Who gave him the name "the Baptist" and why?

Whether the name was of divine or human origin cannot be determined from the texts. Regardless of its origin, it was very appropriate since it described the central act of his ministry, the baptizing of the repentant in anticipation of the coming of God's kingdom.

2. What Old Testament prophecies are cited as being fulfilled in John's ministry?

There are two cited in these passages: Isaiah

> John - Jehohanan
> "Jehovah's gift" or "Jehovah is gracious."

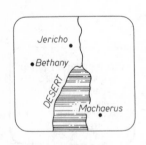

Jericho

Bethany

DESERT

Machaerus

40:3-5 and Malachi 3:1. Matthew and Luke refer to the Isaiah passage and Mark mentions both. In his announcement to Zechariah, Gabriel quoted yet another passage, Malachi 4:5, 6 (Luke 1:17). See also Matthew 11:14 and Luke 7:27.

3. How was John dressed and what did he eat?

John, like Elijah in whose spirit and power he came, wore rough clothing and ate wild food (see 2 Kings 1:8). His tunic, or coat-like shirt, was made from the long, shaggy hair of the camel, woven into a coarse, cheap cloth. His leather girdle was probably between two and six inches wide, and served to bind his garment at the waist. Such girdles were also used to carry various items which were placed under them. The locusts, or grasshoppers (the terms are interchangeable), are members of the Acrididae family. The law permitted the Jews to eat them (Leviticus 11:21, 22). Palestine was called "the land flowing with milk and honey" (Exodus 3:8, 17). John evidently secured his honey from the holes in the rocks in the wilderness, where it is said there was an abundance.

Camel hair coat

4. What was the purpose of John's baptism?

It is called "the baptism of repentance for the remission of sins" (Mark 1:4; Luke 3:3). Only the repentant were to be baptized (Luke 3:7-14), all others being harshly reprimanded. The remission of sins promised by John, like forgiveness elsewhere under the old dispensation, was in promise, and was dependent upon Jesus' future death on Calvary.

5. Should men confess their sins to each other today?

Those who hearkened to John were "baptized of him in Jordan, *confessing their sins*" (Matthew 3:6). This confession was public and general and had the benefit of preparing the heart of the confessor for the spiritual nature of the kingdom which was to come. As far as the Scriptures are concerned such a confession would be appropriate today. See James 5:16. This type of confession is not to be confused with auricular confession which is not Scriptural.

An Example of John's Preaching ... Matthew 3:7-12; Mark 1:7, 8; Luke 3:7-18

1. What is "the wrath to come"?

This is a reference to the future punishment that shall come upon the wicked. See 1 Thessalonians 1:10 and 2 Thessalonians 1:7-10.

29

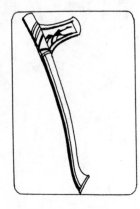

2. What did John mean by the statement: "God is able of these stones to raise up children unto Abraham"?
"John meant that their being children of Abraham by natural descent gave them no more merit than children of Abraham made out of stones would have."—J.W. McGarvey, P.Y. Pendleton, *The Fourfold Gospel*, p. 75.

3. What is the meaning of the reference to the ax?
When an ax is laid at the root of a tree it is generally for the purpose of cutting it down. That is obviously the meaning in this text. The picture is of a woodman examining his orchard and cutting and burning the unprofitable trees. Similarly, God was about to strike the proud and pretentious whose lives produced no fruit.

4. To whom did John compare himself?
John compared himself to the lowest household servant whose duty it was to unloosen and bind on sandals. The expression is one of sincere humility.

5. Does the expression, "he shall baptize you with the Holy Ghost, and with fire," refer to the same or different baptisms?
Different. The baptism of the Holy Spirit has occurred but twice, once in Acts 2 and again in Acts 10. The baptism of fire refers to the future punishment of the wicked. Because of the absence of the preposition "in" before "fire" in John's statement, some assume that John spoke of only one baptism. Those who hold this view believe that the baptism in Acts 2 and 10 is a baptism of the Holy Spirit *and* fire. Evidence favors the former view, especially considering the context of the next verse.

6. What did John say the people should do to show their repentance?
He required them to produce the fruits of repentance. When particular groups inquired what they should do, he gave specific answers: the "haves" were to share with the "have-nots," the tax-collectors were told to be honest, the soldiers were informed that they should be fair and content.

7. To whom does John compare Jesus?
In Luke 3:17 John compares Jesus to a farmer who is winnowing his crop, separating the wheat from the chaff. The wheat represents the righteous; the chaff, sinners.

WHEN AND WHERE

Neither Matthew nor Mark attempts to date the beginning of John's ministry. Luke, however, is very specific, using six historical points of reference to give an accurate dating. It was in the fifteenth year of the reign of Tiberius Caesar; when Pontius Pilate was governor of Judea; Herod, tetrarch of Galilee; Philip, his brother, tetrarch of Ituraea and Trachonitis; Lysanias, tetrarch of Abilene; Annas and Caiaphas being the high priests. At that point in time John began his preaching and baptizing (Luke 3:1-3). According to Samuel J. Andrews, who has written a thorough discussion of this question, it was the summer of A.D. 26 (779 U.C.) that John began his work.— Samuel J. Andrews, *The Life of Our Lord Upon the Earth*, p. 29. This was a sabbatic year. If we are correct in our dating, this fact would account for the large multitudes of people. Being free from agriculture and business, they could flock to John to hear his message.

The place of John's birth is difficult to determine. From the Scriptures we learn that it was "a city of Judah" located somewhere in "the hill country" (Luke 1:39, 65). A number of spots have been suggested, including Hebron, Juttah, Jerusalem, Beth Zacharias, Khirbet el Yahud, and Ain Karim. The weight of evidence seems to favor either Juttah or Ain Karim. Find these two places on the map.

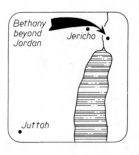

The scene of John's early ministry is described as being "in the wilderness of Judea" (Matthew 3:1), and at the Jordan River (Matthew 3:6). In other words, a place in the wilderness through which the Jordan flowed. Both of these requirements are met in the territory just north of the Dead Sea.

PROJECTS AND PLANS

Find a description of the Holy Place and of the Holy of Holies, and draw a scale model of them, indicating the various pieces of furniture and their exact location. See 1 Kings 6, Exodus 26, and Hebrews 9. Be prepared to explain where you think the angel, Gabriel, stood when making his announcement.

Read "Date of the Lord's Baptism"—Samuel J. Andrews, *The Life of our Lord Upon the Earth*, pp. 21-35, and the article by W. Ewing on "Capernaum" in *The International Standard Bible Encyclopedia*, pp. 566, 567.

THE BEGINNING OF CHRIST'S MINISTRY

TOPICS AND TEXTS

The Baptism of Jesus . . . Matthew 3:13-17; Mark 1:9-11; Luke 3:21, 22
The Temptation of Jesus . . . Matthew 4:1-11; Mark 1:12, 13; Luke 4:1-13
John's Defense of His Ministry . . . John 1:19-28
John's Identification of Jesus as the Christ . . . John 1:29-34
The First Disciples of Jesus . . . John 1:35-51
The First Miracle . . . John 2:1-11
The Change of Residence to Capernaum . . . John 2:12

CONTEXT AND CONTINUITY

The preceding lesson bears a relationship to this book similar to that of a parenthetical statement to a sentence: it breaks the line of thought, but supplies additional essential information. Now we may begin again our investigation of Jesus' life. Since our last view, some eighteen years of time have elapsed. No doubt many important events occurred during these years, but of them we have no record. Our knowledge of this period is restricted to what can be deduced from the kind of person we know Jesus to have been and from the situation existing when the Gospel writers again take up His life's story.

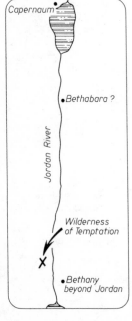

Capernaum

Bethabara ?

Jordan River

Wilderness of Temptation

X

Bethany beyond Jordan

We can be sure that there were some family changes. Apparently Joseph died during these years, for there is no further reference to him in the Gospels. As previously mentioned, there were half-brothers and half-sisters in the family (Matthew 13:55). It is not known when they were born nor consequently how old they were when Jesus began His ministry. If Joseph's death occurred while they were still young, then Jesus, as the eldest son, had the responsibility of rearing them. The attitude of these children toward their unusual brother during this time is not known, and we can therefore only speculate. Later we read of their unbelief and their attempt to interrupt Jesus' ministry (John 7:5; Matthew 12:46-50).

Jesus was twelve when the Passover recorded in Luke 2 took place. He was about thirty years old when the next known event in His life occurred. At that time He left Nazareth, never to return there as a permanent resident, and journeyed to the Jordan River to be baptized by John. The Holy Spirit then led Jesus into the wilderness where He spent forty days fasting and being tempted. He then returned to the scene of John's baptizing, enlisted His first disciples, and journeyed to Cana where He performed His first miracle. He then took up residence in Capernaum, which thereafter is spoken of as "his own city" (Matthew 9:1).

Thus was launched Jesus' ministry which lasted about three-and-a-half years, and which took Him from Nazareth to Jerusalem, from a workman's bench to a crudely made cross on a hill. The remaining chapters of this book will be devoted to the study of that brief but dynamic ministry.

INQUIRIES AND INSIGHTS

The Baptism of Jesus . . . Matthew 3:13-17; Mark 1:9-11; Luke 3:21, 22

1. What was the cause of John's hesitation to baptize Jesus?

Jordan River

One is first inclined to answer that John was divinely informed as to Jesus' identity and therefore felt unworthy. However, a check of John's own testimony reveals that he did not know the true identity of Jesus at this time. The descent of the Holy Spirit upon Him was God's afore-promised sign to John that He was the One who would baptize in the Holy Spirit (John 1:32-34), and that did not occur until after Jesus was baptized (Matthew 3:16). It seems that John had heard enough about Jesus from those closely associated with Him to be convinced of His greatness and of his own unworthiness to baptize Him. John's personal evaluation was then corroborated by the Holy Spirit.

2. What is the meaning of Jesus' statement: "Suffer it to be so now: for thus it becometh us to fulfil all righteousness"?

The following, though not a translation of this troublesome statement, seems to express its true meaning: "Permit it now, for it is fitting that we should observe all of God's methods for constituting men righteous." This does not imply that Jesus was not already righteous, but merely that as God's Son it was proper for Him to do all that God had commanded. (See John 6:38.)

3. How was the multitude affected by Jesus' baptism?

Evidently the multitude did not understand the voice nor grasp the significance of the dove's presence. As on a similar occasion (John 12:28, 29), perhaps these people thought that it had thundered. Still, John's attitude toward Jesus, the strange sound, and the sudden appearance of a dove probably told the multitude that there was something unique about Jesus. Later John confirmed their guess (John 1:29).

4. After the baptism what happened?

After He was baptized Jesus "went up straightway out of the water" (Matthew 3:16; see also Mark

33

1:10). Some artists have interpreted this to mean that Jesus was raised above the water and suspended in mid-air. The texts do not say this. The statement simply refers to Jesus' exit from the river to one of its banks. While standing on the shore, still dripping with the waters of His own baptism, and with His head humbly bowed in prayer (Luke 3:21), the Holy Spirit descended upon Him and the voice of God spoke words of praise: "Thou art my beloved Son, in whom I am well pleased" (Mark 1:11).

The Temptation of Jesus ... Matthew 4:1-11; Mark 1:12, 13; Luke 4:1-13

1. Was Jesus tempted throughout the forty days or only at the end of the period?
He was tempted throughout the period. This fits with what Mark (1:13) and Luke (4:2) state and does not contradict Matthew's statement (4:2). Numerous temptations were probably employed by Satan but to no avail. After forty days of fasting and struggling, Jesus was physically weak and weary. Then Satan hurled his three greatest temptations at Him.

2. Did Jesus literally fast forty days or merely abstain from certain foods?
The answer is found in Luke 4:2: "And in those days he did *eat nothing.*" Jesus is not the only Bible character to fast for forty days. Both Moses (Exodus 34:28) and Elijah (1 Kings 19:8) fasted the same length of time.

3. In what ways do these accounts differ?
There are a number of minor differences. Mark is much more concise than Matthew or Luke. He devotes only two sentences (two verses in our Bibles) to the entire event, whereas Matthew uses nine sentences (eleven verses) and Luke eleven sentences (thirteen verses). Only Mark mentions the presence of wild animals. His purpose in this is not clear; perhaps the reference indicates Jesus' loneliness or perhaps His danger. Mark states that the Spirit *drove* Jesus into the wilderness, whereas Matthew and Luke say He was *led* by the Spirit. With Matthew, Mark relates that the angels ministered to Jesus, but unlike Matthew, who places the ministering after Jesus' struggle, Mark makes it a general statement as to with no consideration as to time. Matthew and Luke mention that Jesus fasted for forty days, but Mark does not. Only Luke mentions that after the temptations Satan departed from Jesus for a season. One other difference is discussed in the following section.

OTHERS FASTED

Moses: "And he was there with the Lord forty days and forty nights; he did neither eat bread, nor drink water" (Exodus 34:28).

Elijah: "And he arose, and did eat and drink, and went in the strength of that meat forty days and forty nights" (1 Kings 19:8).

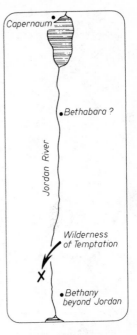

Capernaum

Bethabara ?

Jordan River

Wilderness of Temptation

X

Bethany beyond Jordan

4. What difference is there in the order of the temptations?

According to Matthew, the temptations occurred in the following order: (1) stones to bread, (2) pinnacle of the temple, (3) the kingdoms of the world. Luke reverses the latter two, making it impossible to determine which is the correct order. The important point is that Jesus was tempted in all of the three ways that are mentioned. The order of the temptations is relatively unimportant.

5. What is the significance of the temptations?

The real struggle which Jesus had in these temptations often is missed. Underlying each of them is the question concerning the type of Messiah Jesus was to be. Was He to use His power for self-gratification or for others? Was He to be a spectacular leader, gaining His followers through clown-like stunts, or was He to win them by the power of His message? Should He make an alliance with the devil to gain the kingdoms of this world which the devil controls, or should He consider Satan His eternal enemy, resist him, and cause him to flee? These were the battles Jesus fought and from which He emerged victorious.

6. Was Jesus literally taken up onto the pinnacle of the temple?

Yes, for both Matthew (4:5) and Luke (4:9) so declare. Evidently the place called a pinnacle in the records was the highest part of Solomon's Porch, a part of the temple. From this spot to the bottom of the Kedron Valley below was some 450 feet. Josephus says that from this place one could scarcely look down into the valley without a feeling of giddiness (*Antiquities of the Jews,* Book XV, Ch. XI, Sec. 5).

7. Does Satan own all of the kingdoms of the world?

Certainly not, for if he owned them he would have ceased long ago in his attempt to gain possession of them.

8. What comfort does the Christian gain from the temptations of Jesus?

"For we have not an high priest which cannot be touched with the feeling of our infirmities; but was in all points tempted like as we are, yet without sin. Let us therefore come boldly unto the throne of grace, that we may obtain mercy, and find grace to help in time of need" (Hebrews 4:15, 16). Jesus was tempted as we all will be: He was triumphant as we all should be.

Pinnacle of Temple

35

Capernaum

• Bethabara ?

Jordan River

Wilderness of Temptation

X

• Bethany beyond Jordan

John's Defense of His Ministry . . . John 1:19-28

1. Is this text parallel to Matthew 3:1-12?

Although there are similarities between these accounts, they cannot be parallel, for the event recorded in Matthew 3 happened before Jesus was baptized, whereas this one took place some forty days after that event.

2. Who did the Jews think John was?

No fewer than seventy times John's Gospel refers to the Jews, and always they are represented as Jesus' opposition. Here, the specific Jews are priests and Levites, representatives perhaps of the Sanhedrin, the great council of the nation. Obviously rumors concerning John's identity were widespread. Some believed that he was the Messiah, others, Elijah, and still others, "that prophet" (meaning perhaps Isaiah or Jeremiah, but more likely the prophet whose coming Moses predicted in Deuteronomy 18:15).

3. Why ask John about baptism?

Baptism was the main feature of John's ministry and since it was new in its application it aroused much interest. Why should John baptize? What was his authority? These and similar questions were upon the lips of the religious leaders. John refused to give them the kinds of answers they wanted. Rather, he kept both his identity and his authority clothed in an air of mystery.

John's Identification of Jesus as the Christ . . . John 1:29-34

1. How many days are mentioned in John 1:29—2:11?

In this text John has outlined, in typical time-conscious fashion, the days of an entire week, the first great week of Jesus' ministry after His victory over Satan. The days are mentioned in the following verses: first day—1:19-28; second day—1:29-34; third day—1:35-42; fourth day—1:43-51; fifth and sixth days—not specifically mentioned; seventh day (the third day following the four already mentioned)—2:1-11.

2. What is the significance of the title "the Lamb of God"?

To a Jew this title would be full of significance. It would recall the annual Passover feast as well as the daily sacrifices in the temple. Furthermore, the lamb was an emblem of patience and meekness. Isaiah 53, with its predictions of a suffering Savior, was as familiar to these Jews as it is to present-day

Christians. We can reasonably assume that some who heard John speak would associate the "Lamb of God that taketh away the sin of the world" with this famous Messianic prophecy.

The First Disciples of Jesus . . . John 1:35-51

1. What is the import of Jesus' question to the two disciples of John?

When the two followed Jesus, He turned and asked: "What seek ye?" At face value the meaning is obvious. The question, however, has a deeper significance: "For what are you seeking *in life?*" Rather than give a direct answer, the two asked Jesus their own question: "Where dwellest thou?" They implied that they desired some time with Him for discussion. Jesus granted their wish by saying, "Come and see."

2. Who were the two?

Only one of them, Andrew, is named. The other man was most likely John, the author of the fourth Gospel. It is a characteristic of his writing that whenever possible he doesn't identify himself (13:23; 18:15; 19:26; 20:2; 21:7, 20-24). Andrew immediately called his brother, Simon, and very likely John similarly called his brother, James.

3. What other disciples were called at this time?

When Jesus made ready to depart from Judea to go into Galilee, He found Philip and invited him to be His disciple. Philip then brought Nathanael to Jesus. This is evidently the Bartholomew of the synoptics, for *Bartholomew* is actually a second name, meaning, "son of Tholomai (Ptolemy)."

4. What kind of place was Nazareth?

From Nathanael's question, "Can there any good thing come out of Nazareth?" we conclude that the reputation of Nazareth was bad. A description of the city's location is given by J.W. McGarvey in his *Lands of the Bible* on pages 522 and 523.

5. What is the significance of Jesus' statement about Nathanael?

Jesus said of Nathanael, "Behold an Israelite indeed in whom is no guile." The title "Israel" was first used of Jacob (Genesis 32:28) and thereafter of his descendants. Jacob, as a young man, was noted for his guile. It was through his deceit that he secured the birthright from his brother, Esau (Genesis 25:27-34), and the parental blessing from Isaac (Genesis 27:1-29). Jesus was saying, "Here is a descendant of Jacob who is unlike his

> **FIRST DISCIPLES**
>
> Andrew/Simon
> John?/James?
> Philip/Nathanael

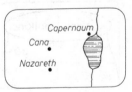

37

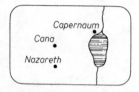

ancestor in that he has none of his guile." Jesus made further reference to Jacob in verse 51 (see Genesis 28:10-22).

The First Miracle . . . John 2:1-11

1. Where did this miracle occur?
Jesus chose to perform His first miracle in an insignificant village in Galilee called Cana. The exact location of this village is uncertain, but opinion favors the present Kefr Kenna, a few miles northeast of Nazareth.

2. Was Jesus rude to His mother?
Mary was at the wedding feast and, from the important role she played, it is concluded that she was in some way related to those in charge of the feast. When she informed Jesus of the wine shortage, He addressed her with the term, "Woman," which some, judging from present-day usage, have considered a term of disrespect. However, there is no evidence that it was such in Jesus' day. He used the same term when He spoke to His mother from the cross (John 19:26), and after His resurrection when He addressed Mary Magdalene (John 20:15). Barclay states:

> So far from being a rough and discourteous way of address, it was a title of respect. We have no way of speaking in English which exactly renders it; but it is better to translate it *Lady* which gives at least the courtesy in it.— William Barclay, *The Gospel of John*, p. 83.

In His question, "What have I to do with thee?" there seems to be a slight rebuke for her attempt to dictate His program.

3. How much wine did Jesus make?
The stone jars which were available were used for purification purposes. This means that they were used for the washing of human bodies, utensils, and even furniture to make them ceremonially clean. Each jar would hold two or three firkins (evidently the Hebrew "bath" is meant). A firkin is thought to equal from seven and one-half to nine gallons. This means each pot would hold from fifteen to twenty-seven gallons. Jesus had all six filled with water to exclude the possibility of deception. By changing all the water into wine Jesus demonstrated that with God there is always an abundance.

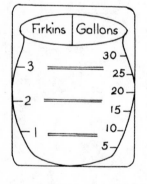

4. Was the wine intoxicating?
In the light of the strong interdicts against drinking and drunkenness found elsewhere in the Word of

God (Proverbs 20:1; 23:31; 1 Corinthians 6:10) the question is unnecessary. Of course the wine wasn't intoxicating, and there is nothing in the text to indicate that it was.

The Change of Residence to Capernaum . . . John 2:12

1. What was the purpose of this trip to Capernaum?

Jesus went there to take up residence. (See Matthew 4:13 and 9:1.) Situated on the northwestern shore of the Sea of Galilee, Capernaum was a better center for Jesus' operations. Capernaum is repeatedly mentioned in the Gospels. It is not, however, mentioned in the Old Testament. This has led some to conclude that it was not founded until after the captivity.

2. Who were "his brethren"?

This question is answered in Lesson Ten.

WHEN AND WHERE

Tradition has long accepted January 6 as the date of Jesus' baptism. Although there is no evidence to verify the date, neither is there any to negate it. Beginning with the first Passover of Jesus' ministry (April 11th A.D. 27) and working backward, we conclude His baptism must have occurred sometime in the three-month span of December to February, A.D. 26 or 27 (779 or 780 U.C.). This date allows ample time for the early ministry of John the Baptist which began in the summer of A.D. 26, and also gives sufficient time for the events in Jesus' life which followed His baptism and preceded that first Passover of His ministry.

The exact spot of Jesus' baptism is not known. The Bible states that Jesus, after His temptation, visited John at "Bethabara, beyond Jordan" (John 1:28, 29). We are uncertain as to the location of Bethabara (or "Bethany" according to the most ancient reading), nor do we know that Jesus was baptized there. The text merely states that John was baptizing there when Jesus returned from His temptation.

PROJECTS AND PLANS

Work together as a class to make flannelgraph backgrounds and characters to illustrate the baptism, temptation, and first miracle of Jesus.

Using a concordance, make a list of all the New Testament references to Samaria. Write a sentence explanation concerning each reference.

39

IN JERUSALEM AND SAMARIA

TOPICS AND TEXTS

The First Cleansing of the Temple . . . John 2:13-22
The Conversation With Nicodemus . . . John 2:23–3:21
Jesus' Growing Ministry in Judea and John's Waning Ministry at Aenon . . . John 3:22-36
The Ministry in Samaria . . . John 4:1-42
The Arrest of John the Baptist . . . Luke 3:19, 20

CONTEXT AND CONTINUITY

Having changed His residence from Nazareth to Capernaum, Jesus set out on a journey to Jerusalem. It was springtime in Palestine, the Passover was at hand, and Jesus felt the need to be in the capital city for the feast.

Apparently four Passovers are mentioned by John as occurring during the ministry of Jesus: 2:23; 5:1; 6:4; and 11:55. (There is some question concerning the feast mentioned in John 5:1 as to whether it was Passover or another feast.) Three of these Passovers found Jesus in the Holy City. We are indebted to John for these references, for it is through them that we are able to determine that Jesus' ministry was somewhat more than three years in length.

The task of harmonizing the Gospels and presenting a valid chronology of Jesus' life is a major one. In addition to the uncertainty concerning the number of Passovers, other problems arise. Did Jesus cleanse the temple once or twice? Were there two rejections at Nazareth, or was there only one? Is the sermon on the plain of Luke 6 the same as the Sermon on the Mount of Matthew 5—7? It is not easy to answer these questions. With reference to the cleansing of the temple, it appears that this happened twice, once near the beginning of Christ's ministry and once near its end. Although the same procedure was used by Jesus for both cleansings there are a sufficient number of differences to justify this conclusion. It would be well to compare the two events and note the similarities and differences: first cleansing—John 2:13-22; second cleansing—Matthew 21:12-17, Mark 11:12-18, Luke 19:45-48.

Shortly after the first cleansing—and perhaps partially because of it—one of the rulers of the Jewish people, a man named Nicodemus, came to see and talk with Jesus. Nicodemus had heard of the signs performed by this teacher in Jerusalem and/or Galilee, and it is not unlikely that he himself had witnessed the cleansing of the temple. If so, he must have detected something of the power and majesty of this unusual man who had marched into the temple and by His actions informed the priests, to whom God had entrusted temple oversight, that they were operating it poorly!

Perhaps it was mere curiosity that took Nicodemus out on his night journey to visit Jesus. Or perhaps—and we would rather believe it—Nicodemus was motivated by a desire for the truth, and by a belief that one so spiritually powerful as Jesus must have some knowledge of it. Nor was Nicodemus disappointed, for he discovered that Jesus could not only act with power, but speak with authority as well, answering not only spoken questions but unuttered ones too.

After this Passover visit to Jerusalem, Jesus remained in Judea for a number of months. Unfortunately we know but little concerning this Judean ministry.

At this time John the Baptist was preaching and baptizing in Aenon near Salim. During these days a question concerning purification (and apparently baptism's connection with it) arose between the Jews and the Baptist's disciples who turned to their teacher for help. Instead of asking forthright the question on their hearts, they chose to speak of the success of Jesus in making disciples. John, discerning the intent of their statement, delivered a sermon concerning Jesus and his own relationship to Him.

In the early months of winter, Jesus and His disciples left Judea and journeyed to Galilee, passing on the way through Samaria. It was in December, or possibly January, when Jesus and His party arrived at Sychar. Here Jesus remained for two days, experiencing a great deal of success, largely because of the evangelistic efforts of a once sinful woman whom Jesus personally converted. From here Jesus went on northward into Galilee where He launched a great campaign. At this time John the Baptist was put in prison by Herod Antipas, where he remained until his death, approximately fourteen months later.

Time was moving swiftly for Jesus. It had been a year since His baptism. This means that almost one-third of His ministry was behind Him. Much had been accomplished, but many other things needed to be done. Feelings of urgency must have been constantly keen.

INQUIRIES AND INSIGHTS

The First Cleansing of the Temple ... John 2:13-22

1. Why was Jesus angry?

John cites two things that were happening in the temple that produced Jesus' righteous indignation:

FOUR PASSOVERS

"Now when he was in Jerusalem at the passover, in the feast day, many believed in his name, when they saw the miracles which he did" (John 2:23).

"After this there was a feast of the Jews; and Jesus went up to Jerusalem" (John 5:1).*

"And the passover, a feast of the Jews, was nigh" (John 6:4).

"And the Jews' passover was nigh at hand: and many went out of the country up to Jerusalem before the passover, to purify themselves" (John 11:55).

* It is not certain that this is a reference to Passover.

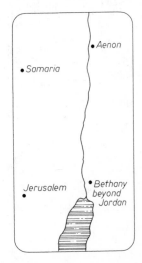

41

Galilean shekels

(1) certain animals (oxen, sheep, doves) were being sold; (2) money was being changed. In Palestine in Jesus' day many kinds of money were in circulation (Roman, Grecian, Egyptian, Persian, Tyrian, Syrian), but to pay the temple tax—which every Hebrew and proselyte male had to pay—only half-shekels of the sanctuary or ordinary Galilean shekels could be used. The money changers took whatever coins were offered them and exchanged them for proper temple money. For this service they charged exorbitant rates of their almost-captive customers. Many of the Jews who assembled for the Passover would naturally desire to offer sacrifices to God, and the sellers of animals were in the temple to facilitate this. Here again, however, a great injustice was being performed. Since the animals offered to God had to be perfect, and since there were inspectors who conveniently rejected the animals purchased outside the temple, the temple salesmen had a near monopoly on the business. This allowed them to charge huge prices and thus fleece the people. Operated properly, and in an acceptable place, both of these businesses probably would have been recognized by Jesus as essential services that aided the Jewish worshipers. Performed as and where they were, they caused Him to be filled with "zeal for His Father's house."

2. In what part of the temple did this scene occur?
The temple proper was enclosed by a number of courts that derived their names from the worshipers permitted within them. Nearest to the Holy Place was the Court of the Priests; next, the Court of Israel; then the Court of Women; and on the outer extremity, beyond the Sacred Enclosure, was the Court of the Gentiles. It was in this latter court that Jesus had His encounter with the merchants. One can well imagine with what difficulty the Gentiles endeavored to worship God, for all about them were noise and confusion.

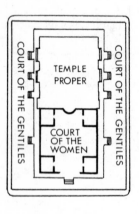

3. Did Jesus use the scourge on the people or on the animals?
Since it doesn't harmonize with the character of Jesus that He should beat humans, it appears most likely that the scourge was for the animals. His forceful words and actions were sufficient to repel the merchants.

4. Why did the Jews ask for a sign?
The Jews did not say that Jesus was wrong in what He did. Rather they sought from Him a sign of

authority to justify His unusual conduct. When Elijah condemned the priests of Baal he called down fire from Heaven, and now the Jews wanted some similar indication that Jesus was acting by the power of God. The sign which He gave did not satisfy them, and that day marked the beginning of a deadly feud between the Jewish rulers and Jesus, which finally culminated in His crucifixion.

The Conversation With Nicodemus ... John 2:23–3:21

1. What is known about Nicodemus?

He was a ruler of the Jews, that is, a member of the Sanhedrin or great council of the nation. After this conversation he apparently became a secret follower of Jesus. Two other times he is mentioned in the Scriptures: John 7:50, where he spoke out against the injustice of his fellow rulers in condemning Jesus without hearing Him; and John 19:39, where, with Joseph of Arimathea, he took the body of Jesus and prepared it for burial.

2. Why did Jesus speak to Nicodemus concerning the new birth?

Jesus realized that upon this man's heart was a question concerning the nature of the kingdom of God. Recognizing in him a capacity for understanding deep spiritual truths, Jesus went right to the heart of the whole matter, declaring the impossibility of seeing the kingdom of God apart from a new birth. Nicodemus did not fully comprehend all that was said to him, but the teaching must have lingered with him and challenged his thoughts for years to come.

3. According to Jesus, how is the new birth to be accomplished?

Jesus said a man must be born of water and of the Spirit. That cannot be called the new birth which lacks either. Notice other teaching of Jesus concerning the new birth in Matthew 28:19, 20 and Mark 16:15, 16.

4. How was the Son of man in Heaven at this time?

Although bodily on earth, Jesus' spirit was in direct communication with the Father in Heaven. So intimate and complete was this relationship that it was proper to say the Son of man was in Heaven.

5. To what serpent is reference made?

As the Israelites journeyed from Mount Hor by way of the Red Sea, they became discouraged and began to complain against God and Moses. As a

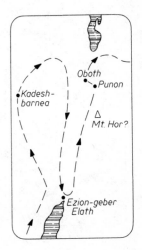

43

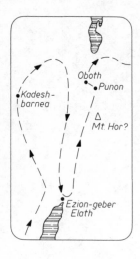

punishment the Lord sent fiery serpents among the Israelites which bit many of them, causing their death. The word, "fiery," probably refers to the inflammatory effect of the snakes' bites. Or, it could have reference to their color and/or design. When the people repented, Moses was instructed by God to erect a pole and place a fiery serpent upon it. He made the serpent of brass, placed the pole in the midst of the camp, and instructed those who were bitten to look upon it and live. (See Numbers 21.) Similarly, the Son of man was to be lifted up (on the cross) so that all who would look to Him in obedient faith would not perish but have eternal life.

6. Where do Jesus' words cease and John's begin?

We cannot be certain. Quotation marks would have eliminated this problem, but they were not used by the Greeks. The beginning of a quotation was indicated with a capital letter, but there was no means of marking its end.

Jesus' Growing Ministry in Judea and John's Waning Ministry at Aenon . . . John 3:22-36

1. Did Jesus ever baptize anyone?

Not in water, although John 3:22 might be understood as affirming that He did. John 4:2, however, serves as a commentary on this verse: "Jesus himself baptized not, but his disciples." Only through His disciples did Jesus baptize. The reason for this is apparent—any baptized by Jesus might have considered themselves superior. (See 1 Corinthians 1:14-16 where Paul was beset with this problem. See also Matthew 3:11 and Acts 2:1-4.)

2. Why was John baptizing in Aenon?

He baptized in Aenon because there was much water there, and baptism requires much water.

3. What question was there between John's disciples and the Jews?

All that can be learned from the text is that it was a question about purification. The fact that John's disciples spoke to him about baptism would indicate that the question dealt with baptism's relationship to purification.

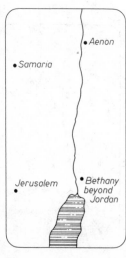

4. What relationship did John bear to Jesus?

John said he bore a relationship to Jesus similar to that of a friend to the bridegroom. As such a friend would rejoice at the bridegroom's wedding, so John declared that his joy was fulfilled in the successes of Jesus.

The Ministry in Samaria . . . John 4:1-42

1. Why "must" Jesus go through Samaria?

Probably no more is meant by this statement than that geographically it was the nearest way from Judea to Galilee. It was not, however, the popular route. The majority of the Jews, wishing to avoid all contact with the Samaritans, would take a longer route, one which took them on the eastern side of the Jordan.

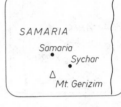

SAMARIA

Samaria
Sychar
△
Mt. Gerizim

2. Who were the Samaritans?

When Sargon of Assyria captured the northern kingdom (Israel) in 722 B.C., he followed the practice of many ancient conquerors, moving many of the nationals to another land (2 Kings 17:6) and replacing them with other people (2 Kings 17:24). In violation of God's law, the remaining Jews intermarried with the pagans who had been brought into their land. The Jews in the southern kingdom, who themselves were later conquered but did not succumb to the same practice, never forgave their northern brothers, and would have nothing to do with them. When Nehemiah made it clear that those people had "no portion, nor right, nor memorial, in Jerusalem" (Nehemiah 2:20), they countered by erecting their own temple on Mt. Gerizim. Over the years the hatred between these two peoples increased until in Jesus' day there were literally no dealings between them (John 4:9). The Samaritans have retained their identity through the centuries and continue to exist as a distinct people with their own religion. In 1930 they were nearly extinct, but now there are several hundred of them.

3. What kind of water did Jesus have?

Jesus didn't speak about literal water, H_2O, but about figurative water, spiritual water. His water was the water of life. The thirst which it would quench was the thirst of the soul. The well whence it came was the well of salvation, adequate to satisfy every spiritual desire

4. Why did Jesus mention her husband?

Jesus introduced a very unpleasant subject and did so purposely. He wanted the woman to examine her life and see how shallow and dissatisfying it was. He hoped to create within her a genuine desire for something better. The reference to her unsuccessful marital life accomplished this. The first step in the right direction is often motivated by a dissatisfaction with one's present condition. This was true of the Samaritan woman.

45

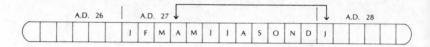
SAMARIA
Samaria
• Sychar
△
Mt. Gerizim

5. According to Jesus, where were the people of that day to worship?
The Samaritans contended that Mt. Gerizim was the proper place to worship. A temple had been erected there in the days of Sanballat (5th century B.C.), and although it was later destroyed by John Hyrcanus (2nd century B.C.), the Samaritans continued to worship there. Jesus made it clear that the Samaritans' worship was wrong, and that salvation was from the Jews (John 4:22).

6. Where and how are true worshipers to worship today?
No longer is there one particular spot to which people must make a pilgrimage in order for their worship to be acceptable. Jesus' declaration in John 4:21 indicates that under the new dispensation, not only on Mt. Gerizim or in Jerusalem, but from *anywhere* acceptable worship can rise to God. Such worship has two components: (1) It must be in spirit, which indicates that it must be sincere. (2) It must be in truth, or in harmony with God's revelation.

7. What meat did Jesus have to eat?
From this account we learn that Jesus had both water (v. 10) and meat (v. 32), but the woman could not see the water, nor could the disciples see the meat. In verse 14 Jesus explained that the water of which He spoke was spiritual water. In verse 34 He described His meat: "My meat is to do the will of him that sent me, and to finish his work." Jesus, in His attempt to help this unnamed woman, forgot the hunger and exhaustion that wearied His physical body, and found strength and nourishment in doing the will of His heavenly Father.

8. To what harvest did Jesus refer?
Jesus looked beyond the fields, which had but recently been sown and would not be harvested for four months, to the large number of Samaritans who, in response to the woman's invitation, were coming to see and talk with Him. It is to this harvest of souls that Jesus referred.

9. What caused the Samaritans to believe?
Two reasons are cited: (1) Many believed because of the testimony of the woman; (2) others, because they heard Jesus themselves. The fact that one woman could so profoundly influence a whole community indicates something concerning the strength of her personality. Although she was a social outcast whose conduct was widely con-

demned, it is apparent that she was respected for her intelligence and discernment. It would be interesting to know what happened to this woman after her contact with Jesus. Unfortunately we have no further information.

The Arrest of John the Baptist . . . Luke 3:19, 20

1. Is this the correct time for the arrest?
Yes, for so Matthew (4:12) and Mark (1:14) declare. Luke's statement concerning the arrest of John is placed at a much earlier time. It was not, however, intended by Luke to be understood as having occurred at the time he mentioned it, for he has it preceding Jesus' baptism by John! While discussing the Baptist in 3:7-18, Luke merely adds the fact that Herod (at a later time) put him in prison.

2. Which Herod was this?
The word *Herod* was a family name, used of many rulers who were the descendants of Herod the Great. The one who arrested and later beheaded John was Herod Antipas, son of Herod the Great and his fourth wife, Malthace. It was before this same man that Jesus was tried. He is never called Antipas in the Gospels, only Herod.

WHEN AND WHERE
The period of time covered by this lesson was about nine months, from the Passover of A.D. 27 (which fell on April 11 in that year), to the time of the arrest of John the Baptist. Just exactly when this event occurred is not known, but it was probably in January of A.D. 28.

According to Josephus *(Antiquities,* XVIII:5:2) the place of John's imprisonment was the castle of Machaerus, located in the southern part of Perea. McGarvey says of it: "It was a very strong fortress, on an almost inaccessible mountain-top, built originally by Hyrcanus, and afterward greatly strengthened and enlarged by Herod."—J.W. McGarvey, *Lands of the Bible,* p. 371. Locate Machaerus on the map which is provided.

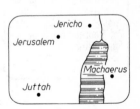

PROJECTS AND PLANS
Prepare a lesson concerning Nicodemus, emphasizing the desirable traits which he possessed. In addition to the John 3 passage check John 7:50 and 19:39.

Read chapter VII, "Places in Galilee"—J.W. McGarvey, *Lands of the Bible.* This will help prepare you for study of the great Galilean campaign of Jesus which begins in the following lesson.

Lesson Seven

JESUS THE ITINERATE PREACHER

TOPICS AND TEXTS

CONTEXT AND CONTINUITY

FEAST OF TABERNACLES

—to commemorate the wanderings of the Israelites in the wilderness; also called feast of Booths, feast of Ingathering.

With this lesson we begin an investigation of Jesus' great Galilean campaign which lasted for about half of His entire ministry. It was probably in the early part of January, approximately one year after His baptism, that Jesus began this effort. It was in October, some twenty-one months later that He concluded it. At that time He attended the feast of Tabernacles (John 7:10-52) and remained in Judea for a two month's campaign.

Not all of this time was spent in Galilee. There was an excursion to Jerusalem to attend a Passover feast (John 5:1-47), another to Phoenicia (Matthew 15:21-28; Mark 7:24-30), and four recorded visits to the eastern side of the Sea of Galilee into Gaulanitis and the Decapolis area. Although there were these brief interruptions, the great campaign continued, reaching its climax in the feeding of the five thousand. Immediately thereafter it collapsed because of Jesus' refusal to be a political Messiah.

In this one brief lesson we are attempting a study of the first five or six months of this period, months that were filled with thrilling incidents as Jesus healed and taught and debated. Coming into Galilee, Jesus went first to Cana where He performed a second miracle. This one was upon a subject some twenty-five miles away, in Capernaum. From Cana He proceeded to Nazareth where He preached and was rejected by the people. He then traveled to the Sea of Galilee and called the four fishermen. Next He went into Capernaum where He taught and performed a number of miracles. After that He conducted a general tour of Galilee, "teaching in their synagogues, and preaching the gospel of the kingdom, and healing all manner of sickness and all manner of disease among the people" (Matthew 4:23). Two miracles were then performed as Jesus cleansed a leper and healed a paralytic. These miracles were followed by the call of Matthew, which subsequently led to a controversy about eating with sinners. Then came another controversy, one regarding fasting.

At this time Jesus left Galilee and journeyed to Jerusalem to attend "a feast of the Jews" (evidently the second Passover of Jesus' ministry, the one of A.D. 28). In Jerusalem He became engaged in a debate concerning His relationship to the Father. This was followed by still further controversy regarding the Sabbath day and man's relationship to it. Realizing that He had greatly incensed the Pharisees, Jesus withdrew from them and went again into Galilee where great multitudes followed Him. This lesson comes to an end in the summer of A.D. 28, with Jesus again in Galilee where, after a night of prayer, He called the twelve apostles.

INQUIRIES AND INSIGHTS

Statements Introducing the Galilean Ministry . . .
Matthew 4:12-17; Mark 1:14, 15; Luke 4:14, 15;
John 4:43-45

1. What Old Testament prophecy was fulfilled in Jesus' Galilean ministry?
A prophecy recorded in Isaiah 9:1, 2 was fulfilled.

2. What message did Jesus preach?
The same message which John the Baptist preached: "Repent: for the kingdom of heaven is at hand."

Healing of the Nobleman's Son . . . John 4:46-54

1. Who was this nobleman?
His identity is not known. The title, "nobleman," means that he was an officer, either civil or military. Some assume he was Chuza, Herod's steward, whose wife ministered to Jesus of her substance (Luke 8:3). Others incorrectly identify him with the centurion of Matthew 8 and Luke 7.

FEAST OF PASSOVER

—to commemorate the deliverance of the Israelites from Egyptian bondage. The name Passover was derived from the fact that God "passed over" (spared) the firstborn of obedient Israelites during the last of the Egyptian plagues; sometimes called feast of Unleavened Bread, due to strict abstinence from leaven during observance.

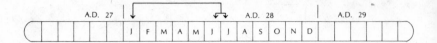
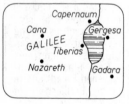

GREEK AND ROMAN HOURS	JEWISH
6:00 p.m.	Sunset.
6:20 "	Stars appear.
10:00 "	First watch ends.
12:00 "	Midnight.
2:00 a.m.	Second Watch ends.
3:00 "	Cock crow.
4:30 "	Second cock crow.
5:40 "	Column of dawn.
6:00 "	Sunrise (third watch ends).
9:00 "	1st hour of prayer.
12:00 m.	Noon.
1:30 p.m.	Great vesper.
3:30 "	Small vesper.
6:00 "	Sunset.

Map: Galilee — Capernaum, Cana, Gergesa, Tiberias, Nazareth, Gadara

2. When did this miracle occur?

John says it was at the seventh hour. Since he used Roman time that would be 7:00 p.m. Reconstructing the account, it appears that the nobleman left his home early one morning, traveled up a mountain road to Cana, met and talked with Jesus who granted his request by healing his son. Remaining in Cana that night, he left for home early the next morning. On the way he was met by his servants who told him at what hour the previous day the boy's fever left him.

His First Rejection at Nazareth . . . Luke 4:16-30

1. How many times was Jesus rejected at Nazareth?

From the evidence it is not possible to give a dogmatic answer. Most writers seem to favor the view that He was twice rejected: this time, and a little more than a year later as recorded in Matthew 13 and Mark 6.

2. Why did the Jews become so angry with Jesus?

Jesus' reading of the passage from Isaiah, emphasizing the word "me," would irritate them. Likewise, His statement, "This day is this scripture fulfilled in your ears," would incense them. Nor did He endear himself to His former, unbelieving neighbors by His reference to the widow of Zarephath and Naaman of Syria, both of whom were Gentiles.

3. What is the meaning of, "Physician, heal thyself"?

This was probably a common proverb in Jesus' day based upon the conviction that a doctor, suffering from a particular disease, should first heal himself before attempting to heal others of the same disease. The application in this incident is not easy to make. The following seems to be correct: "You are thinking that since it is reported I have performed miracles in Capernaum, I should perform some here in order to create confidence in me and my message."

The Calling of Four Fishermen . . . Matthew 4:18-22; Mark 1:16-21; Luke 5:1-11

1. Had Jesus previously known these four men?

We know that He knew Peter and Andrew before this call (see John 1:40, 41). If we are correct in identifying the unknown disciple of John 1:40 as John, the son of Zebedee, then it is most likely that all four of these men were already His disciples. Until this time there had been only a loose, informal relationship between them, but now a definite call is extended and accepted.

2. What were these men doing when Jesus called them?

It would appear that we have in the three accounts the events of a good portion of a day. Evidently when Jesus arrived it was early morning, and the fishermen were just ending an unsuccessful night on the sea. Entering Simon's ship, Jesus requested him to thrust out a little from the land. When this was done, Jesus sat in the ship and taught the people who had assembled on the shore. After this there was a miraculous draught of fishes. Sometime during this busy day Jesus extended His invitations to the four men.

3. What details are given by Mark? Luke?

Mark mentions that Zebedee had hired servants which indicates he was a man of some means. Luke says that James and John were partners of Simon.

Teaching and Miracles in Capernaum ... Matthew 8:14-17; Mark 1:21-34; Luke 4:31-41

1. What miracles did Jesus perform during this ministry?

He cast out a spirit of an unclean devil from a man in the synagogue, healed Simon's mother-in-law of a fever, cured many that were ill with various diseases, and cast out many other devils.

2. Which Simon was this?

Simon Peter, the brother of Andrew. Both of these men later became apostles of the Lord. Peter's wife is also mentioned in 1 Corinthians 9:5 where Paul states that other apostles were also married.

3. What does the Bible teach about demons?

For an answer to this question see Lesson Ten.

The First General Tour of Galilee ... Matthew 4:23-25; Mark 1:35-39; Luke 4:42-44

1. What were the characteristics of this campaign?

Teaching, preaching, and healing (Matthew 4:23).

2. Why did Jesus leave the multitude?

It seems strange that Jesus, at a time when the multitudes were flocking to Him, should turn from them and seek other places to minister. Jesus realized, however, that His time was limited and that He must cover as much territory as possible.

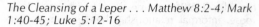
The Cleansing of a Leper . . . Matthew 8:2-4; Mark 1:40-45; Luke 5:12-16

1. Was leprosy known in the Old Testament?
The disease of leprosy was well known and dreadfully feared in Old Testament times. In fact, it was so widespread that two chapters of the Old Testament (Leviticus 13 and 14) are devoted to a description of its characteristics and to the rites and ceremonies that had to be employed in the cleansing of lepers. Miriam (Numbers 12) and Naaman (2 Kings 5) are well-known examples of those who were healed of the disease.

2. Why did Jesus send the leper to the priest?
In addition to their religious functions, Jewish priests served as health officers of the people. To them God gave the responsibility of examining and determining the condition of those suspected of having leprosy and those who claimed to be cleansed of it. In compliance with this Old Testament teaching Jesus sent the man to see a priest.

3. Why did the man disobey Jesus?
Jesus charged the leper to tell no one about the miracle, but no sooner had he departed from Jesus than he began "to publish it much, and to blaze abroad the matter." Probably the man didn't intend to disobey the Lord, but circumstances made it impossible for him to keep the healing a secret. The priest, the man's family and former friends, as well as his numerous leprous associates, would have been aware of the man's changed condition. They would have insisted he give them an explanation concerning the manner of his healing. Each one told would tell others until the story would spread throughout the land. Even if the man had refused to tell, those who saw the miracle would speak of it, with the same result. Jesus could no longer escape the multitudes and concentrate on teaching His disciples, for people came to hear Him from every area.

The Healing of the Paralytic . . . Matthew 9:1-8; Mark 2:1-12; Luke 5:17-26

1. Where did this miracle occur?
Mark states that it was in Capernaum, in "the house" (evidently Peter's house) that the miracle was performed.

2. Whose faith brought about this miracle?
All three texts use the pronoun, "their." It was "their" faith which Jesus saw that caused Him to say: "Son, thy sins be forgiven thee." The an-

For information regarding leprosy in the Old Testament, see Leviticus 13 and 14.

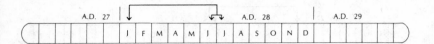
tecedent of the pronoun includes the four who showed faith, persistence, and ingenuity in getting the man before Jesus, as well as the palsied man who permitted these novel and strength-consuming plans to be carried out.

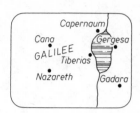

3. Were the Pharisees correct in their accusation?

They made two observations concerning Jesus' pronouncement, one of which was right and the other, wrong. In their question, "Who can forgive sins but God only?" they expressed a Bible truth. But in their charge that Jesus spoke blasphemously, they erred. Jesus proved this by demonstrating that what power He professed to have, He actually possessed.

4. Was the house damaged?

The uncovering and breaking up of the roof (Mark 2:4) and the lowering of the man's bed through the tiling (Luke 5:19) would certainly have caused some damage. Who stood the cost for this we are not told. Perhaps it was the owner, or the four, or the family of the palsied man.

The Call of Matthew and the Controversy About Eating With Sinners . . . Matthew 9:9-13; Mark 2:13-17; Luke 5:27-32

1. Was this Matthew's first contact with Jesus?

The Gospels do not tell us there had been a previous acquaintanceship between Jesus and Matthew, but there probably had been. It seems illogical that Matthew should respond to such a call as Jesus extended if they were strangers. As in the case of the four fishermen who followed Jesus before being specifically called by Him, Matthew may have been His disciple previously. After this call a more binding relationship existed. In connection with this question, read the qualifications of an apostle in Acts 1:21, 22.

2. Who were the publicans?

To the Jews in general, and the Pharisees in particular, no group of men was more detestable than the tax collectors (or publicans as they are called in the King James Version). This hatred stemmed in part from their being servants of Rome, a heathen power. It was also produced by the quality of men they were—most were unjust men, noted for their extortion and oppression. Edersheim explains that there were two types of publicans: the Gabbai (tax-gatherers in general) and the Mokhes (custom-house officials), and that Matthew belonged to the latter, which was the more

PUBLICANS

Gabbai: tax gatherers in general;
Mokhes: custom-house officials.

hated of the two.—Alfred Edersheim, *The Life and Times of Jesus the Messiah*, Vol. I, pp. 516, 517.

3. What was the purpose of this feast?
Perhaps it was a farewell party given by Matthew as he made ready to travel with Jesus. To it he invited his friends and former associates. No doubt he presented Jesus to them hoping they could be influenced by the Master as he had been.

4. How did Jesus answer the question of the scribes and Pharisees?
It was difficult for the Pharisees to understand how Jesus could associate with such people as were at Matthew's feast. When they asked His disciples concerning His conduct, Jesus responded: "They that be whole need not a physician, but they that are sick." The application of His statement was apparent, and the logic underlying it none could question. We should not conclude that Jesus hereby affirmed that the scribes and Pharisees were whole or righteous—only that they considered themselves to be such.

The Controversy About Fasting ... Matthew 9:14-17; Mark 2:18-22; Luke 5:33-39

1. Who introduced the fasting question to Jesus?
Although the disciples of the Pharisees as well as the disciples of John had discussed the question, it was the latter who came to Jesus inquiring concerning the conduct of His disciples.

2. What answer did Jesus give them?
Jesus employed three illustrations (one of which is called a parable by Luke) in order to answer their question. All three teach the same lesson: "Things which do not harmonize should not be put together." In effect He said: "It is incongruous that my disciples should fast at this time." He indicated that the time would come when they would fast and in so saying gave the first clear intimation of His death.

The Healing and Controversy at the Pool of Bethesda ... John 5:1-47

1. When did this event happen?
If we are correct in assuming that the feast mentioned is a Passover, then this was the second one of Jesus' ministry and commenced on March 30, A.D. 28.

2. Did an angel really trouble the water?
The answer to this question rests upon whether the fourth verse (John 5:4) is a part of John's work

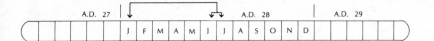
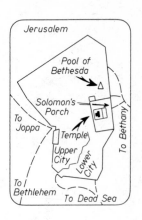

or a later scribal addition. Apparently it is the latter, for the best manuscripts do not contain it. From verses 3 and 7 it is clear that the people thought there was some relationship between the troubled waters and healing. They probably felt that God was in some way involved. Such miracles, however, would be out of harmony with the Bible's teaching regarding miracles.

3. How many claims did Jesus make for himself in this controversy?
At least thirteen separate claims were made by Jesus in this controversy. Note especially His claims that God was His Father and that He, like the Father, could raise the dead.

Another Controversy About Breaking the Sabbath . . . Matthew 12:1-8; Mark 2:23-28; Luke 6:1-5

1. What kind of grain?
Although the word corn is used, the reference is to barley or wheat, for maize was unknown until the discovery of America.

2. Did the disciples steal the grain?
No, for according to the law they were permitted to pluck their neighbor's grain with their hands (Deuteronomy 23:25).

3. How were the disciples supposedly violating the Sabbath?
According to the Pharisees they were laboring. The labor consisted of reaping, thrashing, and winnowing the grain and preparing a meal. All four of these acts were considered work and were forbidden on the Sabbath.

4. How did Jesus answer their charge?
He cited the action of David in eating the shewbread (1 Samuel 21), and the weekly labor of the priests in the temple. Jesus did not mean to justify David's action, but by His reference cast the problem back into His critics' laps. "You condemn my disciples," He reasoned, "but you are not consistent, for you neither condemn David nor the priests." He wanted them to see that the Sabbath was made for man, not man for the Sabbath.

The Healing of a Man With a Withered Hand and Further Controversy . . . Matthew 12:9-14; Mark 3:1-6; Luke 6:6-11

1. What affliction did the man have?
His right hand had withered, i.e., atrophied, probably as a result of palsy or paralysis (the terms are synonymous).

55

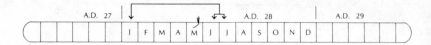

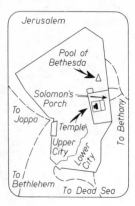

Jerusalem

Pool of Bethesda

Solomon's Porch

To Joppa

Temple

Upper City

Lower City

To Bethlehem

To Bethany

To Dead Sea

2. How did Jesus answer their question?

Jesus answered their question by citing a practice that was evidently common—the rescuing of a sheep from peril on the holy day. "It would be inconsistent," He argued, "to help a sheep on the Sabbath and to refuse to help a man, for a man is more valuable than a sheep." Who could dispute that logic?

3. Who were the Herodians?

This question is answered in Lesson Twenty.

Jesus and the Multitudes: Teaching and Healing . . . Matthew 12:15-21; Mark 3:7-12

1. What prophecy does Matthew cite?

A prophecy in Isaiah 42.

2. From where did the multitude come?

By this time Jesus' fame had spread throughout the entire section. People from every area were flocking to Him to hear His message and to be healed by His power. From Judea and Galilee, from Idumea and beyond Jordan, even from the Phoenician cities of Tyre and Sidon they came. "And he healed them all" (Matthew 12:15).

The Calling of the Twelve Apostles . . . Mark 3:13-19; Luke 6:12-16

1. Why pray all night?

The selecting of the twelve apostles was a major decision in Jesus' life, and He felt the need of communion with His heavenly Father before making the choice.

2. Who were the men that He selected?

All of the twelve men were faithful disciples who had been associated with Jesus since the baptism of John (Acts 1:21, 22). There were, of course, more than these twelve who had proven themselves to be faithful. That is why it was necessary to make this choice. The word apostle means "one sent forth."

3. Where else can a list of the apostles be found?

In addition to these lists there is one to be found in Matthew 10 and another in Acts 1. The names of the apostles are the same in these lists, with the exception of the one whom Mark calls Thaddeus. Luke, in both of his accounts (Luke 6:16; Acts 1:13), calls this man Judas, the brother (or perhaps father) of James. Matthew calls him Lebbeus but explains that he was surnamed Thaddeus.

TWELVE APOSTLES

Simon (Peter)
James and John
(Boanerges)
Andrew
Philip
Bartholomew
Matthew
Thomas
James
(son of Alpheus)
Thaddeus
Simon the Canaanite
Judas Iscariot

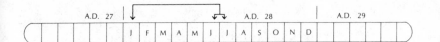

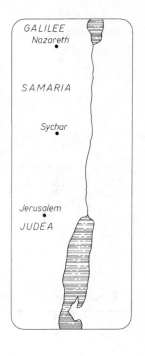

WHEN AND WHERE

It was January of A.D. 28 when Jesus launched His Galilean campaign, and it was summertime of the same year—possibly June or July—when Jesus called the twelve apostles. This one lesson is concerned with approximately five or six months, or one-seventh of Jesus' ministry.

In New Testament days, Palestine proper was divided into three provinces—Judea, Samaria, and Galilee. The latter was the most northerly of the three. This section was approximately fifty miles north and south by thirty miles east and west. The northern part of it is rugged, mountainous country. The southern part is less hilly and possesses a milder climate. In Jesus' day, Galilee was heavily populated, due in part to the rich fertility of the soil and the profitableness of the fishing business on the sea. Many of the inhabitants were of a mixed race, partly Jewish and partly heathen. The territory was governed by Herod Antipas from the time of his father's death in 4 B.C. until A.D. 39. Using the map which is provided, familiarize yourself with Galilee and the surrounding areas.

PROJECTS AND PLANS

Make a classroom-size chart of the twelve apostles. Check the various lists (Matthew 10:1-4; Mark 3:13-19; Luke 6:12-16; Acts 1:13) and other Scripture references to see by what different names the twelve were called.

Read the Sermon on the Mount in its entirety as recorded by Matthew.

THE SERMON ON THE MOUNT

TOPICS AND TEXTS

The Sermon on the Mount . . . Matthew 5:1–8:1; Luke 6:17–49

CONTEXT AND CONTINUITY

On the same day that Jesus called the twelve apostles He also taught the Sermon on the Mount. This famous lesson, containing many of the standards of His kingdom, is recorded in an abbreviated form by Luke, but in a much fuller fashion by Matthew. This is as would be expected, for Matthew gives special emphasis to the Lord's discourses. In addition to this sermon, which fills three chapters, there are six other major addresses of Jesus in Matthew: (1) the commission of the twelve (10:1-42); (2) the parables by the sea (13:1-52); (3) the message concerning humility, stumbling blocks, and forgiveness (18:1-35); (4) denunciation of hypocrisy (23:1-39); (5) Olivet discourse concerning the destruction of Jerusalem and eschatology (24:1—25:46); (6) the Great Commission (28:18-20). These discourses comprise about three-fifths of his Gospel.

The importance of the Sermon on the Mount has been recognized from the day of its delivery. Following as it does the calling of the apostles, one writer has designated it, "The Ordination Address to the Twelve." Others have referred to it as "The Compendium of Christ's Doctrine," "The Magna Charta of the Kingdom," "The Manifesto of the King." Edersheim compares it to the law of Moses. He says:

> We will not designate the "Sermon on the Mount" as the promulgation of the New Law, since that would be a far too narrow, if not erroneous, view of it. But it certainly seems to correspond to the Divine Revelation in the "Ten Words" from Mount Sinai.—Alfred Edersheim, *the Life and Times of Jesus the Messiah,* Vol. I, p. 527.

Many pages have been written concerning the contents of this sermon. One particularly good summation is by R.C. Foster:

> The sermon on the Mount gives an unparalleled analysis of the principles upon which righteousness is based; a unique series of illustrations of how these principles are to be applied to the problems of everyday life; a critical study of the motives of human conduct and their influence upon the quality of our deeds and words; a picture of the earthly and eternal results of human conduct that is transcendent. —*Studies in the Life of Christ,* pp. 287, 288.

MAJOR ADDRESSES OF JESUS IN MATTHEW'S GOSPEL

Chapters 5, 6, 7
10:1-42
13:1-52
18:1-35
23:1-39
Chapters 24 and 25
28:18-20

SERMON ON THE MOUNT

1. Introduction
2. Beatitudes
3. Influence and Duties of Kingdom Men
4. Old and New Teaching
5. Sincerity in Religion
6. Security of Heavenly Treasures
7. Concerning Judging
8. Concerning Prayer
9. The Golden Rule
10. Two Ways and False Prophets
11. Conclusion and Application

It would be profitable to study, and if possible, to memorize the following outline of the sermon:

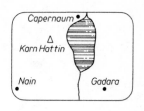

Capernaum
Δ
Karn Hattin
Nain   Gadara

   I. *Introductory Statement . . . Matthew 5:1, 2; Luke 6:17-20*
  II. *Beatitudes: Promises to Messiah's Subjects . . . Matthew 5:3-12; Luke 6:20-26*
 III. *Influence and Duties of Messiah's Subjects . . . Matthew 5:13-16*
 IV. *Relation of Messianic Teaching to Old Testament and Traditional Teaching . . . Matthew 5:17-48; Luke 6:27-30, 32-36*
  V. *Almsgiving, Prayer, and Fasting to be Performed Sincerely, Not Ostentatiously . . . Matthew 6:1-18*
 VI. *Security of Heavenly Treasures Contrasted with Earthly Anxieties . . . Matthew 6:19-34*
 VII. *Law Concerning Judging . . . Matthew 7:1-6; Luke 6:37-42*
VIII. *Concerning Prayer . . . Matthew 7:7-11*
 IX. *The Golden Rule . . . Matthew 7:12; Luke 6:31*
  X. *The Two Ways and the False Prophets . . . Matthew 7:13-23; Luke 6:43-45*
 XI. *Conclusion and Application: Two Builders . . . Matthew 7:24-29; Luke 6:46-49—J.W. McGarvey, P.Y. Pendleton, The Fourfold Gospel, pp. 227-270.*

INQUIRIES AND INSIGHTS

Introductory Statement . . . Matthew 5:1, 2; Luke 6:17-20

1. Are Matthew's and Luke's accounts reports of the same occasion?

There are differences between the accounts which have led some to conclude that they are records of separate, but similar, events. The following four differences must be reconciled if it is maintained that the two records are of the same event: (1) *Difference of place* (Matthew, a mountain; Luke, a plain); (2) *Difference of time* (Matthew has it preceding the healing of a leper; Luke, before the healing of the centurion's servant); (3) *Difference of audience* (Matthew's audience was from Galilee, Decapolis, Jerusalem, Judea, and from beyond Jordan; Luke's from all Judea, Jerusalem, and the seacoast of Tyre and Sidon); (4) *Difference of content* (Matthew's account is 111 verses in length, Luke's only thirty-three). The first two of these problems are dealt with in the "When and Where" section of this lesson. Problem three is hardly a problem at all. Neither Matthew nor Luke claims to tell whence all the audience came, only that it was a multitude representative of the entire area. The difference in length between the accounts must not be permitted to carry too much weight. The same beginning and ending, similarity in order, and identity of many expressions reinforce the position that the two accounts describe the same event.

2. Was this a sermon or a lesson?

Jesus was both a teacher and a preacher (Matthew 4:23); His method varied with His audience and purpose. Although this discourse is widely called a sermon, there is no textual evidence in favor of the view. From Matthew 5:2 it is clear that this is a lesson He taught rather than a sermon.

Beatitudes: Promises to Messiah's Subjects . . . Matthew 5:3-12; Luke 6:20-26

1. What does the word "beatitude" mean?

This word does not appear in the English Bible, but in the Latin Vulgate. It means "happy" or "blessed." Since there are many pronouncements of blessedness in both Testaments, it is proper to say there are many beatitudes in the Bible. However, since the fourth century, the word has had special reference to the promises with which Jesus began this lesson.

2. How does Luke's account of the beatitudes differ from Matthew's?

Matthew has nine beatitudes whereas Luke has only four. (There is no parallel to the third, fifth, sixth, seventh, and eighth beatitudes of Matthew). Matthew has the sayings, with the exception of the ninth one, in the third person, while all of Luke's are in the second person. Matthew states the spiritual content more clearly than Luke, but only Luke gives the contrasting woes.

3. Is any interpretation of the beatitudes necessary?

If each beatitude is considered as complete in itself and in need of no interpretation, Jesus is made to say some ridiculous things. Are all the poor to receive the Kingdom of God as Luke states? Are all who mourn—regardless of *why* or *for what* they mourn—to be comforted as Matthew records? No. Neither will the meek inherit the earth, nor the peacemakers be called the children of God, unless they bear a proper relationship to God and possess other Christian virtues. In these beatitudes Jesus was not describing separate types of Christian character. Rather, He was setting forth qualities and experiences that are to be found in the ideal person.

THE BEATITUDES

"Blessed are the poor in spirit: for theirs is the kingdom of heaven. Blessed are they that mourn: for they shall be comforted. Blessed are the meek: for they shall inherit the earth. Blessed are they which do hunger and thirst after righteousness: for they shall be filled. Blessed are the merciful: for they shall obtain mercy. Blessed are the pure in heart: for they shall see God. Blessed are the peacemakers: for they shall be called the children of God. Blessed are they which are persecuted for righteousness' sake: for theirs is the kingdom of heaven. Blessed are ye, when men shall revile you, and persecute you, and shall say all manner of evil against you falsely, for my sake. Rejoice, and be exceeding glad: for great is your reward in heaven: for so persecuted they the prophets which were before you" (Matthew 5:3-12).

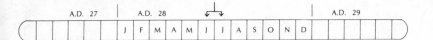

*Influence and Duties of Messiah's Subjects . . .
Matthew 5:13-16*

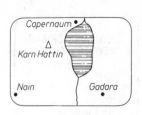

1. What qualities of salt are needed by Christans?

Salt is useful for two things—preservation and seasoning. In both ways Christians must affect the society in which they live. They must, by their godly lives, keep that society from becoming putrid with the corruption of sin. They must also, by their continuous happiness and wholesome outlook, give real spice and flavor to life.

2. How are Christians the "light of the world"?

Christ is the supreme light (John 8:12), and His followers are imperfect reflections of His glory. Light dispels darkness, destroys germs, and reveals the way; Christians have the power to dispel the darkness of sin, destroy the germs of evil, and reveal the way to glory.

*Relation of Messianic Teaching to Old Testament
and Traditional Teaching . . . Matthew 5:17-48;
Luke 6:27-30, 32-36*

1. What was Jesus' relationship to the law?

This question probably was on the minds of those in Jesus' audience as He began this lesson. Instead of dodging it, Jesus came immediately to grips with it. First He made it clear that He had not come to destroy the Old Testament but to fulfill it. Having established this, He launched into a discussion of a number of its teachings. Here as elsewhere, both by attitude and declaration, Jesus showed himself to be superior to the law.

2. Is the Old Testament still in force?

Jesus said that not one jot (smallest Hebrew letter) or tittle (a small point used as a part of some Hebrew letters) should pass from the law *until* all was fulfilled. However, He did not say that it would never pass away. From the following passages it is clear that the Old Testament is no longer in force: Jeremiah 31:31-34; Hebrews 8:7-13; Colossians 2:14; Acts 15:22-29; Ephesians 2:15.

3. How can a man's righteousness exceed that of the scribes and Pharisees?

The scribes and Pharisees considered themselves as models of righteousness, but it was a righteousness that centered in outward observances (offering sacrifices, fasting, tithing, etc.) instead of inward holiness (Matthew 23:23). Jesus demands that His followers have pure hearts which, in turn, produce pure living.

61

JEWISH TEACHINGS REVISED BY JESUS

Murder
Adultery
Divorce
False Swearing
Retaliation
Human Relations

4. How many Jewish teachings were discussed by Jesus in this sermon?
Jesus specifically discussed the following six teachings: prohibition against killing, prohibition against adultery, law regarding divorce, prohibition against false swearing, teaching concerning retaliation, teaching concerning one's attitude toward his neighbor and toward his enemy. To each of these doctrines Jesus gave a new and richer meaning. He taught that sin is committed not only by evil acts, but also by evil thoughts which precede and produce the act.

5. How can a man be perfect?
According to Matthew, Jesus requires perfection like God's in every aspect of life (5:48), whereas Luke specifies imitation of the Father in only one thing—His mercy (6:36). Apparently Jesus elaborated upon the point in His lesson, declaring that the goal of His followers should be perfection like God's in everything, and citing His mercy as an example.

The Greek word means "full grown," "complete," or "mature." Originally it was used to describe a machine that was complete in all its parts. This is the meaning of Matthew. Jesus was saying that no part of His followers' lives should be defective, that their characters should be wanting in no area. Like God, they must be consistent in everything. One way they are to show this completeness is by loving their enemies as well as their friends.

Almsgiving, Prayer, and Fasting to be Performed Sincerely, Not Ostentatiously . . . Matthew 6:1-18

1. What are alms?
The word *alms* is found fourteen times in Matthew, Luke, and Acts. To do alms is to perform deeds of kindness toward the unfortunate.

2. Did Jesus forbid all public prayer?
No, only that which is pretentiously done. Notice in Matthew 6:9, "Our Father" at the beginning of a public prayer taught by Jesus. Notice also Matthew 26:26 and John 11:41-43 where Jesus prayed publicly, and Acts 4:23-31 and 12:5 where the early church did the same.

3. Is this the Lord's Prayer?
More correctly it is the "Disciples' Prayer." It is not a prayer which Christ prayed, but one by which He taught His disciples to pray. The prayer of Jesus recorded in John 17 can more appropriately be identified as personally *His*.

MODEL PRAYER

"Our Father which art in heaven, Hallowed be thy name. Thy kingdom come. Thy will be done in earth, as it is in heaven. Give us this day our daily bread. And forgive us our debts, as we forgive our debtors. And lead us not into temptation, but deliver us from evil: For thine is the kingdom, and the power, and the glory, for ever. Amen" (Matthew 6:9-13).

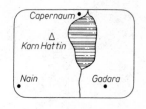

4. Should Christians fast?

Christians should fast when the act is the natural expression of the grief or the concern of their hearts. They should not fast to demonstrate their superior piety or to call attention to themselves. See Matthew 4:2; Acts 13:2; Acts 14:23; and 1 Corinthians 7:5.

Security of Heavenly Treasures Contrasted With Earthly Anxieties . . . Matthew 6:19-34

1. How can treasure be laid up in Heaven?

Treasures are laid up in Heaven by the merciful acts performed and the sacrificial gifts presented in the name of Christ. Such treasures are not laid *at* Heaven's door as the price of admission, but are amassed *in* Heaven by those who have already gained the right to enter by the blood of Christ.

2. What is Mammon?

Originally this word was spelled with only one "m" where the two are now together and had a good meaning—"to entrust." In time the word came to mean "that in which one puts his trust" rather than "that which is entrusted to another." Spelled with a capital "M" it came to be used as the name of the god of riches.

3. Is "take no thought" a correct translation?

William Barclay has written:

> It is not ordinary, prudent foresight, such as becomes a man, that Jesus forbids; it is worry. Jesus is not advocating a shiftless, thriftless, reckless, thoughtless, improvident attitude to life: He is forbidding a care-worn, worried fear, which takes all the joy out of life."—William Barclay, *Gospel of Matthew,* p. 258.

"Be not anxious" is a better rendering of the Greek word.

4. What did Jesus mean: "Sufficient unto the day is the evil thereof"?

Since each day produces its own cares and anxieties, it is best to use today's strength for today's trials without borrowing trouble from tomorrow. The same God who helps conquer today's problems will also help conquer tomorrow's.

Law Concerning Judging . . . Matthew 7:1-6; Luke 6:37-42

1. Is all judging prohibited?

"Judge not" is a general command which must be interpreted in the light of other Scriptures. It does not forbid all judging, only that which is hasty and

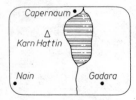

harsh. It seeks to eliminate a fault-finding spirit that condemns without due examination and without charity toward the offender. Notice the sixth verse of this same chapter in Matthew where judging is commanded. See also the following passages: Matthew 7:15-20; 2 Thessalonians 3:6; Titus 3:10. In understanding this command, as well as many other Bible passages, a little common sense is needed.

2. What is a mote? A beam?
A mote is any light substance such as a tiny chip or a speck of wood dust. A beam is a large piece of timber. The illustration has an element of humor. It presents a man with a log jutting out of his eye endeavoring to get a speck out of another's eye.

3. How does Luke 6:38 fit into the context?
If instead of harshly judging others an attempt is made to help them by giving them what they need, then with this same measurement will blessings be returned. With what standard we judge others, we will be judged; with what standards we aid others, we will be aided.

Concerning Prayer . . . Matthew 7:7-11

1. Will a mere asking secure anything a Christian wants?
A prayer, in order to receive an affirmative answer from God, must be offered in a proper spirit; it must be for such as is consistent with the will of God; it must be for that which will prove a blessing to its receiver. The Greek verbs used here are present imperatives and should be rendered, "Keep on asking, seeking, knocking." Perseverance in prayer is being taught.

2. To whom did Jesus compare God?
God is compared to an earthly father to whom certain requests are made by his son. Similar words are found in Luke 11:9-13 where three requests are cited: the bread and fish of Matthew's account plus a request for an egg.

3. Are all humans evil?
Man is not evil by nature but by choice. All who reach the age of accountability eventually make a wrong choice and lose their moral innocence. There is a sense in which they then may be called evil. (See Romans 3:23 and 1 John 1:8-10.) Jesus' reasoning is: "If fallible human fathers will answer reasonable requests of their children, surely the infallible heavenly Father can be expected to do the same."

The Golden Rule . . . Matthew 7:12; Luke 6:31

1. Was Jesus the first to teach this principle?
This rule had already been taught, in a negative form, by others (Buddha, Confucius, Socrates, Hillel, Tobias), but Jesus was the first to teach it in its positive form.

2. Why is it called the Golden Rule?
As gold is more precious than other metals, so is this superior to other rules. Barclay says that this is very probably the most universally famous statement that Jesus ever made. He calls it "the Everest of all ethical teaching."—William Barclay, *Gospel of Matthew*, pp. 276, 277.

> **GOLDEN RULE**
>
> "Therefore all things whatsoever ye would that men should do to you, do ye even so to them: for this is the law and the prophets" (Matthew 7:12).

The Two Ways and the False Prophets . . . Matthew 7:13-23; Luke 6:43-45

1. To what did Jesus compare life?
In Matthew 7:13, 14, Jesus compared life to two roads, one broad and the other narrow. To enter the wide gate and walk the broad way to destruction, no effort is required, no discipline is necessary, and no thought is needed. In contrast, the way that leads to life can be entered and followed only with forethought and diligence.

2. How are false prophets to be recognized?
A tree must be judged, not by its appearance, but by the fruit it yields. In like manner men are not to be judged by their claims, but by their conduct. One who claims to be a prophet must substantiate his claim by what he produces.

3. Are the speakers in Matthew 7:22 telling the truth?
That these workers of iniquity claimed to have performed miracles should not be taken as proof that they actually had done so. Jesus said to them (v. 23), "I never knew you." It is certain that if Jesus didn't know them they hadn't performed miracles.

Conclusion and Application: Two Builders . . . Matthew 7:24-29; Luke 6:46-49

1. How did Jesus conclude this famous lesson?
Jesus brought this lesson to a conclusion with an illustration about two builders, one who wisely built on a rock foundation and one who foolishly built on the sand. The wise builder is secure, the foolish, a failure. Notice the claim of Jesus that a man's attitude toward His sayings determines whether he is a wise or foolish builder.

2. Why were the people astonished?

Matthew cites two reasons: (1) the message He taught, and (2) the manner of His teaching. After nearly two thousand years the world is still thrilled by the wonder of this famous lesson.

WHEN AND WHERE

Assuming the sermon recorded by Matthew is the same as that recorded by Luke, it then must be determined which, if either of the two authors, has placed it in proper chronological order. An almost unanimous consensus favors Luke's arrangement. Matthew arranged his Gospel topically, grouping examples of Christ's teaching and healing. Apparently he has taken this sermon out of its time sequence and placed it in the early part of his Gospel to give his readers an introduction to the teaching of Jesus. In this way Matthew prepares his readers for that which follows.

Matthew states that the sermon was taught on a mount, whereas Luke, some claim, says it was taught on a plain. Actually Luke doesn't say where He taught the sermon, only that He came down to the plain after calling the twelve (see Luke 6:17). Perhaps He then returned to the mountain and taught there. Another possible solution to this hypothetical problem is that the plain of Luke's Gospel was a plateau in a mountain. There the multitude assembled and was instructed by Jesus who had gone up a little higher in the mountain so as to be seen when He sat down and taught.

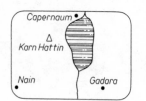

As to which mountain it was, there is a great difference of opinion. From the days of the Crusades, Karn Hattin (Horns of Hattin), located about four or five miles southwest of Tiberias, has been the choice of many. Others reject this mountain as unsuitable, pointing out other, more likely places in the area.

PROJECTS AND PLANS

Plan a debate on the subject: "Resolved that the Sermon on the Mount of Matthew 5—7 is the same as the Sermon on the Plain of Luke 6."

Read chapters 1 through 4 of the Introductory Remarks in *Notes on the Parables* by R.C. Trench, pp. 3-26.

FURTHER PREACHING AND TEACHING IN GALILEE

TOPICS AND TEXTS

Healing the Centurion's Servant . . . Matthew 8:5-13; Luke 7:1-10
Raising the Widow's Son at Nain . . . Luke 7:11-17
John's Doubt and Jesus' Sermon on John . . . Matthew 11:2-19; Luke 7:18-35
Condemnation of Unbelief of Surrounding Cities: The Great Invitation . . . Matthew 11:20-30
Scene and Sermon in the House of Simon the Pharisee . . . Luke 7:36-50
Second Preaching Tour of Galilee . . . Luke 8:1-3
Blasphemous Charge of Pharisees That Jesus was in League With the Devil . . . Matthew 12:22-37; Mark 3:19-30*
Scribes and Pharisees Demand a Sign . . . Matthew 12:38-45*
Attempt of Jesus' Mother and Brethren to Interrupt His Ministry . . . Matthew 12:46-50; Mark 3:31-35; Luke 8:19-21
The Great Sermon in Parables . . . Matthew 13:1-35; Mark 4:1-34; Luke 8:4-18
Further Private Instruction in Parables . . . Matthew 13:36-53
   * To be considered in Lesson Fifteen.

CONTEXT AND CONTINUITY

After teaching the Sermon on the Mount, Jesus returned to Capernaum. Upon His arrival, He was met by some of the elders of the city who asked Him to heal the servant of a certain centurion who had endeared himself to the people by erecting a synagogue for them. Because of the man's great faith, Jesus answered their request.

The next day Jesus, accompanied by a large crowd, traveled to the city of Nain, a distance of some twenty-five miles. As they approached the city from the northeast, they met a funeral procession of a young man, the only son of a widow of that city. Jesus stopped the sad procession and, to the great astonishment of all, commanded the young man to arise. Life returned to the corpse, and the command was obeyed! After this stupendous miracle, Jesus probably remained in the vicinity of Nain for several days, teaching and preaching. He then returned to Capernaum.

At this time the disciples of John arrived with their leader's question concerning the identity of Jesus. It was a question born not so much of doubt about Jesus as of impatience with Him. Christ's answer introduced a sermon about John and his greatness. This was followed by a message of condemnation of the cities of that area because of their unbelief.

At the invitation of a Pharisee named Simon, Jesus went into his house to dine. While there, an unnamed woman of the street entered, washed His feet with her tears, and anointed them with ointment. The Pharisee's attitude toward Jesus for permitting the woman to so act called forth from Him a sermon concerning forgiveness and genuine love.

Luke states that Jesus then went throughout the area, preaching and showing the glad tidings of the kingdom in every city and village. On this, the second preaching tour of Galilee, Jesus was accompanied by the twelve apostles, certain named women, and many other disciples.

While Jesus and His followers were working so strenuously, His mother and brethren came and tried to interrupt His ministry. They felt He was working too hard and risking what we would call a "breakdown." Soon Jesus left Capernaum (where He had returned after the second preaching tour), sat in a ship in the Sea of Galilee, and taught a number of parables to a great multitude on the shore. When He had finished teaching He was requested by His disciples to explain the meaning of one of the parables, the one about the tares. After doing so, He gave them some additional private instruction.

INQUIRIES AND INSIGHTS

Healing the Centurion's Servant ... Matthew 8:5-13; Luke 7:1-10

1. What was a centurion?

A centurion was an officer in the Roman army who had the command of one hundred men. This particular one, although a Gentile, had come to have great respect for the Jewish religion. Other centurions are mentioned in Matthew 27 and Acts 10, 22, 23, and 27.

2. Did the centurion actually go to Jesus?

There is a difference between Matthew's and Luke's accounts. Matthew represents the centurion as going to Jesus personally. Luke says that he sent elders of the Jews and then later some friends to speak to Jesus. Perhaps he did both. He may first have approached Jesus through others and then on his own.

3. What is the meaning of Jesus' prediction in Matthew 8:11?

Observing the faith of this Roman centurion, Jesus took occasion to speak of the future conversion of other Gentiles. The phrase, "east and west," was used by the Jews to describe the entire world.

Raising the Widow's Son at Nain ... Luke 7:11-17

1. What were the burial customs of the Jews?

In order to avoid unpleasant odors and possible ceremonial pollution (Numbers 19:11-22), it was customary to bury the dead on the day of their death. The body was prepared by cutting the hair

> CENTURIONS
>
> Matthew 8
> Matthew 27
> Acts 10
> Acts 22
> Acts 23
> Acts 27

and nails, washing, anointing, and then wrapping in a cloth. Coffins were rarely used. Instead the body was carried to the grave on a bier, perhaps better described as a wicker basket. There was great lamenting by friends, relatives, neighbors, and professional mourners. The crying was accompanied by flutes, cymbals, and trumpets as the group went to the burial place. It was this kind of procession that Jesus stopped and turned back to Nain.

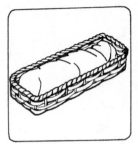

Wicker bier

2. Why did Jesus touch the bier?
Jesus touched the bier as a signal to the bearers to halt. It may also have served as a suggestion to His disciples that He intended to use His power to help this bereaved widow.

3. Had Jesus previously raised the dead?
There is no record of His having done so. A check of the Old Testament will reveal that this is the first recorded instance of a dead person's being restored to life since the days of Elisha (2 Kings 13:21). It is little wonder that the people were filled with fear.

John's Doubt and Jesus' Sermon on John . . . Matthew 11:2-19; Luke 7:18-35

1. What motivated John to ask his question?
Luke says that the disciples of John showed their leader "all these things." The phrase evidently alludes to Jesus' teaching and miracles, including the raising of the dead. Matthew makes a similar reference (11:2). With so much evidence indicating that Jesus was the Messiah, it is difficult to believe that John's question came from doubt. Apparently John asked the question to force Jesus to declare himself and establish the kind of kingdom that John and the rest of the Jews expected.

2. How did Jesus answer John's question?
In the presence of John's messengers, Jesus performed a number of cures and spoke of others He had wrought. He then sent the messengers back to their leader to tell him all they had seen and heard. In effect Jesus said: "John, the works that I am performing should answer your question. If I were not the Messiah, could I do such things?"

3. To what did Jesus compare His and John's ministries?
Jesus likened His generation unto two groups of children, one of which desired to play while the other refused to do so. Although the first group changed its game from one extreme to another,

69

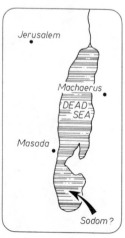

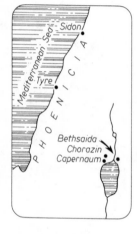

A.D. 27 | A.D. 28 | A.D. 29

J F M A M J J A S O N D

the second group would not cooperate. Similarly John's and Jesus' ministries had been different, and yet neither had been accepted by many of the Jews.

4. Was John in the kingdom?

From Jesus' statement, "He that is least in the kingdom of heaven is greater than he," it is clear that John was not in the kingdom. The reason is that the kingdom of heaven ("of God," according to Luke) had not yet begun. Jesus' message, like John's, was that the kingdom was "at hand" and that preparation should be made for its coming. McGarvey and Pendleton state: "The least born of the Holy Spirit (John 1:12, 13 and 3:5) is greater than the greatest born of women. They are greater in station, privilege and knowledge."—J.W. McGarvey, P.Y. Pendleton, the Fourfold Gospel, p. 283.

Condemnation of Unbelief of Surrounding Cities: The Great Invitation ... Matthew 11:20-30

1. What miracles did Jesus perform in these cities?

Capernaum was the site of several of His wonders (Matthew 8:14-17; Mark 2:1-12; Luke 7:1-10; John 4:46-54). No mention is made in the Gospels of any miracle having been performed by Him in Chorazin or Bethsaida. Jesus' statement, however, makes it clear that there had been some. We are reminded of John 20:30: "Many other signs truly did Jesus in the presence of his disciples, which are not written in this book."

2. How will it be more tolerable?

Tyre and Sidon were Phoenician cities that had not been blessed by the presence and power of Christ. (He later visited in the vicinity of these cities and performed a miracle; see Matthew 15:21-28 and Mark 7:24-30). Sodom had been one of the cities of the plain which had been utterly destroyed by God in Abraham's time because of its extreme wickedness. Jesus did not state that these wicked cities would escape punishment in the judgment. He said that the degree of their punishment would be less, comparatively, than that of the more favored cities. The standard of judgment here as elsewhere in the Bible is one of opportunity.

3. For what did Jesus give thanks?

Jesus thanked His Father because He had hidden certain things from the wise and had revealed them unto the simple and the humble. The text

70

does not state how God did the hiding. To harmonize this passage with the nature of God as revealed elsewhere in His Word, we must conclude that He did it through the natural operation of their own evil hearts and corrupted minds.

4. Had all things been delivered unto Jesus?
As yet they had not, but He spoke by anticipation. It was not until after His ascension and coronation that all power was given unto Him by the Father.

5. To whom did Jesus extend this invitation?
Although Jesus spoke directly and specifically to those in His audience, the full scope of the invitation includes the burdened and oppressed in all the world in all ages.

Scene and Sermon in the House of Simon the Pharisee . . . Luke 7:36-50

1. What was Simon's motive?
The motive of this man's inviting Jesus into his house is not revealed. His lack of genuine hospitality, however, leads us to conclude that his intentions were not purely good. Possibly he invited Jesus into his house that he might observe Him at close range.

2. Who was this woman?
Her identity is unknown. Some confuse her with Mary Magdalene, but there is no evidence to support this view. It is based upon the coincidence that Mary Magdalene is introduced by Luke in the next paragraph of his account (8:1-3). Notice, however, that she is there introduced as a new character. Others, with equally slight evidence, identify her as Mary of Bethany, sister of Martha and Lazarus.

3. How did Jesus answer Simon's accusation?
Simon implied two things in his criticism: (1) Jesus had been unable to discern the character of this woman and was therefore no prophet; (2) If He had known her character, He would not have permitted her to touch Him. Jesus answered him by the use of two of His favorite teaching methods: a parable (this one with an obvious application), and a question that required a self-incriminating answer. Although not the first to use either of these methods, Jesus became the unequaled master of them both.

4. Was Simon better than this woman?
From the parable of the two debtors (vv. 41, 42), one might conclude that Jesus affirmed that Simon

71

was in need of only a little forgiveness, whereas the woman was in need of much. This, of course, Jesus did not teach. His parable was designed to help Simon who *felt the need* of less forgiveness, and who would hence love less if forgiven.

5. How did Jesus reward the woman?

As a reward for her faith, Jesus gave her the greatest of all gifts, the forgiveness of sins. This was accompanied by that marvelous peace which comes to the forgiven.

Second Preaching Tour of Galilee . . . Luke 8:1-3

1. When did Jesus conduct His first tour?

His first preaching tour of Galilee is recorded in Matthew 4:23-25 and in parallel passages in Mark and Luke. It occurred shortly after the launching of His great Galilean campaign, in the early part of A.D. 28, the second year of His ministry.

2. Who accompanied Jesus on this second tour?

Jesus' entourage consisted of the twelve apostles, certain women whose names are given, and other disciples. Among the women were Mary Magdalene, Joanna, the wife of Chuza (steward or administrator of Herod Antipas), and a certain Susanna, about whom nothing more is known. Mary Magdalene is remembered as the first person to see the resurrected Christ (Mark 16:9).

Blasphemous Charge of Pharisees That Jesus Was in League With the Devil . . . Matthew 12:22-37; Mark 3:19-30

This event is difficult to place chronologically. Matthew has it after the teaching and healing in Galilee which followed the healing of a man with a withered hand. Mark has it following these same events and immediately after the calling of the twelve apostles (not recorded by Matthew). Luke places it much later, during Jesus' Judean ministry, immediately following His discourse on prayer. To complicate the matter further, Matthew has a similar event recorded in 9:32-34 (which apparently is out of chronological order). Some feel there were three separate but similar events (Matthew 12 and parallel text in Mark 3; Matthew 9; Luke 11); others, that there were but two events (Matthew 12, Mark 3, and Luke 11; Matthew 9). The evidence seems to favor this latter view. Whether the Matthew-Mark placement or Luke's is correct is still another problem. We prefer Luke's, thus this event will be discussed in Lesson Fifteen.

Scribes and Pharisees Demand a Sign . . . Matthew 12:38-45

This event, like the preceding one, is placed by Luke at a later time. Evidently his account, instead of Matthew's, is chronological. This event, therefore, will also be considered in Lesson Fifteen.

Attempt of Jesus' Mother and Brethren to Interrupt His Ministry . . . Matthew 12:46-50; Mark 3:31-35; Luke 8:19-21

1. Who were Jesus' brethren?
This question is answered in Lesson Ten.

2. Why had they come?
Mark 3:21 contains the answer to this question. The text speaks of "his friends," but the Greek actually reads, "they who were of him," i.e., His relatives. These relatives (apparently the same as those mentioned in Mark 3:31-35 and parallel texts) came to lay hold on Jesus because they felt He was beside himself. This explains why Jesus refused to go out to them. The expression, "beside himself," means, "the absence of self-possessedness." They felt His zeal for God was consuming Him, and they wanted to make Him rest.

3. Who, according to Jesus, are His relatives?
Jesus declared that those who do the will of His Father are to Him as a brother, sister, or mother. Spiritual ties are thus raised above physical ones. All who unduly exalt Mary, the mother of Jesus, should study this text.

The Great Sermon in Parables . . . Matthew 13:1-35; Mark 4:1-34; Luke 8:4-18

1. What is a parable?
The word is derived from two Greek words which literally mean "to throw alongside." A parable is a story "thrown by the side" of a spiritual truth to help make its meaning clear. Although Jesus was not the first to employ parables in teaching, He is the only user of them in the New Testament.

2. How many parables did Jesus teach in this sermon?
Matthew records four as having been taught to the multitude (also four later ones, in private to the disciples). Mark includes three, two of which are the same as Matthew's. Luke shares only one, the parable of the sower, which is recorded in both of the other synoptics. This brings the total to five different parables.

> "Is not this the carpenter's son? is not his mother called Mary? and his brethren, James, and Joses, and Simon, and Judas? And his sisters, are they not all with us? Whence then hath this man all these things?" (Matthew 13:55, 56).

> **PARABLE**
>
> para—"alongside"
> ballo—"throw"

> **PARABLES HERE**
>
> "The Sower"
> "The Tares"
> "The Mustard Seed"
> "The Leaven"
> "The Harvest"

73

3. Why did Jesus teach in parables?

Jesus explained that His purpose in using parables was two-fold, the two at first appearing to be contradictory. For the simple-hearted and trusting, the parable was a means of clarifying deep spiritual truths. For the arrogant and haughty who did not desire to learn, the parable served only to obscure the truth.

4. What is the teaching of each of these parables?

The Sower. Not all who hear the Word make the same response to it: some do not understand it; some quickly accept it and then as quickly reject it when tribulation or persecution arises; some accept it only to have it choked out by the care of this world and the deceitfulness of riches; others understand and internalize the Word with the result that it bears fruit in their lives.

The Seed Growing Secretly. As a seed has an orderly process of growth, from the blade to the ear to the full corn in the ear, so the Word of God grows in a man's heart according to a similar, definite plan. Man does not fully comprehend the growth process whether it is of natural or spiritual seed. Eventually harvesttime comes.

The Tares. In the world, growing side by side, are wheat (the children of the kingdom) and tares (the children of the wicked one). In the harvest (end of the world) the tares will be gathered and burned (Hell), and the wheat will be gathered and placed in the barn (Heaven).

The Grain of Mustard Seed. There is a great difference in size between a mustard seed and its mature plant. Similarly, the kingdom, which had a small beginning, has now grown to a tremendous size.

The Leaven. The gospel, like leaven, is noted for its permeating quality. Wherever it goes, its influence is felt in every life, family, and community it touches.

Further Private Instruction in Parables . . . Matthew 13:36-53

1. What was the purpose of this private instruction?

Matthew relates how a question of the disciples concerning the interpretation of the parable of the tares brought on this teaching session. Jesus then used the occasion to give additional instruction to His disciples. Realizing His time was limited, Jesus took advantage of every opportunity to prepare His apostles and other close disciples for the leadership which was to be theirs.

2. What parables did Jesus teach at this time?

The Hidden Treasure. The kingdom, with its offer of eternal life, is more valuable than any treasure. To attain it, no sacrifice is too great.

The Pearl of Great Price. Here is another parable concerning the great value of the kingdom. In the former parable the man accidently found the treasure, whereas in this one he sought it diligently.

The Net. As a net cast into the sea may catch both good and bad fish, so the church will have good and bad people. The end of the world will be the time of separating the wicked from the just.

The Householder. As a householder will employ both old and new possessions when they are needed, so every disciple should not keep hidden the truth he has learned, whether it is old or new, but should bring it forth and use it at proper times.

PRIVATE PARABLES

"The Treasure"
"The Pearl"
"The Drawnet"
"The Householder"

WHEN AND WHERE

The events of this lesson happened in the late summer and fall of A.D. 28 (781 U.C.), the second year of Jesus' ministry. Beyond this general dating it is impossible to be specific, for there are no references to time in the material covered in this lesson.

The following cities are mentioned in this lesson: Capernaum, Nain, Chorazin, Bethsaida, Tyre, and Sidon. Locate these on the map.

PROJECTS AND PLANS

Using a concordance, check the various references to the centurions mentioned in the Scriptures. As a whole, were they good or evil men? Be prepared to discuss this subject.

Read "At Geresa—The Healing of the Demonised"—Alfred Edersheim, *The Life and Times of Jesus the Messiah,* Vol. I, pp. 606-615.

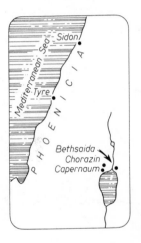

GOING AND SENDING

TOPICS AND TEXTS

A Conversation About Following Jesus . . . Matthew 8:18-22; Luke 9:57-62
Stilling the Tempest . . . Matthew 8:23-27; Mark 4:35-41; Luke 8:22-25
Healing the Gadarene Demoniacs . . . Matthew 8:28-34; Mark 5:1-20; Luke 8:26-39
Healing of Woman Who Touched Christ's Garment, and Raising of Jairus' Daughter . . . Matthew 9:18-26; Mark 5:21-43; Luke 8:40-56
Healing of Two Blind Men and a Dumb Demoniac . . . Matthew 9:27-34
Last Visit to Nazareth . . . Matthew 13:54-58; Mark 6:1-6
The Twelve Sent on Evangelistic Campaign: Jesus' Third Tour of Galilee . . . Matthew 9:35—11:1; Mark 6:7-13; Luke 9:1-6
Herod's Conscience Stricken: Confusion of John the Baptist and Jesus . . . Matthew 14:1-12; Mark 6:14-29; Luke 9:7-9

CONTEXT AND CONTINUITY

It is not possible to determine which was the busiest day of our Lord's ministry, but the one on which He taught the seaside parables deserves consideration. After teaching the multitude from a boat, He entered a house where He gave further instruction to His disciples. Then, "when the even was come" (Mark 4:35), He gave commandment to His disciples "to depart unto the other side" (Matthew 8:18). Before entering the boat He had a conversation with three men, a scribe and two disciples. Then He set sail for the eastern shore of the Sea of Galilee. Exhausted from the strenuous activities of the day, He fell asleep in the boat, only to be awakened by the passionate pleading of His disciples, "Lord, save us: we perish" (Matthew 8:25). Arising, He majestically rebuked the winds and the sea, causing a great calm.

The time when they arrived on the eastern shore is not easy to determine. There are two possibilities, each based on the uncertain time of departure. Mark's statement, "when the even was come," is not clear as to whether the Jewish first evening (3:00—6:00 p.m.) or second evening (6:00—9:00 p.m.) is meant. If the reference is to the first evening, the arrival would have been on the same day, for the crossing of the sea, even allowing for a delay because of the storm, would not have taken all that evening and night. That it was daytime when He arrived is based on the statement that He was seen afar off (Mark 5:6). On the other hand, if the departure was during the second evening perhaps the arrival was on the next day. Edersheim favors the former view, which appears to harmonize better with the texts. If this is correct, then it was almost dusk when Jesus was met by two demoniacs of the area. That time of day would have enveloped the incident with an eeriness which would have further etched

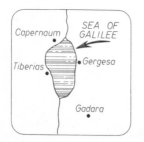

Capernaum — SEA OF GALILEE
Tiberias — Gergesa
Gadara

the drama upon the memories of those who witnessed it. Jesus expelled the demons from the men, bringing to an end a very busy day.

The following morning, some of the citizens of the area, having been aroused late on the previous evening, came to Jesus requesting that He leave their country. They were unhappy with Him because He had indirectly caused the death of two thousand of their pigs by allowing them to be possessed of the demons He had expelled from the two men. Setting sail, He and His disciples returned to the western side of the lake, probably arriving in the vicinity of Capernaum about noon. There He was met by a great crowd of people. In the multitude was a ruler of a synagogue who urged Jesus to go with him and heal his only daughter, a girl of about twelve. As He went, He met and healed a woman who had suffered from hemorrhaging for twelve years. He continued His journey to Jairus' house (apparently in Capernaum), where He restored life to the girl who by this time had died.

Sometime after this, two blind men, addressing Him with the Messianic title, "Son of David," asked for and received His mercy. Then a dumb man with a devil was brought to Him, and He cast out the devil, restoring the man's speech.

If there were two rejections at Nazareth (a point which is subject to debate; see Lesson Seven), apparently the second one occurred at this time. At least Mark places it here. After this Jesus began His third tour of Galilee. Upon seeing the vast unreached multitudes, He commissioned the twelve apostles to go and labor with the lost sheep of the house of Israel, while He continued His own labors.

During this period of intensive evangelism, John the Baptist was put to death by Herod Antipas. Word of this great tragedy was brought to Jesus by John's disciples, who apparently arrived in Capernaum with their sad news at approximately the same time the apostles returned from their successful mission. It was therefore a time of mixed emotions: a time of sadness because the great Harbinger had been silenced; a time of rejoicing because of the victories that had been won.

INQUIRIES AND INSIGHTS

A Conversation About Following Jesus . . . Matthew 8:18-22; Luke 9:57-62

1. How many men spoke to Jesus on this occasion?
Matthew mentions only two but Luke tells us

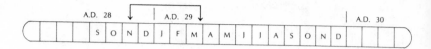
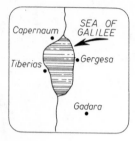

Capernaum

SEA OF GALILEE

Tiberias • Gergesa

Gadara

about three—the two of Matthew plus another man. Obviously there were three (or perhaps more), each writer mentioning those whom he considered important.

2. How can the dead bury the dead?

Since it is impossible for the dead to bury the dead literally, we must seek for a figurative meaning. "Let the spiritually dead (those who are not my disciples) bury the physically dead," appears to be the meaning. Some question if the father of this man was yet dead. According to this view the man's request was to remain at home until his father died.

3. What conclusion can be reached from these conversations?

No matter how plausible one's excuse may sound, there is no acceptable reason for not following Jesus.

Stilling the Tempest . . . Matthew 8:23-27; Mark 4:35-41; Luke 8:22-25

1. At what time of day did this event occur?

This question is discussed in the section, "Context and Continuity." Probably it was during the first Jewish evening (3:00—6:00 p.m.).

2. Why did Mark mention the "other little ships"?

These ships no doubt belonged to some of Jesus' disciples who wanted to follow Him. It has been suggested that Mark, the author of this statement, was in one of them. If so, he was a witness to this miracle.

3. Why rebuke the winds and the waves?

This is one of a group of miracles in which Jesus demonstrated His power over the forces of nature. His speaking to the elements is an example of personification. Jesus treated them like people and reproved them because of their actions. Barclay has an interesting rendering of Mark 4:39: "He spoke sternly to the wind and said to the sea, 'Be silent! Be muzzled!' and the wind sank to rest and there was a great calm."—William Barclay, *The Gospel of Mark*, p. 113.

Healing the Gadarene Demoniacs . . . Matthew 8:28-34; Mark 5:1-20; Luke 8:26-39

1. Where did this miracle occur?

Manuscript differences create a problem for us. The place is called Gadara, Gerasa, and Gergesa. Considering the evidence, it appears that the scene of the miracle was near the small town of Gergesa, midway between the north and south ends of the sea, on its eastern side, near the mouth of Wady Semak. Gadara was a city, some sixteen miles away, which gave its name to the entire area. The variant reading, "Gerasa," is thought to be a manuscript error.

2. How many demoniacs were healed?
Matthew mentions two; Mark and Luke, one. Since neither of the latter two claims there was *only one* man, we conclude there were actually two. For some unknown reason (perhaps the greater prominence of the one) Mark and Luke omit any reference to the second man.

3. What does the Bible teach about demons?
The expression, "demon possession," which is widely used to describe the New Testament phenomenon, is not a Bible term. It comes from the writings of Josephus. In the New Testament, men are described as having an unclean spirit or a demon, or more often, as being *demonised*. This term is found nine times in Matthew, three times in Mark, fourteen times in Luke, and six times in John. The Old Testament doesn't refer to the condition (unless Saul is an exception; 1 Samuel 16), nor does the Apocrypha. John's Gospel records no cases of demon expulsion, but from such texts as 7:20, 8:40-52, and 10:19-21, it is apparent he recognized that men could be possessed by demons. The concept of demon possession cannot be equated with physical illness, for both are mentioned, often in the same texts. Nor did the Jews confuse it with mental illness (Matthew 4:24). Since small children could have evil spirits (Mark 9:14-29) the cause was not always moral. As to the origin and exact nature of demons, the Bible is not clear. Evidently demon possession was restricted to the period surrounding the life of Jesus on earth, and was the result of the devil's bold attempt to meet and defeat Jesus in battle.

4. Were these men insane?
Although being demonised is not to be equated with insanity, it is obvious from the irrational actions of these men prior to the exorcism, and from the description of their changed state afterwards (Mark 5:15; Luke 8:35), that one of the effects of the demons (in their case, at least) was insanity.

5. Why did Jesus honor the demons' request?
His motive is not known. Probably it had something to do with the fact that the swine were un-

DEMONS IN THE GOSPELS	
Matthew —	9
Mark —	3
Luke —	14
John —	6

clean animals and should not have been kept by Jews, nor by Gentiles in Jewish territory.

6. Why the request of the citizens?
Like the Philippians mentioned in Acts 16, who cared more for money than for the well-being of a maiden, the Gadarenes could not appreciate the good that had been done to two fellow human beings. They were thinking primarily about the loss of two thousand pigs.

Healing of Woman Who Touched Christ's Garment, and Raising of Jairus' Daughter . . . Matthew 9:18-26; Mark 5:21-43; Luke 8:40-56

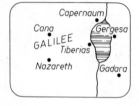

1. Was the girl already dead when Jairus came to Jesus?
Mark quotes Jairus as saying, "My little daughter lieth at the point of death." Luke uses the third person: "He had only one daughter . . . and she lay a dying." Matthew, however, represents Jairus as saying, "My daughter is *even now dead.*" Mark and Luke tell of a later visit by certain ones from Jairus' home with news of the girl's death, but Matthew makes no mention of it. Obviously the girl was still alive when Jairus left his home, but died before Jesus' arrival. Matthew condensed his account but still retained the essential truth.

2. Was the woman healed without the knowledge of Jesus?
No, nor is there any indication in the texts that she was. In fact, just the opposite is true. Both Mark and Luke state that no sooner had she laid her hand in faith upon the hem of His garment than Jesus indicated that He knew what had happened. Nor should it be assumed that He was in ignorance concerning the identity of the woman. His inquiry concerning who touched Him was not to secure information but to develop faith.

3. What did Jesus mean in His statement concerning virtue going out of Him?
The Greek word means "power." He knew that healing power had gone out of Him.

4. Was the girl really dead?
Jesus said, "The maid is not dead, but sleepeth." These words should not be taken literally, for the texts make it clear that she was actually dead. His meaning is that the girl had not ceased to exist, that her spirit was still alive, that she would soon live again. Notice the same figure in other passages: John 11:11; Acts 7:60; 1 Corinthians 15:6, 18, 51; 1 Thessalonians 4:13-15; 2 Peter 3:4.

Healing of Two Blind Men and a Dumb Demoniac . . . Matthew 9:27-34

1. Why did Jesus touch the eyes of the blind men?
He probably wanted to indicate to them that the healing power proceeded from Him.

2. To what event in Jesus' life is the healing of the dumb demoniac similar?
On one or two occasions (see discussion in Lesson Nine), Jesus performed a similar miracle with comparable criticism from His antagonists. Unable to deny His miracles, and unwilling to accept that He performed them by the power of God, they accused Him of being in league with Satan.

Last Visit to Nazareth . . . Matthew 13:54-58; Mark 6:1-6

1. Why were the people of Nazareth astonished?
They recognized Jesus. They had known Him as a humble carpenter (Mark 6:3), and knew that the other members of His family were just normal people, so they couldn't account for His superhuman ability.

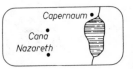

2. Did Jesus have brothers and sisters?
He had four half-brothers and at least two half-sisters, the children of Joseph and Mary. These two passages invalidate the doctrine of the perpetual virginity of Mary.

3. Why didn't Jesus perform many works in Nazareth?
Matthew states (v. 58) and Mark implies (v. 6) that the reason was the unbelief of the people. This doesn't mean His power was limited by their lack of faith. He could have performed miracles but chose not to. The purpose of miracles would have gone unaccomplished because of the people's prejudice against Him. "He did, therefore, only those things which were the proper work of benevolence, and which could not easily be charged on the devil."—William Barclay, *The Gospel of Matthew,* p. 150.

The Twelve Sent on Evangelistic Campaign: Jesus' Third Tour of Galilee . . . Matthew 9:35–11:1; Mark 6:7-13; Luke 9:1-6

1. Did Jesus heal every sickness and every disease?
The American Standard translation of Matthew 9:35 reads "all *manner* of disease and all *manner*

81

Palestinian sheep

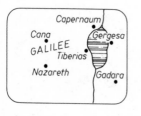

Capernaum
Cana
GALILEE Gergesa
Tiberias
Nazareth Gadara

of sickness." This more correctly expresses the thought of the passage.

2. Why compare the people to sheep?
The helplessness of sheep is proverbial: they depend upon others for food and water; they are easily lost; they lack the instinct for finding their way home; they are almost totally unequipped to defend themselves. The people whom Jesus saw about Him were like such sheep.

3. In what ways do the three accounts differ?
Matthew's account is much longer than the other two (47 verses as compared with seven in Mark and six in Luke) because he devotes more space to Jesus' speech (38 verses as compared with four in Mark and three in Luke). There is a difference concerning whether Jesus said to take one staff (Mark 6:8) or none (Matthew 10:10; Luke 9:3), and to go shod with sandals (Mark 6:9) or without shoes (Matthew 10:10). Jesus' meaning is clear. They were not to take extra supplies, but only essential equipment. Only Mark mentions that they were sent out by twos (v. 7), and that they anointed the sick with oil (v. 13). Matthew says nothing concerning what the twelve actually did on this campaign, whereas Mark in two verses, and Luke in one, speak of their efforts and successes.

4. What commission did Jesus give?
Briefly, the commission was as follows: *extent*—the lost sheep of the house of Israel; *work*—heal the sick, cleanse the lepers, raise the dead, cast out demons; *message*—a call to repentance because "the kingdom of heaven is at hand," to be preached on the housetops; *equipment*—only that which was essential; *conduct*—above reproach; *warning*—to be delivered up to councils, scourged in synagogues, brought before governors and kings, hated of mankind, families divided; *assurance*—the guidance and help of God.

5. Had the apostles previously performed miracles?
There is no record of it, nor of their doing so after this while with Jesus. Later, when the seventy were sent out, they performed miracles, but apparently the twelve were not included in this mission (Luke 10:1; note the word *other*).

6. Which coming of the Son of man did Jesus mean?
Several plausible answers have been offered by various writers. The following two seem to be the

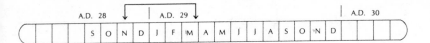

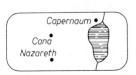

more logical: (1) The coming of Jesus in redemptive power on Pentecost to establish His kingdom; (2) His coming in destructive power in A.D. 70 to destroy the city of Jerusalem. It is difficult to choose between these two.

7. Who is able to destroy both body and soul?
The reference is to God, for He alone possesses such power. If we fear men and follow the devil we will be destroyed with him, but the destruction will be by God.

8. Why would Jesus set members of a family at variance?
The attitude that various members of a household may have toward the Christ often will set them at variance with each other. It is an inevitable consequence of following the Master of men.

9. Was this commission restricted to this one campaign?
No, for some of the predictions of Jesus were not fulfilled until after the Great Commission was issued (Matthew 28:19, 20). Like Old Testament prophets who mingled the present with the future, Jesus, in this commission, blended promises and warnings that were pertinent at that point in time with those that are still applicable today.

Herod's Conscience Stricken: Confusion of John the Baptist and Jesus . . . Matthew 14:1-12; Mark 6:14-29; Luke 9:7-9

1. How could Herod confuse Jesus with John?
The mind of man is capable of creating many fantasies. This is especially true when a guilty conscience attacks a superstitious person such as Antipas must have been. Knowing that John had been a righteous man, and being burdened with guilt at having put him to death, Antipas made an incorrect assumption. He reasoned that God had raised John from the dead and sent him back in the person of Jesus to haunt and torment him. Such a rumor must have been widespread (see Matthew 16:14).

2. Which Herod and which Philip?
Both of these men were of the Herodian family. The one called Herod in these texts is Antipas, the tetrarch of Galilee, son of Herod the Great and Malthace. Philip was his half-brother, son of Herod the Great and Mariamne. He should not be confused with another son of Herod, by Cleopatra, who had the same name, and was tetrarch of East Jordan. To distinguish between these

See page 237.

A.D. 28   A.D. 29   A.D. 30

| | | | S | O | N | D | J | F | M | A | M | J | J | A | S | O | N | D | | | |

two, the Philip of our texts is commonly called Philip of Rome. Herodias was the daughter of yet another of Herod's sons, Aristobulus. She first married her uncle, Philip of Rome, but deserted him to live with Antipas, another of her uncles. It was because John condemned this illicit relationship that he was decapitated.

3. When did John's death occur?
As nearly as can be calculated, John was executed in March or April of A.D. 29 (782 U.C.).

4. Was Herod impressed by John?
Mark 6:20 says he feared him, and observed him (kept him safely), and heard him gladly. Unfortunately, however, he did not obey John's message.

WHEN AND WHERE

It was probably in the late fall of A.D. 28 (781 U.C.) that Jesus, while crossing the Sea of Galilee, stilled the tempest. It was some four months later, in the spring of A.D. 29, that the twelve returned from their evangelistic campaign. As was true in the preceding lesson, the dating of these events is to a great extent arbitrary, for there are no references to the time of year in any of the Scriptures handled. However, the very next topic for consideration, the feeding of the five thousand, is dated by John (6:4) as being near the Passover. Starting from this event, the Passover of A.D. 29 (which in that year fell on the 17th of April), and going backward in time, we are able, with a fair degree of accuracy, to determine when the events of this lesson happened.

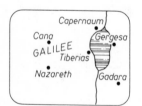

During this four month period, Jesus was in Capernaum, the land of the Gadarenes, Nazareth, and a number of unnamed Galilean cities. Locate these known places on the map.

PROJECTS AND PLANS

Have a round-table discussion of the value of sending out workers two by two. Organize a calling campaign following this practice to help win others to Christ.

Read the four accounts of the feeding of the five thousand, and prepare a chronology of the various phases of the event.

FEEDING THE FIVE THOUSAND

TOPICS AND TEXTS

Retirement of Jesus With the Apostles: Feeding the Five Thousand . . . Matthew 14:13-21; Mark 6:30-44; Luke 9:10-17; John 6:1-14
Jesus Refusing the Crown: Walking on the Water . . . Matthew 14:22-33; Mark 6:45-52; John 6:15-21
Miracles at Gennesaret . . . Matthew 14:34-36; Mark 6:53-56
Collapse of Galilean Campaign Because of Jesus' Refusal to Be a Political Messiah . . . John 6:22-71

CONTEXT AND CONTINUITY

We come now to an investigation of one of the more widely known events in Jesus' life, the feeding of the five thousand. That all four of the Gospel writers recorded this event indicates something of its importance, for it is the only event in Jesus' life prior to the "triumphal entry" that received such treatment. With this miracle Jesus' ministry in Galilee reached its climax; immediately after it His popularity with the multitude waned. This is not to say that His ministry in Galilee lost all of its effectiveness at this time. It did not. As a matter of fact there were other highlights during the next six months (e.g., feeding the four thousand, Peter's confession, the transfiguration), but He was never again the focal point of such widespread interest and enthusiasm.

There were several reasons for His popularity at this time:

1. The twelve had just returned from a very successful evangelistic effort in many of the towns and villages of Galilee. Their efforts had increased Jesus' fame.

2. The death of John the Baptist had caused many of his disciples to turn to Jesus for leadership (Matthew 3:11, 12; John 3:30).

3. The Passover, one of the three annual feasts with required attendance for all male Jews who were able, was soon to be observed. This made it an excellent time for assembling a great multitude, for many of the people already would have their work so arranged as to be free to make a pilgrimage to Jerusalem. They could, therefore, the more easily be caught up by the enthusiasm of the occasion.

From all over Galilee and the surrounding areas happy, enthusiastic people came and assembled in a grassy, deserted area overlooking the Sea of Galilee. There Jesus taught them and healed their sick and labored with them throughout the day. Realizing they had been a long time without food, He showed His compassion by miraculously multiplying five loaves and two fishes so that there was enough food to feed every person present.

> **GALILEAN CAMPAIGN**
>
> Began Jan., A.D. 28
> (Lesson 7)
> Ended Oct., A.D. 29
> (Lesson 13)
> Events of this lesson:
> Apr., A.D. 29

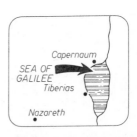

85

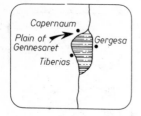

Capernaum
Plain of Gennesaret
Gergesa
Tiberias

The crowd included five thousand men, besides women and children! This miracle, added to the other factors already mentioned, raised the enthusiasm-thermometer of the multitude to the exploding point. The people, therefore, determined to make Jesus their king. To prevent this, Jesus sent away His apostles by ship, attempted to dismiss the multitude, and departed into a nearby mountain for private prayer.

Later that night (between 3:00 and 6:00 a.m.) Jesus walked on the water to join the apostles, whose crossing of the Sea of Galilee had been delayed by a storm. When they arrived in the Plain of Gennesaret they probably spent what little remained of that night in much-needed sleep. Rest now was at a premium for Jesus and His company. Wherever they went great throngs flocked to them. In fact, it had been to gain rest after their tiring evangelistic campaign that they had crossed from Capernaum to Bethsaida Julias in the first place (Mark 6:31). There they had been met by the multitude of five thousand. Now, upon re-crossing, they were confronted by the people of the area who brought Him their sick to be healed.

On this day, a part of the multitude that Jesus had left on the eastern shore of the lake followed Him to the vicinity of Capernaum. There He delivered a discourse on the bread of life and debated with some of them concerning His identity. The exact time and place of this meeting are not clear. From John 6:59 we learn that part, if not all, of Jesus' speech was delivered in the synagogue of Capernaum. In the debate it became apparent that the majority of the multitude was more concerned with the bread He gave them than with the bread He is.

Jesus' refusal to cooperate with the people and become a political Messiah brought to an end His Galilean campaign. John says: "Many of his disciples went back, and walked no more with him" (6:66). Seeing this, Jesus turned to His apostles and inquired, "Will ye also go away?" Peter, demonstrating some of his characteristic rocklikeness, responded, "Lord, to whom shall we go? thou hast the words of eternal life" (John 6:68).

INQUIRIES AND INSIGHTS

Retirement of Jesus With the Apostles: Feeding the Five Thousand . . . Matthew 14:13-21; Mark 6:30-44; Luke 9:10-17; John 6:1-14

1. In what sense was it a desert place?
The Greek word means an uninhabited, desolate, uncultivated section of land. The same word is

used of the "wilderness" of Judea (Matthew 3:1). Such places had grass, as is evident from our texts (Matthew 14:19; Mark 6:39; John 6:10), and were suitable for pasturing flocks. Tenney states: "It must not be thought that the deserts known to the Israelites were merely wastes of sand, like the Sahara. They were mostly latently fertile lands, needing only rain to make them fertile." Merrill C. Tenney, *Pictorial Bible Dictionary*, p. 213.

2. What was the sequence of events leading up to the miracle?

Apparently Jesus suggested the shortage of food to Philip (John 6:5), who in turn called the fact to the attention of the other apostles. Later, when their hunger pangs had increased, the apostles turned to the Lord with their own solution: "Send the multitude away, that they may . . . buy themselves victuals." In response He commanded what appeared to be the impossible: "Give ye them to eat." Since the apostles had no food they considered going and buying some. They estimated that more than two hundred pennyworth (Greek danarion; in the Roman world one denarius represented a day's pay for a laborer) of bread would be required to feed the people. When Jesus asked, "How many loaves have ye?" Andrew discovered a lad with five barley loaves and two small fishes. The multitude was seated in groups, thanks was offered, and the food was multiplied and distributed to the happy people.

3. At what time of day was the miracle performed?

Matthew says, "when it was evening"; Mark, "the day was now far spent"; Luke, "when the day began to wear away." It is not possible to determine the exact time, but obviously it was "a late hour" (literal meaning of Mark 6:35) in the day.

4. Why have the people sit in groups?

Several reasons suggest themselves: (1) It was a means of extending the expectancy of the apostles to the multitude, and thus creating faith in His power; (2) it was a logical step to facilitate the dispensing of the food; (3) it was an aid in estimating the size of the multitude.

5. How many women and children were present?

Only Matthew mentions women and children, and he offers no hint as to their number. Many writers feel that the number was negligible. Others contend that it may have equaled that of the men.

Denarius of Augustus

In the Roman world, one denarius represented a day's pay for a laborer.

Barley grain is considered the most universally cultivated cereal. Barley bread was a basic food among the Hebrews.

"So when they had rowed about five and twenty or thirty furlongs, they see Jesus walking on the sea" (John 6:19).

Furlong is an English word translated from the Greek stadion. It is a distance of 600 feet (Greek), or somewhat less than ⅛ of a mile. Twenty-five or thirty furlongs would be about 3½ miles.

Jesus joined His apostles in the "fourth watch of the night" (Matthew 14:25). The watches were:
1st . . . 6:00—9:00 p.m.
2nd . . . 9:00—12:00 p.m.
3rd . . . 12:00—3:00 a.m.
4th . . . 3:00—6:00 a.m.

Jesus Refusing the Crown: Walking on the Water . . . Matthew 14:22-33; Mark 6:45-52; John 6:15-21

1. Why did Jesus dismiss the multitude?
Matthew and Mark mention the dismissal, whereas John, who doesn't refer to it, explains Jesus' motive. Jesus sent away the multitude to prevent them from carrying out their plan to forcibly make Him king. This is a good example of how the Gospel records complement each other.

2. How did Jesus see the apostles, "toiling in rowing"?
Whether natural or supernatural sight is meant is not clear. It was probably the latter, for this happened at nighttime when the boat was twenty-five or thirty furlongs (about three and one-half miles) from the eastern shore where Jesus was.

3. At what time of night did Jesus join the apostles?
Matthew says it was *in* the fourth watch of the night, and Mark that it was *about* the fourth watch. It was roughly between 3:00 and 6:00 a.m.

4. For what did the apostles mistake Jesus?
Unable to give a reasonable explanation for what they saw, they concluded it was an apparition. Strangely, the translators of the King James Version, who regularly use the term Holy *Ghost* instead of Holy *Spirit,* use the word *spirit* here where we expect the term *ghost.* Thus has the English language changed in 350 years.

5. How was Peter able to walk on the water?
Matthew, who alone records this incident, attributes Peter's ability to his faith in the Lord. When he shifted his focus from Jesus to the boisterous waves, fear destroyed his faith.

6. Why did the wind cease when Jesus entered the ship?
The way Matthew and Mark introduce this fact seems to indicate that a miracle was involved. Neither writer, however, calls it such. A similar problem exists with John 6:21: "And immediately the ship was at the land whither they went." Probably a supernatural interpretation fits better with this text also.

7. What is the meaning of Mark 6:52?
This verse contains a reprimand of the apostles for their slowness in comprehending the power of

Jesus. Although they had just witnessed the miraculous feeding of five thousand, they hadn't grasped the significance of the event. If they had understood that Jesus possesses power over the elements of nature, they wouldn't have been so amazed by these further miracles.

8. What effect did the miracles have on the apostles?

Having witnessed the various miracles—the feeding of the five thousand, the walking on the water, the rescuing of Peter, and the calming of the wind—the apostles acknowledged the deity of Jesus, addressing Him as the Son of God.

Miracles at Gennesaret . . . Matthew 14:34-46; Mark 6:53-56

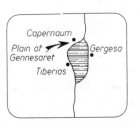

1. How did the people know Jesus?

By this time the popularity of Jesus had spread throughout all of Galilee. His name was known in every home, and His teaching was the chief topic of conversation among the masses. As is true of present-day celebrities, probably every phase of Jesus' life was discussed. There was interest in His dress, mannerisms, appearance, companions, etc. When He disembarked at Gennesaret with a dozen men (some of whom would be personally known by their fellow Galileans) it would have taken only a little while for that fact to spread throughout the entire plain.

2. Why send for all of the diseased?

The healing ability of Jesus was widely known. Unfortunately, by many it was considered to be of more importance than His teaching. Although faith was shown in sending for the physically ill, the spiritually ill should have been sent for.

3. Was there healing power in Jesus' clothing?

The garment referred to probably was the square garment worn over the shoulders, called a "cloak" in Matthew 5:40. The hem was the fringe mentioned in Numbers 15:38, 39 and Deuteronomy 22:12. There was nothing miraculous about Jesus' garments. The healing power was in the person of Jesus. Only when He permitted it were those healed who touched His clothing. This is indicated in a similar passage in Mark 5 where the healing of a woman with an issue of blood is described. After the woman touched His garment and was healed, Mark explains, "Jesus . . . knowing in himself that virtue *had gone out of him* . . . said, Who touched my clothes?" (Mark 5:30).

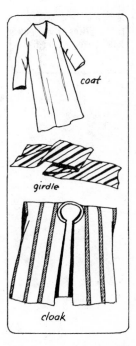

coat

girdle

cloak

Collapse of Galilean Campaign Because of Jesus' Refusal to Be a Political Messiah . . . John 6:22-71

1. What did Jesus mean in John 6:26?

Jesus criticized the people because they had failed to grasp the significance of His miracles. They ate the loaves which He provided and were satisfied, but did not understand the power or purpose of the miracle. They followed Him because of what He did for them, not because of who He was.

2. In what sense had God sealed the Son of man?

"To seal is to confirm or approve as *ours* . . . So God the Father, by the miracles which had been wrought by Jesus, had shown that he had sent him, that he approved his doctrines, and ratified his works. The *miracles* were to his doctrine what a *seal* is to a written instrument."—Albert Barnes, *Notes on the New Testament, Luke and John,* p. 244.

> "But without faith it is impossible to please him: for he that cometh to God must believe that he is, and that he is a rewarder of them that diligently seek him" (Hebrews 11:6).

3. How is believing, "the work of God"?

Faith is often set at antithesis to *works* by theologians who advocate salvation by one or the other. Jesus, however, taught that believing is itself a work. In fact, He called it, *"the* work of God." The man who has had to wrestle through doubt to come to a saving faith can testify to that. (See Hebrews 11:6.)

4. Why should the people ask for a sign?

"How could they?" might be a better question, for they had just witnessed the miraculous multiplication of food. They were not, however, satisfied with that. Instead they sought some other stupendous sign, like the fire of Elijah's day, or the manna of Moses' time. It has been suggested that they were only sparring for time, being convinced of the messiahship of Jesus, but unwilling to surrender their worldly ambitions.

5. How is Jesus the bread of life?

As bread is the staff of the physical life, so is Jesus of the spiritual. Every soul that fails to feed on Him will suffer spiritual malnutrition. The manna provided through Moses sustained only the physical body, and that for only a while. In contrast, one who feasts his soul on the bread of life shall live forever (John 6:58). (Compare John 4:14.)

6. What did Jesus say is the Father's will?

Jesus spoke concerning the Father's will in verses 39 and 40. He presented two aspects of it: First, it

was not God's will that any of those who had become followers of Jesus would be lost. Second, it is the will of God that all who from that time forward should see the Son and believe in Him should have everlasting life.

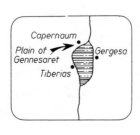

7. What statement of Jesus angered the Jews?
Verse 41 explains that it was His claim to be the bread which came down from Heaven (see vv. 33-36) that irritated the Jews and caused them to murmur against Him. There are other, more startling claims to be found in verses 37-40. These statements seem more likely to have caused the murmuring. Thus Edersheim concludes that the material found in these verses was not spoken to the multitude, but privately to Jesus' apostles.

8. How do men come to Jesus?
Only through a divine drawing is it possible for men to come to Jesus (vv. 44 and 65). This drawing comes through His Word as the Spirit works upon the hearts of those who hear. Two things therefore are necessary for a sinner to come to Christ: (1) the divine calling, and (2) the human willingness.

Two saving essentials:
1. Divine call;
2. Human will.

9. How do men eat the flesh and drink the blood of the Son of man?
As men believe in the Son of man and accept Him into their lives, they may be said to be eating His flesh and drinking His blood. This is the primary meaning of Jesus' words. A secondary meaning makes these words applicable to the Lord's Supper. Surely Jesus had the latter, as well as the former, in mind in making this claim. Although it could not then be understood as applying to an ordinance not yet given for a church not yet established, Jesus realized that the secondary meaning would become clear in the future. In the same way His statement to Nicodemus relative to the new birth was not understood until after the Holy Spirit had given additional light.

10. Why were many of the disciples offended?
Unable to comprehend His claims and unwilling to accept them by faith, most dismissed the truth from their minds as hard sayings, and forsook Him.

11. Why did Jesus ask the question, "Will ye also go away?"
This question, containing what some call "the saddest words of Jesus," was not asked for the

purpose of gaining information (v. 64). It was asked to make the disciples analyze their own conduct and reaffirm their faith.

12. In what sense was Judas a devil?
This is a metaphorical statement. Jesus called him a devil because his actions were devilish.

WHEN AND WHERE

The events of this lesson happened in the spring of A.D. 29 (782 U.C.), almost certainly in the month of April. John enables us to be rather positive in our dating for he declares that "the passover, a feast of the Jews, was nigh" (6:4). In that year the Passover fell on the 17th of April. This is the third Passover of Jesus' ministry. Only one more, that one at which He was crucified, remains to be considered. All of the material yet to be dealt with is concerned with the year leading up to His death, burial, and resurrection, and the forty post-resurrection days.

> Passover, A. D. 29:
> April 17

There were two Bethsaidas in the time of Christ. Both of them were near the Sea of Tiberias, only a few miles apart. Both cities are mentioned in connection with Jesus' ministry. One, the western, was in Galilee, and was called by John "Bethsaida of Galilee" (12:21). The other, the eastern, was in Gaulanitis, and was named Bethsaida Julias after Augustus Caesar's daughter. According to Josephus, Philip the Tetrarch, who gave the city its name, advanced it from a village unto the dignity of a city (*Antiquities,* 18:2:1). Jesus and His apostles crossed the Sea of Galilee from the western to the eastern shore and came into "a desert place belonging to the city called Bethsaida" (Luke 9:10). After feeding the five thousand "he constrained his disciples to get into the ship, and to go to the other side before unto Bethsaida, while he sent away the people" (Mark 6:45). The former was Bethsaida Julias, and the latter, Bethsaida of Galilee.

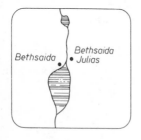

PROJECTS AND PLANS

In addition to walking on the water, Jesus performed several other "nature miracles." Working together as a class, find all of these miracles, and then discuss the subject: "Nature, One of God's Revelations."

Read as many commentators on Matthew 16:13-20 as are available and as time permits.

THE GREAT CONFESSION

TOPICS AND TEXTS

Attack of Jerusalem Pharisees Concerning Traditions . . . Matthew 15:1-20; Mark 7:1-23; John 7:1
Retirement to Phoenicia and Healing of Syrophoenician Woman's Daughter . . . Matthew 15:21-28; Mark 7:24-30
Third Retirement and Ministry in Decapolis . . . Matthew 15:29-38; Mark 7:31—8:9
Brief Visit to Magadan and the Demand for a Sign From Heaven . . . Matthew 15:39—16:4; Mark 8:10-12
Fourth Withdrawal to Eastern Side of Lake: Warning to the Disciples . . . Matthew 16:5-12; Mark 8:13-26
Peter's Great Confession at Caesarea Philippi . . . Matthew 16:13-20; Mark 8:27-30; Luke 9:18-21
First Distinct Prediction of His Death . . . Matthew 16:21-28; Mark 8:31—9:1; Luke 9:22-27

CONTEXT AND CONTINUITY

Some Pharisees and scribes from Jerusalem, seeing an opportune moment, attacked Jesus' disciples because they transgressed the tradition of the elders. At this time Jesus' spirit was at a low. So was that of the apostles. They had just witnessed the abandonment of Jesus by many disciples whose interest was more physical than spiritual. Such timing was typical of the scribes and Pharisees who were ever lurking in the shadows awaiting opportunities to disarm and discredit Jesus.

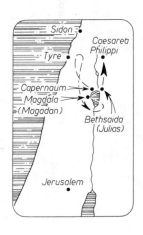

It is interesting to note that the debate recorded by John (John 6:22-71; see the previous lesson) is not mentioned by either Matthew or Mark. Both of these writers place this present attack immediately after Jesus' ministry in Gennesaret. It may be that part of the agitation seen in the John 6 passage was caused by these men from Jerusalem. Arriving in Capernaum at the time when the multitude was dissatisfied with Jesus because He wouldn't be their kind of king, they capitalized on the situation. First they stirred up the people causing the debate of John 6. Then they brought their charge against the disciples of Jesus. Although just speculation, the events could quite conceivably have occurred in that order.

Jesus heard the complaints against His disciples, and then turned the situation to His own advantage by exposing the hypocrisy of the scribes and Pharisees. After this He departed into Phoenicia, "into the borders of Tyre and Sidon." There He healed the daughter of a Greek woman by casting out an unclean spirit. He and His companions then moved in a southeasterly direction, passed through Galilee, entered the Decapolis area, and came to the sea. There Jesus healed

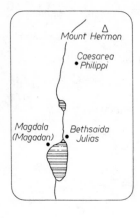

Mount Hermon △

Caesarea Philippi •

Magdala (Magadan) •   Bethsaida Julias •

countless people who were lame, blind, dumb, and maimed (Matthew 15:30). One, whose healing is given special attention, was a deaf man with a speech impediment (Mark 7:32-35). It was at this time that Jesus miraculously fed a multitude of four thousand men, besides women and children.

Entering into a ship, Jesus and His apostles crossed the sea to Magadan (Magdala or Dalmanutha) where they were met and challenged by some Pharisees and Sadducees who pretended to seek a sign from Heaven. Following this encounter, Jesus again withdrew to the eastern side of the lake. During this crossing He warned His apostles against the influence of the Pharisees, Sadducees, and of Herod. Upon arrival at Bethsaida Julias, Jesus restored sight to a blind man in an unusual and dramatic way. From there He and His apostles journeyed approximately 25 miles northward into the vicinity of Caesarea Philippi.

The discussion which took place at this time is one of the better known events in Jesus' life. In answer to a question concerning His identity, the apostles appraised Him of the various rumors which were circulating. When asked whom they held Him to be, Peter responded with his famous confession: "Thou art the Christ, the Son of the living God" (Matthew 16:16). No sooner had Peter made the good confession and Jesus promised the establishment of His church than He began to speak of His forthcoming death. Unable to reconcile the victorious beginning of the kingdom with the death of its King, Peter attempted to correct his Master's thinking. This resulted in Jesus' rebuking Peter as an agent of the devil.

INQUIRIES AND INSIGHTS

Attack of Jerusalem Pharisees Concerning Traditions ... Matthew 15:1-20; Mark 7:1-23; John 7:1

1. What charge was made against Jesus' disciples?

They were charged with transgressing the traditions of the elders. These traditions were oral explanations by famous Jewish scholars of Old Testament laws. The specific charge against the disciples was that they ate with unwashed hands. It was not made out of regard for sanitation, but in the interest of ceremonial cleanliness. The charge against the disciples was actually an attack upon Jesus for permitting their conduct.

2. What countercharge did Jesus make against the Pharisees?

Some Pharisees, in order to receive a little praise, would dedicate to God the money which by right should have been used for the support of their aged parents *(corban* means "given to God"). By so doing they violated the fifth commandment and were guilty of a gross sin. This practice Jesus condemned.

"Honor thy father and thy mother: that thy days may be long upon the land which the Lord thy God giveth thee" (Exodus 20:12).

3. How was Isaiah's prophecy fulfilled by the Pharisees?

Isaiah's words were spoken directly of the people of his own day, but indirectly of the nation at other times. There is ever the tendency to obey externally God's commands while inwardly ignoring their meaning.

4. Is a man ever defiled by that which goes into his mouth?

Yes, for narcotics, alcohol, etc.,—items consumed through the mouth—have an effect upon the mind and hence upon the soul of man. The desire to partake of such pollutants is produced in the heart. It is this desire which must be changed if one is to be helped.

5. What Old Testament teaching did Jesus alter?

Once it came into effect, Jesus' teaching destroyed the Mosaic distinction between clean and unclean meat. It was not until Jesus' death on the cross that the Old Testament ceremonial laws were repealed. Even after the church began, the relationship of the Old Testament to the New was not grasped immediately (Acts 10:14, 15; Colossians 2:13-17). (See also Acts 15: 29, 1 Timothy 4:1-5.)

See Leviticus 11 for Old Testament teaching regarding clean and unclean meat.

6. What did Jesus say defiles a man?

Matthew's list includes: evil thoughts, murders, adulteries, fornications, thefts, false witness, and blasphemies. Mark has six of these in his list (he omits false witness and has only the singular, *blasphemy),* and includes an additional seven: covetousness, wickedness, deceit, lasciviousness, an evil eye, pride, and foolishness.

These defile a man:
    evil thoughts,
    murders,
    adulteries,
    fornications,
    thefts,
    false witness,
    blasphemies,
    covetousness,
    wickedness,
    deceit,
    lasciviousness,
    an evil eye,
    pride, and
    foolishness.

Retirement to Phoenicia and Healing of Syrophoenician Woman's Daughter . . . Matthew 15:21-28; Mark 7:24-30

1. Who were the Phoenicians?

The Phoenicians were Semites who lived along the Mediterranean coast north of Mt. Carmel and west of upper Galilee. They are remembered for

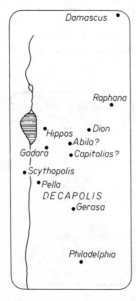

their nautical ability. Many consider them the most notable sailors of the ancient world.

2. Who was this woman?
She is called a woman of Canaan (Matthew 15:22), a Greek, and a Syrophoenician (Mark 7:26). Apparently she was a Phoenician by birth who lived in Canaan (a term applied to Phoenicia as well as to other sections of Palestine). By the Jews she would be considered a Greek, since her people had absorbed the Greek culture.

3. Was Jesus unkind to her?
Two parts of the record might cause one to conclude that He was unkind: (1) He at first refused to speak to her although she addressed Him with the Messianic title, son of David, and pleaded for His help; (2) He compared her and her people to dogs. Properly understood, neither action was unkind. In fact, His motive in both was just the opposite. He refused to speak that He might more fully develop her faith. The diminutive for the word dog was used, indicating He had in mind the tame, household pet which must depend on others for its food and care, rather than the mongrel dog which was both unclean and undesirable.

4. How did she show her faith?
Her faith was indicated by her use of the Messianic title, by her persistence while being spurned, and by her worship of Jesus. Note especially her quick and faith-filled response to Jesus' words.

Third Retirement and Ministry in Decapolis . . . Matthew 15:29-38; Mark 7:31—8:9

1. How account for such a large multitude?
The scene of this gathering was in the Decapolis area where Jesus had done very little evangelistic work. However His fame had spread there too, and many would be anxious to see this miracle worker about whom they had heard so much. The work of the Gadarene demoniac healed by Jesus would have contributed to His popularity and undoubtedly helped swell the crowd (see Mark 5:18-20).

2. Why did Jesus use such a dramatic method to heal the deaf man?
Since the man was deaf it was necessary for Jesus to use pantomime to communicate His plan to the man. From Mark's wording it can't be determined whether Jesus put His fingers in His own or the deaf man's ears, nor whose tongue was touched.

The spitting was a part of the pantomime. Later Jesus employed a similar method in healing a blind man in Bethsaida Julias (Mark 8:23) and another in Jerusalem (John 9:6).

3. What differences are there between the feeding of the four thousand and the feeding of the five thousand?

There are the following differences: (1) the time and place performed; (2) the length of time the multitude was with Jesus; (3) the size of the multitude; (4) the amount of food on hand; (5) the quantity of fragments gathered; (6) the attitude of the multitude after the feeding.

Brief Visit to Magadan and the Demand for a Sign From Heaven . . . Matthew 15:39—16:4; Mark 8:10-12

1. Where did Jesus go after feeding the four thousand?

Matthew states He came into the coasts of Magdala *(Magadan,* American Standard Version). Mark says He came into the parts of Dalmanutha (evidently a village adjoining Magadan). Magadan was probably the place formerly called Migdalel (Joshua 19:38) and today called Mejdel. It was located on the western shore of the Sea of Galilee, south of the Plain of Gennesaret.

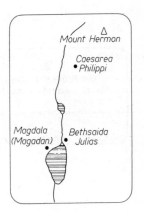

2. Did Jesus mean that the weather signs were always correct?

No, only that they are often true, that generally speaking certain weather is preceded by certain signs. We make similar judgments today. We say: "Red sky at night, sailor's delight; Red sky in the morning, sailors take warning." Or we say: "Evening red, morning gray, lights the traveler on his way; Evening gray, morning red, the rains come pouring on his head."

3. Why should the Pharisees be able to discern the signs of the times?

The evidence that Jesus was the Messiah was overwhelming. His sinless life, marvelous miracles, and tremendous influence, coupled with HIs stupendous claims, should have convinced them that He was the Messiah. It was because they refused to see that they remained in unbelief.

4. What was the sign of Jonah?

Jesus referred to His resurrection, which is the supreme miracle of Christianity, the conclusive proof of all His claims. See Matthew 12:40 and Luke 11:29, 30.

97

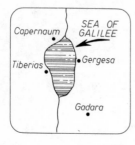

Fourth Withdrawal to Eastern Side of Lake: Warning to the Disciples ... Matthew 16:5-12; Mark 8:13-26

1. Why did Jesus issue this warning?

Jesus detected His enemies' influence was beginning to be felt among His apostles. Questions were arising in their minds concerning His conduct. Such things as His open condemnation of the national leaders (Matthew 15:12) and His refusal to produce a sign from Heaven (Matthew 16:1) bothered them. Jesus' warning was given to offset this tendency.

2. Why the confusion in the apostles' minds?

Jesus' reference to leaven was figurative, but the apostles interpreted it literally. They assumed His criticism was because of their lack of preparation. Leaven was a form of yeast used in making bread.

3. How did Jesus correct their thinking?

He recalled the two miracles involving the feeding of great multitudes. Thus He reminded them that His power was adequate to supply food if the need for it should arise. When He explained that His reference was not to bread, they understood the figurative meaning of His warning.

4. What were the doctrines of the Pharisees, Sadducees, and Herod?

The Pharisees were noted for their formalism, pretentious display, and traditionalism. The Sadducees were known for their rationalistic unbelief, free thought, and worldliness. The Herodian court was characterized by irreligion, sensuality, and corrupt living.

> For additional information about the Pharisees and Sadducees, see Lesson 20.

5. What is unusual about Jesus' method of healing in this case?

This is the only recorded instance of a miracle performed by Jesus which was done gradually by degrees rather than totally in an instant. Various explanations for this are offered by different writers.

Peter's Great Confession at Caesarea Philippi ... Matthew 16:13-20; Mark 8:27-30; Luke 9:18-21

1. How account for the various rumors concerning Jesus' identity?

Some, influenced by Herod Antipas, confused Jesus with John the Baptist, whom they felt had been raised from the dead (Matthew 14:2). Others identified Jesus with the prophet Elijah whose coming had been predicted by Malachi (4:5, 6).

The apocryphal book 2 Esdras predicted the return of Isaiah and Jeremiah (2:18). It was commonly believed among the Jews that at the Messiah's coming the prophets would rise again. "The nearer still the 'kingdom of heaven' came, by so much the more did they dream of the resurrection of the prophets."—Lightfoot on John 1:25, as quoted by Samuel J. Andrews, *The Life of Our Lord Upon the Earth*, p. 352.

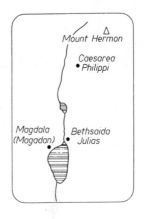

2. What is the meaning of Peter's confession?
Two truths stand out: (1) Jesus is the long anticipated Messiah (Greek, *Christos*, "Anointed One"); (2) He is the Son of the living God. Mark mentions only the first (8:29); Luke uses the expression, "Christ of God" (9:20); Matthew clearly presents both factors (16:16). It is clear from his later conduct that Peter didn't fully comprehend the meaning of his words.

3. What was the source of Peter's knowledge?
His source was not "flesh and blood" (a common Jewish expression denoting man in contrast to God), but the heavenly Father. The method used by the Father in making known to Peter this revelation is not explained. No doubt it was through the words and deeds of Christ, which were really not His own but the Father's who sent Him. The same signs which convinced Peter of the messiahship of Jesus led the Pharisees and scribes to conclude that He was an imposter. Peter sought the Father's guidance; they relied on their own human (and in this case *prejudiced*) opinion.

4. What are the various interpretations of Matthew 16:18?
There are at least three: (1) the reference is to Peter; (2) to the confession which he made; or (3) to Christ himself. Roman Catholicism accepts the first view, whereas Protestantism is fairly well divided between the other two. Perhaps all three are necessary to exhaust Jesus' meaning. There is a sense in which the church is built upon Christ, for He is the "chief cornerstone." It is also correct to say that the church is built upon Peter *and all others like him* who believe and openly confess their faith in Jesus Christ. The following Scriptures throw additional light on this difficult verse: Isaiah 28:16; Matthew 18:15-20; Acts 4:11; Ephesians 2:19-22; 1 Peter 2:1-8.

5. How does Jesus picture the church?
"He represents: 1. His kingdom as a city about to be built upon a rock. 2. Himself as a builder of this

"Behold, I lay in Zion for a foundation a stone, a tried stone, a precious corner stone, a sure foundation: he that believeth shall not make haste" (Isaiah 28:16).

"Now therefore ye are no more strangers and foreigners, but fellow citizens with the saints, and of the household of God; and are built upon the foundation of the apostles and prophets, Jesus Christ himself being the chief corner stone; in whom all the building fitly framed together groweth unto a holy temple in the Lord: in whom ye also are builded together for a habitation of God through the Spirit" (Ephesians 2:19-22).

99

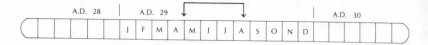
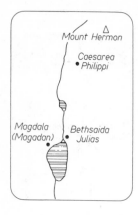

Mount Hermon

Caesarea • Philippi

Magdala (Magadan) • Bethsaida • Julias

JESUS FORETELLS DEATH

"From that time forth began Jesus to show unto his disciples, how that he must go unto Jerusalem, and suffer many things of the elders and chief priests and scribes, and be killed, and be raised again the third day" (Matthew 16:21).

---

city. 3. Simon Peter as the one who holds the keys to the gates by which egress and regress is had to the city. 4. The gates or powers of the opposing city of Hades are not able to prevail against this kingdom city."—J.W. McGarvey, P.Y. Pendleton, *The Fourfold Gospel*, p. 412.

6. What power was promised to Peter?
He was given the keys of the kingdom by which he could open its gates and allow the lost to enter and be saved. He used these keys in Jerusalem on Pentecost, A.D. 30, to admit the Jews, and about seven years later in Caesarea to admit the Gentiles (Acts 10). Similar power was promised to all of the apostles (Matthew 18:18). Their binding and loosing was to be in harmony with the Holy Spirit's plan and was to originate in Heaven rather than on earth.

First Distinct Prediction of His Death . . . Matthew 16:21-28; Mark 8:31—9:1; Luke 9:22-27

1. Why must Jesus go to Jerusalem?
A divine necessity was laid upon Him that required His going there to die. Only through denying the will of His heavenly Father and His own purpose for taking on human flesh could He avoid Jerusalem's cross.

2. What was the meaning of Jesus' rebuke?
Peter's proposal recalled the devil's temptation of Jesus to become a spectacular Messiah rather than a suffering Savior (Matthew 4:1-11). At that time Jesus commanded Satan to depart. Now, addressing Peter with the same name, that he might know whose agent he was, Jesus commanded Peter to get behind Him. Peter was not "savoring" (literally, "thinking upon") the things of God, but the things of men.

3. What is cross-bearing?
The cross-bearing of which Jesus spoke is not synonymous with having a few bad breaks or enduring the normal hardships of life. Rather, it is the enduring by the Christian of whatever afflictions come upon him as he labors for his Master. The Christian should not seek after trouble or delight in opposition, but when they come, he must accept them in the spirit of Him who bore His cross for all.

4. How does one find his life?
The man who places all of his emphasis upon this life and seeks only fleshly gratification will lose the spiritual reward which could be his. By way of

contrast, the one who, like Paul, can say truthfully, "I am crucified with Christ: nevertheless I live; yet not I, but Christ liveth in me" (Galatians 2:20), will enjoy the best this world has to offer and ultimately will inherit the paradise of God.

5. To which of His comings did Jesus refer?
Jesus came in heavenly splendor in the transfiguration, in resurrection glory following His ordeal on the cross, in Pentecostal power after His ascension, and in divine judgment on Jerusalem in A.D. 70. He is yet to come in great majesty in His second advent. It is not clear which coming Jesus meant in this passage. Probably He combined two of them. Matthew 16:27 (and comparable texts in Mark and Luke) refers to the second coming of Jesus, whereas verse 28 describes His Pentecostal advent.

> "Comings" of Jesus:
> His birth,
> His transfiguration,
> His resurrection,
> Pentecost, A.D. 30 (in Spirit),
> Jerusalem, A.D. 70 (in judgment),
> His "coming again."

WHEN AND WHERE

Jesus fed the five thousand near Passover time in April of A.D. 29. The next chronological reference is the feast of Tabernacles (John 7), which was held in October. The former event was considered in the preceding chapter, the latter will be in the following one. The events of this lesson must be fitted into this interval of six months, most likely between the last of April and the middle of August, A.D. 29.

In this lesson Jesus was on the move—from Capernaum to Phoenicia, into the Decapolis area, across the sea to Magadan, on the sea again to Bethsaida Julias, and then northward to Caesarea Philippi. Locate these places on the map, determine the distances between them, and figure the amount of time required for Jesus to make His journeys.

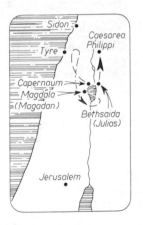

PROJECTS AND PLANS

In this lesson Jesus made the first distinct prediction of His death. Make a list of all of the veiled references to His suffering and death which have been in the material handled thus far.

Read the article, "Transfiguration," by Charles M. Stuart, in *The International Standard Bible Encyclopedia*, p. 3005.

THE TRANSFIGURATION AND SEVERAL DISCUSSIONS

TOPICS AND TEXTS

The Transfiguration . . . Matthew 17:1-8; Mark 9:2-8; Luke 9:28-36
Discussion of the Vision . . . Matthew 17:9-13; Mark 9:9-13; Luke 9:36
Healing of a Demoniac Boy . . . Matthew 17:14-21; Mark 9:14-29; Luke 9:37-43a
Third Prediction of His Death . . . Matthew 17:22, 23; Mark 9:30-32; Luke 9:43b-45
Jesus and the Temple Tax . . . Matthew 17:24-27
Discussion of Who Shall Be Greatest . . . Matthew 18:1-5; Mark 9:33-37; Luke 9:46-48
The Unknown Worker of Miracles . . . Mark 9:38-41; Luke 9:49, 50
The Question of Stumblingblocks . . . Matthew 18:6-14; Mark 9:42-50
Discussion of Mistreatment and Forgiveness . . . Matthew 18:15-35
Jesus and His Unbelieving Brethren . . . John 7:2-9
Private Journey Through Samaria to Jerusalem . . . Luke 9:51-56; John 7:10

Mt. Hermon

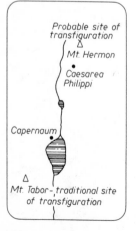

Probable site of transfiguration
△
Mt. Hermon
•
Caesarea Philippi

Capernaum •

△
Mt. Tabor- traditional site of transfiguration

CONTEXT AND CONTINUITY

A week after the good confession Jesus took Peter, James, and John into a mountain and was transfigured before them. We do not know how this intervening week was spent. Perhaps Jesus used the time to correct such false concepts among the apostles as that which Peter had expressed at the time of the good confession (Matthew 16:22).

The day of the transfiguration is also unknown. God didn't consider it significant enough to tell us. However, suppose it was after sunset on a Sabbath Day when Jesus and His trusted trio ascended the mountain, and later that night when the transfiguration took place. Since a Jewish day began at sunset, this would place the event on the first day of a week. Tracing backwards, counting the six days of Matthew and Mark or the eight days of Luke (who counted both the days on which the events took place), the good confession falls on the previous first day of the week. Of course, this is mere speculation; there is no evidence to support it. However, it is possible that Jesus arranged His schedule so as to have both of these great events fall on the day which afterwards would be designated as His. If so, His apostles would later be able to look back and see how He had prepared them for a change from Sabbath to Lord's Day worship.

The rest of that night was spent on the mountainside. Sometime the next day (Luke 9:37), probably quite early, they began their descent to join the apostles who had been left behind. I would like to think that it was a lovely day. Perhaps the sun's first rays were glistening on the snow-covered peaks above them, and the territory below lay in semi-darkness when they arose, spent some time in prayer and meditation, and started down the mountain. There must have been many beautiful days in Jesus' ministry, and perhaps this was one of them.

The three apostles, having had a night to think about the vision, must have been thrilled by its implications. Surely their attitude was greatly improved over that of the previous day when they were still suffering from the shock of Jesus' prediction of His death. Now the three were convinced that, regardless of what happened to Him, He was indeed the Messiah. In the days which followed, the three somehow managed to communicate this new conviction to the other apostles. This confidence was later shaken, but not destroyed.

As the group descended the mountain, they discussed Malachi's prediction concerning the coming of Elijah.

Arriving at the base of the mountain, Jesus found a state of confusion. A man had brought his son, who was possessed, to have the demon cast out. Because of their lack of faith, the apostles had been unsuccessful in their attempt. On hand as usual were some scribes, antagonizing the apostles by their questions, and seeking to alienate the multitude. In a matter of minutes, Jesus had the situation in hand. With a rebuke to the multitude and a word of challenge to the father of the boy, He created an atmosphere of faith, and expelled the demon.

From the mount of the transfiguration, Jesus' company traveled toward Capernaum. Along the way He issued the third distinct prediction of His death. When they had arrived in the city, Peter was approached concerning Jesus' relationship to the temple tax. To avoid embarrassment for Peter and to prevent others from stumbling, Jesus had Peter get the money in a miraculous way and pay the tax for the two of them.

As they made their way from Hermon to Capernaum, a dispute had arisen among the apostles concerning who was the greatest in the kingdom. Afraid that Jesus would be displeased, the apostles didn't want Jesus to know about the argument. He therefore startled them with His question: "What was it that ye disputed among yourselves by the way?" (Mark 9:33). The argument in this way was brought out into the open. Setting a little child in their midst, He lectured concerning humility and its importance in the kingdom. Mark and Luke next introduce a question of John's about an unknown worker of miracles. This is followed by a lengthy discussion concerning stumblingblocks, mistreatment, and forgiveness.

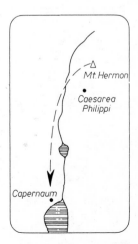

The feast of Tabernacles was now at hand. Jesus, refusing to go up to the feast with His unbelieving brothers, remained for awhile in Galilee. He then made a rather hurried trip through Samaria to Jerusalem. Perhaps He arrived before the feast commenced; we know He got there before it was over (John 7:14).

INQUIRIES AND INSIGHTS

The Transfiguration . . . Matthew 17:1-8; Mark 9:2-8; Luke 9:28-36

1. Why take only Peter, James, and John?
Either because of personal qualifications or exceptional devotion, or likely both, these three received special treatment on several occasions. (See Mark 5:37 and 14:33.)

2. At what time of day did the transfiguration occur?
Three things point to the nighttime: 1. Jesus went into the mountain to pray (which He often did at night); 2. the apostles were sleepy; 3. the descent from the mountain wasn't until the following day. None of these is conclusive; taken together they make a rather strong case.

3. What does the word transfigure mean?
It means "to change the appearance or form." In this case it refers to the transformation which came over Jesus' face and clothing as He assumed a measure of His heavenly glory. Matthew says "his face did shine," and Luke that "the fashion of his countenance was altered." Mark, who mentions no facial change, gives the fullest description of the appearance of His clothing (9:3).

4. Why Moses and Elijah?
These two men, rather than other outstanding Old Testament characters, appeared at the transfiguration because one of them, Moses, represented the law, and the other, Elijah, the prophets. Their conversation about Jesus' approaching death (Luke 9:31) should have helped the three apostles to realize it was in harmony with the Old Testament.

5. Why did Peter make the proposal to build three tabernacles?
Mark says very simply that Peter didn't know what to say (9:6). (See also Luke 9:33.) Thrilled by the scene before his eyes, Peter felt something should be said, but, not knowing what, he blurted out his proposal. What he suggested was unacceptable

Probable site of transfiguration
△
Mt. Hermon
● *Caesarea Philippi*

Capernaum

△
Mt. Tabor - traditional site of transfiguration

Transfigure is translated from the Greek *metamorphäo*, "to change into another form, to transform."

since it elevated Moses and Elijah to an equal position with Jesus.

6. What was the significance of the cloud?
Such a cloud was an accepted symbol of God's presence and had been since the time of the Exodus. Check the following Scriptures: Exodus 14:19, 20; 24:15-18; 1 Kings 8:10, 11; Ezekiel 1:4; 10:4.

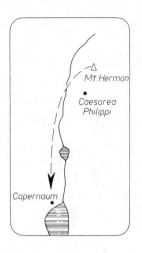

Discussion of the Vision . . . Matthew 17:9-13; Mark 9:9-13; Luke 9:36

1. Of what benefit was the vision since those who saw it couldn't share it with others?
First, the prohibition was not against ever telling the vision. It was only "till the Son of man were risen from the dead" (Mark 9:9). After that they shared it freely. Second, although the other apostles didn't get to see or hear about the transfiguration immediately, they must have detected in the attitude of the three that something tremendous had happened on the mountain.

2. Is there an eyewitness account of the transfiguration?
Matthew, Mark, and Luke—who were not eyewitnesses—record the incident, whereas John, who was present, doesn't. However, it is generally recognized that Mark wrote at the direction of Peter, and Luke states he had access to eyewitnesses (1:2). John 1:14 may be an indirect reference to the event, and 2 Peter 1:16-18 contains a very vivid description by an eyewitness.

Healing of a Demoniac Boy . . . Matthew 17:14-21; Mark 9:14-29; Luke 9:37-43a

1. From what affliction did the boy suffer?
In the King James version of Matthew 17:15 he is called a lunatic. Later translations more accurately refer to him as an epileptic. The cause of his affliction was a demon, called by Mark, "a dumb spirit" (9:17).

2. Toward whom was Jesus' rebuke directed?
Jesus directed His rebuke to the entire generation. He called the people faithless and perverse. The boy's father, the disciples, and the multitude were all included.

3. Why had the disciples failed?
The cause of their failure was unbelief which showed itself in a lack of prayer and fasting, necessary accompaniments to the expulsion of such demons.

Peter's testimony: "For we have not followed cunningly devised fables, when we made known unto you the power and coming of our Lord Jesus Christ, but were eyewitnesses of his majesty. For he received from God the Father honor and glory, when there came such a voice to him from the excellent glory, This is my beloved Son, in whom I am well pleased. And this voice which came from heaven we heard, when we were with him in the holy mount" (2 Peter 1:16-18).

105

Third Prediction of His Death . . . Matthew 17:22, 23; Mark 9:30-32; Luke 9:43b-45

1. Where was Jesus when this prediction was made?
He was on a journey somewhere between Mt. Hermon and Capernaum. The exact place is not given, only that it was in Galilee.

2. Why did the apostles fail to understand His meaning?
Luke says it was hidden from them (9:45). As elsewhere in the Bible, this concealment was self-imposed and for it the apostles would be personally responsible.

Jesus and the Temple Tax . . . Matthew 17:24-27

1. What tax was this?
It was the temple tax which all Jewish men from twenty years of age and upward were required to pay yearly. (See Exodus 30:13 and 38:26; also, Josephus, *Antiquities,* 18:9:1.)

2. How was Jesus' answer appropriate?
As the Son of God, Jesus was exempt from the payment of a tax used for the support of His Father's program in the same way that a king's son is free from the taxes levied by the king.

3. How did the coin get in the fish's mouth?
We are not told. Most likely it got there in a natural way. In any case, catching the fish with the coin was a miracle of omniscience.

Discussion of Who Shall Be Greatest . . . Matthew 18:1-5; Mark 9:33-37; Luke 9:46-48

1. What caused this discussion?
Envy was probably the cause of the dispute. It may have arisen because of Jesus' commendation of Peter at the time of his confession, or because of Jesus' selection of the three to accompany Him into the mountain. McGarvey and Pendleton declare: "The fires of envy that set burning were not easily quenched. We find them bursting forth again from time to time down to the very verge of Christ's exit from the world—Matthew 20:20-24; Luke 22:24."—*The Fourfold Gospel,* p. 430.

2. Who instigated the conversation?
Apparently Jesus did as indicated by Mark (9:33). After He showed His knowledge of their private dispute, the apostles brought it out into the open with their question: "Who is the greatest in the kingdom of heaven?" (Matthew 18:1).

JESUS HINTS AT DEATH

John 2:19-21
Matthew 16:4
Matthew 16:21-28
Matthew 17:9
Matthew 17:22, 23

"This they shall give, every one that passeth among them that are numbered, half a shekel after the shekel of the sanctuary: (a shekel is twenty gerahs:) a half shekel shall be the offering of the Lord" (Exodus 30:13).

Ruins of Capernaum

3. In what ways must Christ's disciples resemble little children?

Little children are characterized by their humility, teachableness, and trust. Also they are noted for their lack of selfish ambition, pride, and arrogance. In these things Christians should imitate them.

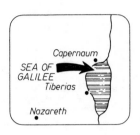

Capernaum

SEA OF GALILEE

Tiberias

Nazareth

The Unknown Worker of Miracles ... Mark 9:38-41; Luke 9:49, 50

1. To whom was this man unknown?

Although called "the unknown worker of miracles," he was certainly not unknown to Jesus. In fact he may have been given a special commission by the Lord at one of those times when the apostles weren't present. They didn't know him, and this upset them. Underlying John's question there seems to be the feeling that because of their close association with the Messiah, the apostles had somewhat of a monopoly on God's power. That someone outside of their company should have miraculous power irritated them. Exclusiveness is still a prevalent sin amongst God's people.

2. What was Jesus' attitude toward the miracle worker?

Jesus explained that he should be permitted to continue with his work since it was the work of God. Notice that this man performed his miracles in the name of Christ (Mark 9:39), and consequently with His permission.

The Question of Stumblingblocks ... Matthew 18:6-14; Mark 9:42-50

1. Are "the little ones" children or disciples?

That Jesus spoke of "little ones which *believe* in me," indicates His reference is to Christians who possess the spirit of little children. Notice the similar usage in 1 John 2:1, 12, 18, 28.

2. Why must occassions of stumbling come?

The devil's constant labor coupled with man's willingness to be led into sin keep the temptations coming. In His famous prayer in John 17, Jesus didn't pray that Christians should be removed from the world (freed from all temptations), but rather that they should be kept from the evil one (not be overcome by his enticements) (John 17:15). This is all that Christians can expect.

3. Is Jesus' advice concerning the treatment of the body to be taken literally?

No. Mutilation of the body doesn't keep a man from temptation nor improve his spiritual status.

Miracle in verse 39 is translated from the Greek dunamin, having the primary meaning of "power." The unknown miracle worker was performing powerful acts of an unusual nature in the name of Christ.

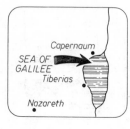

These are figurative expressions used to teach that the most strenuous and painful measures should be taken to avoid the punishment of Hell. (See 1 Corinthians 9:27 and Colossians 3:5.)

4. What do these passages teach about Hell?
(1.) Hell is a place to be avoided at all costs, (2.) into which certain people will be cast, (3.) where there is everlasting, unquenchable fire, (4.) and where "their worm dieth not." This last expression is based on Isaiah 66:24 which should be checked for a proper understanding of the figure. From these passages we conclude that Hell is a miserable place whose inhabitants endure loathsome, dreadful, and eternal suffering.

5. How can one be salted with fire?
Salt is used as a symbol of preservation, and fire of either punishment or purification. Perhaps the meaning is: everyone will be salted; some will be preserved or saved from eternal punishment by the fires of persecution that purify; others will be preserved or kept in the fires of Hell hereafter.

Discussion of Mistreatment and Forgiveness . . . Matthew 18:15-35

1. In resolving differences, what procedure should be followed?
According to the text the wronged man should go privately to his brother and discuss the problem. If it is not resolved he should go again, taking with him one or two to serve as witnesses. If the difficulty still remains, it should be told to the church. If a man will not hear the church he should be looked upon as a heathen. Of course the one seeking reconciliation should go to his brother in a good spirit. In Matthew 5:23, 24 Jesus commanded the one who does the wrong to go to his brother. Both parties, therefore, should make the effort to be reconciled.

> Resolving differences:
> 1. Go privately to the one who has wronged you;
> 2. If problem is unresolved, return with one or two witnesses;
> 3. If still unresolved, reveal the problem to the church;
> 4. If the guilty person will not change, he should be looked upon as a heathen.

2. Are there any restrictions on the promise of Matthew 18:18?
This same promise had been made earlier to Peter alone (Matthew 16:19). Here it is extended to include all of the apostles. It must be understood to mean that what the apostles bind on earth will be in harmony with the divine plan. That plan originated in Heaven, not on earth; it was announced by the apostles, not designed by them.

3. How many times should a brother be forgiven?
As often as a brother genuinely seeks forgiveness,

it must be granted him. This goes beyond the three times as practiced by the Jews of that day, the seven as suggested by Peter, and even the 490 times indicated by Christ.

4. What does the parable of the wicked servant teach?

It is an excellent illustration of Jesus' teaching in Matthew 6:15: "But if ye forgive not men their trespasses, neither will your Father forgive your trespasses." (Notice Matthew 18:35.)

Jesus and His Unbelieving Brethren . . . John 7:2-9

1. What did the feast of Tabernacles commemorate?

This annual feast was held at the end of the harvest season to commemorate the wanderings of the Jews in the wilderness. To remind them of their forefathers' hardships, the people built and lived in tents for the eight days of the feast.

2. Why the suggestion by His brethren?

Evidently out of derision, His half-brothers suggested He should go up to Jerusalem and confirm His Judean disciples in their faith. They appealed to the desire for popularity, supposing that Jesus, like themselves, had such a desire.

3. Why did Jesus refuse to go at that time?

We do not know. Perhaps He didn't want to travel with His unbelieving brethren and the other pilgrims on the usual route. John explains that when He did go up it was "not openly, but as it were in secret" (7:10). From Luke we learn that the journey was made with His apostles and through Samaria (Luke 9:51-56).

Private Journey Through Samaria to Jerusalem . . . Luke 9:51-56; John 7:10

1. Is the journey of John 7:10 the same as that of Luke 9:51?

Apparently so, although there is a great difference of opinion on this question. (For a more complete discussion of this question, check the section, "When and Where," in Lesson Sixteen.)

2. Why were James and John so vindictive?

To refuse to accept a religious teacher was considered by the Jews to be a rejection of his claims. This, as well as their personal attachment to the Savior, made them resentful of the Samaritan attitude, and led to their indignant reaction about calling down fire from Heaven. The animosity of Jews for Samaritans may also help to explain their

> **FEAST OF TABERNACLES**
>
> (1) Also called feast of Booths, feast of In-gathering;
> (2) A harvest festival;
> (3) Commemorated Jews' wandering in wilderness;
> (4) Began 15th of Tishri (about Oct.) and lasted eight days;
> (5) See Exodus 23:16; Leviticus 23:33ff; and Deuteronomy 16:13-15.

attitude. (See 2 Kings 1:5-16.) Mark, who does not relate this incident, gives the surname of James and John, "Boanerges, which is, The sons of thunder" (3:17).

WHEN AND WHERE

The transfiguration and the other events studied in this lesson occurred in the late summer of A.D. 29. They conclude with Jesus' going up to Jerusalem at the time of the feast of Tabernacles, which was held from the eleventh to the eighteenth of October that year. The transfiguration has long been associated with August 6, but there is no evidence to support it as the actual date.

Jesus was transfigured on "an high mountain" (Matthew 17:1), apparently near Caesarea Philippi, outside of Galilee (Mark 9:30). Mt. Hermon, which rises to 9400 feet, and is only a short distance from Caesarea Philippi, fits well these requirements. It is, almost without question, the mountain of transfiguration. Unfortunately, a tradition, dating back to the fourth century, cites Mount Tabor, in the south of Galilee, as the spot. Before the end of the sixth century, three churches (fitting the number of suggested tabernacles, and in complete misunderstanding of the words of God) were erected there. Later a monastery was built there. That Mount Tabor is in the southern part of Galilee, is not an exceptionally high mountain (1,843 feet above sea level), and in the day of Jesus had on its top an inhabited fortress—all argue against its being the correct spot.

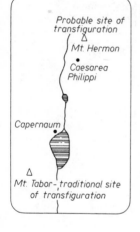

Probable site of transfiguration
△
Mt. Hermon

• Caesarea Philippi

Capernaum
•

△
Mt. Tabor- traditional site of transfiguration

PROJECTS AND PLANS

Working together as a class make "stumblingblocks" by using cardboard boxes, covered and identified with labels such as "Gossip," "Lying," "Drinking," etc. Secure permission, and place these in a conspicuous place in your church building. Perhaps a sermon could be preached or a lesson taught utilizing the blocks as object lessons.

Read the following Scripture references to the feast of Tabernacles: Leviticus 23:33-44; Numbers 29:12-40; Deuteronomy 16:13-17; Nehemiah 8:13-18.

IN AND NEAR JERUSALEM

TOPICS AND TEXTS

Jesus at the Feast of Tabernacles . . . John 7:11-52
Discussion About a Woman Taken in Adultery . . . John 7:53—8:11
Sermon on the Light of the World . . . John 8:12-59
Jesus Heals a Man Born Blind . . . John 9:1-41
Sermon on the Good Shepherd . . . John 10:1-21
The Mission of the Seventy . . . Luke 10:1-24
The Parable of the Good Samaritan . . . Luke 10:25-37
Jesus and Mary and Martha . . . Luke 10:38-42

CONTEXT AND CONTINUITY

During the month of October, A.D. 29, Jesus and His apostles left Galilee and made a hurried trip to Jerusalem to attend the feast of Tabernacles. Although unknown to His disciples, this departure brought to a conclusion His Galilean ministry. (He later passed into the borders of Galilee as He journeyed from Ephraim in Judea through Samaria into Perea, but He spent no great amount of time there. See John 11:54 and Luke 17:11.) It was not until after His death and burial, while in His resurrected body, that He returned to stand again on the shores of the Sea of Galilee to keep a rendezvous with His apostles (John 21).

Jesus' life was fast drawing to a close. It was now October, and within six months the Passover at which He was crucified would come and go. There was still much to be attended to in order to lay the groundwork for God's kingdom, the church. Although much had been done to prepare the apostles for the responsibility which was to be theirs, much still remained to be done. No one was more aware of this than Jesus. He alone bore this burden. His apostles, even the members of the inner group, were unwilling to accept that any tragedy could befall their powerful Master. Therefore, with His usual zeal, Jesus launched this Judean ministry, working the works of Him that sent Him while it was yet day.

This phase of Jesus' ministry, which lasted for better than two months, is not mentioned by either Matthew or Mark. Nor do Luke and John, upon whose accounts we depend, ever refer to the same event. Harmonizing this section of Jesus' life is, therefore, difficult. As would be expected there is a lack of unanimity among the harmonists.

It is John who speaks of Jesus' attendance at the feast of Tabernacles, and of the debate which He conducted with the Jews. It is also John who tells of the unsuccessful attempt of the chief priests and Pharisees to arrest Him, and of Nicodemus' half-hearted defense of Him before the hostile Jewish leaders. John also relates the account of the adul-

Jerusalem

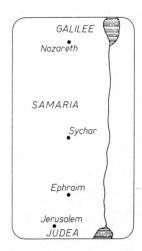

111

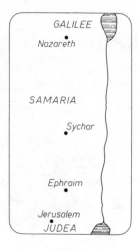

terous woman whom the Jews wished to stone, of the sermon on the light of the world which Jesus preached, of the healing of a man born blind, and of the sermon about the good shepherd. All of these events happened in Jerusalem, apparently in a brief period of time.

John then becomes silent, and Luke takes up the story, relating twelve consecutive events in Jesus' life. The first three of these will be considered in the present lesson, and the other nine in the following one.

Having concluded the sermon on the good shepherd, Jesus called, commissioned, and sent forth seventy disciples to "go into every city and place, whither he himself would come," and prepare the hearts of the people for His coming. After this, Jesus taught the parable of the good Samaritan, one of the most famous of all His parables. This was followed by a trip to the village of Bethany, where He taught an important and enduring lesson relating to the proper values of life.

INQUIRIES AND INSIGHTS

Jesus at the Feast of Tabernacles . . . John 7:11-52

1. What did this feast commemorate?
It commemorated the wanderings of the Israelites in the wilderness. To make more vivid the hardships of their forefathers, the Jews lived in booths (simple, temporary shelters) for the eight days the feast lasted. From this the feast came to be called the feast of Booths. The feast was joyous in nature, and quite popular with the people.

For information about the feast of Tabernacles, see preceding lesson.

2. What claims did Jesus make for himself in this debate?
He claimed that His doctrine was from God (vv. 16, 17), that God had sent Him (v. 29), and that He would return to God (v. 33). Jesus further claimed that they could not come to the place where He was going (v. 34), and that through believing in Him, one would come to have rivers of living water flowing from him (v. 38).

3. What claims did the people make for Jesus?
The claims made for Jesus are in many ways more astonishing than those which He made for himself. There are at least six: (1) He had learning though He had never studied (v. 15); (2) He spoke boldly (v. 26); (3) He worked many miracles (v. 31); (4) He was the Prophet (apparently a reference to Deuteronomy 18:15) (v. 40); (5) He spoke as man never had before (v. 46); (6) He was being judged without a fair hearing (v. 51).

4. How much education did Jesus receive?

From the time of the exile, synagogues had served as educational centers. Jewish boys learned some reading, writing, and arithmetic in synagogues, while being instructed in the principal subject, the Old Testament. That there was a synagogue in Nazareth is clear (Luke 4:16), but whether Jesus, as a boy, attended its school is unknown. Most likely He did. Not that His knowledge couldn't have come directly from God, but that it was more in keeping with His normal childhood that He should have attended school (see Lesson Three, "Context and Continuity" section). The reference in verse 15 is apparently to the fact that He had not received advanced theological training.

> Synagogues were places of assembly which apparently began to be used during the time of the Babylonian captivity. Philo calls the synagogues "houses of instruction, where the philosophy of the fathers and all manner of virtues were taught."

5. Did the people not know where Jesus was born?

Obviously not. They knew that the Messiah was to be born in Bethlehem (as did the chief priests and scribes in Jerusalem over thirty years earlier; Matthew 2:4-6), but assumed that Jesus had been born in Nazareth. Because of this they felt He was disqualified to be the Christ.

6. Had any prophets come out of Galilee?

The Pharisees claimed that none had, but whether their claim was based on truth or was the result of prejudice cannot be determined. Some writers believe that four Old Testament prophets came from Galilee: Elijah, Nahum, Hosea, and Jonah. Others, agreeing with this statement by the Pharisees, contend that none did.

Discussion About a Woman Taken in Adultery . . . John 7:53–8:11

1. In what part of the temple did this encounter take place?

"The Sermon on the Light of the World," which was delivered after this incident, was taught "in the treasury" (John 8:20), located in the Court of the Women. Apparently this encounter occurred there also.

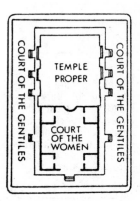

2. Were the Pharisees and scribes interested in seeing the law of Moses upheld?

Had these men been sincere in desiring to see justice executed, they would have brought both guilty parties. Their real motive was to tempt and hence ensnare Jesus (v. 6). They thought they had trapped Him with this dilemma. If, on the one hand, He advocated the death sentence, they would report Him to the Roman officials, for the Jews no longer had the right of capital punish-

> "And the man that committeth adultery with another man's wife, even he that committeth adultery with his neighbor's wife, the adulterer and the adulteress shall surely be put to death" (Leviticus 20:10).

ment. On the other hand, if He refused to honor Moses' law, they would use this to alienate the people from Him.

3. What did Jesus write in the sand?

This is the only time we are told that Jesus wrote anything. Since the writing was in the dust of the pavement in the temple, it did not long endure. We have no way of knowing what word or words He wrote, but there are a number that would have been appropriate. As a lesson to the accusers, He could have written the word, "mercy," or the word, "conscience." Or, for the benefit of the woman, He perhaps wrote, "forgiveness," or "hope." Any of these, or all of them, would have had their effect.

4. Why did no one stone the woman?

Jesus escaped the trap set for Him, and turned the situation against His accusers. As evil as these men may have been, they were not without consciences. Jesus, realizing this, appealed to their inmost thoughts, and by doing so forced them to admit that they were not without sin. In this way Jesus rescued both the woman and himself.

5. Did Jesus excuse the woman's conduct?

No, He did not. He realized she had sinned, told her so, and advised her to sin no more. He had been asked to act as a judge and to condemn her judicially. This He refused to do. Although we are not told that the woman repented, or that Jesus forgave her, we would assume that both are true. The wording of verses 10 and 11 implies as much.

Sermon on the Light of the World . . . John 8:12-59

1. In what sense is Jesus the light of the world?

What the sun is to the physical universe, Christ is to the spiritual. He makes life possible, brightens and purifies all that He contacts, destroys the darkness of ignorance, fear, and sin, and illumines the way to eternity. Through the use of this term, Jesus identified himself as the Messiah, who, according to Isaiah, was to be a great light to the people that walked in darkness (Isaiah 9:2; also Isaiah 60:1).

> "The people that walked in darkness have seen a great light: they that dwell in the land of the shadow of death, upon them hath the light shined" (Isaiah 9:2).

2. What points were debated by Jesus and the Jews?

During this informal debate the following seven points were discussed: (1) the validity of His self-testimony (vv. 13-18); (2) the identity of His Father (vv. 19, 42); (3) His own identity (vv. 25, 28); (4) the

114

nature of the freedom He offers (vv. 31-36); (5) His relationship to the Father (vv. 26-29); (6) the Jews' relationship to their father, the devil (vv. 41-47); (7) His relationship to Abraham (vv. 52-58).

3. What did the Jews understand by Jesus' words, "When ye have lifted up the Son of man"?

The meaning of this prediction of His death at their hands was probably missed or only partially understood by this hostile audience. It was not until after the establishment of the church (Acts 2), when prompted by the sermons of Peter and others, that some of these Jews came to realize that Jesus was the Messiah.

4. How does one show that He is a disciple of Jesus?

By continuing in the Word of Jesus (v. 31). Having believed and practiced His Word in the past is not enough. One must continue in His Word in order to have the hope of eternal life. (See Mark 13:13 and Revelation 2:10.)

5. From what does the truth set one free?

The truth of the Gospel sets a man free from the bondage of the Old Testament, the terror of a guilty conscience, and the slavery of sin. Without Christ these freedoms can never be known. (Read Galatians 5:1 and Romans 6:16-23.)

Jesus Heals a Man Born Blind . . . John 9:1-41

1. Why was this man born blind?

Jesus explained that the man's blindness was not the result of sin, neither the man's nor his parents'. It came upon him through natural causes that the glory of God could be manifested in the miracle performed by Jesus.

2. What admirable qualities did the man have?

Five qualities can be seen: (1) obedience (v. 7), (2) truthfulness (v. 11), (3) discernment (vv. 17, 25), (4) persistence (vv. 25-27), and (5) faith (v. 38). He had a keen mind and a courageous spirit.

Temple exit

3. What tactics were followed by the Pharisees?

They tried to coerce the man into denying that Jesus had given him his sight. Under the threat of being excommunicated from the synagogue, the man's parents had refused to testify that Jesus had restored his sight. The man himself, however, was not so easy to handle. After their threats had failed, the Pharisees actually cast him out (v. 34).

4. What is the meaning of Jesus' words in verse 39?
Jesus said there are two effects of His coming into the world: (1) Many who are blinded by sin will come to see the light He has to offer; (2) Others who think they see, who feel they are righteous, will be blind to His claims and will perish in darkness.

Sermon on the Good Shepherd . . . John 10:1-21

1. Was Jesus the first to use *shepherd* in a figurative way?
No, He was not. The Old Testament offers a number of illustrations: Numbers 27:17; Psalm 23:1; Psalm 80:1; Isaiah 44:28; Jeremiah 31:10; and many others. In these passages the word *shepherd* is applied to both spiritual and temporal overseers. When Jesus said: "I am the good shepherd," He used a phrase His audience understood in a familiar way. What startled the multitude was that He applied the title to himself. The learned people in His audience realized He was implying He was the Messiah. They were acquainted with Ezekiel 34:23 and Zechariah 13:7, both of which are Messianic prophecies.

> Shepherd used figuratively: Numbers 27:17; Psalm 23:1; Psalm 80:1; Isaiah 44:28; Jeremiah 31:10; Ezekiel 34:23; Zechariah 13:7

2. Is sheep tending still practiced in Palestine?
Yes it is, and essentially in the same way it was in the time of Abraham. For an interesting discussion of this point see the article by James A. Patch, entitled, "Sheep Tending," in *The International Standard Bible Encyclopedia,* p. 2758.

3. What is a sheepfold?
The Jewish sheepfold was a simple enclosure into which a shepherd led his sheep for protection at night (Numbers 32:16; Psalm 78:70). An area was walled off with whatever material was at hand. On the top of the wall, thorny brushwood was heaped. Often the shepherd slept at the only entrance so that any animal or man who entered had to cross over his body. In the wintertime caves were often used (1 Samuel 24:3).

Sheepfold

4. How did Jesus describe what a good shepherd does for his sheep?
He knows his sheep (v. 14), cares for them (vv. 4, 9, 12, 13), calls them (vv. 3-5, 16, 27), gives life to them (vv. 10, 28), dies for them (vv. 11, 15, 17, 18).

5. What is a hireling?
The word means "one who serves for hire." It has come to have a contemptuous connotation. Today

it is used of individuals who put their own welfare above that of the group which they serve.

The Mission of the Seventy . . . Luke 10:1-24

1. Who were these seventy?

They are not identified. They must have been faithful disciples who had spent some time with Jesus being prepared for this mission, and for the greater work of evangelizing which followed the establishment of the church. Why the number seventy was chosen is also unknown. Some suggest it was in imitation of the seventy elders appointed by Moses (Numbers 11). Others speculate that seventy were selected to correspond with the number of the Sanhedrin. Both of these are conjectures for which there is no Scriptural basis.

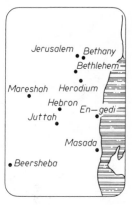

2. Why the similarity between this commission and the one given to the twelve?

The circumstances of the two events were similar. This would necessitate similar commissions. The twelve had labored in Galilee; these seventy were sent to evangelize Judea. (See Matthew 10:5-42; Mark 6:7-11; Luke 9:1-5.)

3. Why should the disciples remain in the same house for the duration of their visit to a particular place?

A man might accept a gracious invitation from people of humble means and later change to a house offering more comfortable quarters. Such a move might destroy the effectiveness of the worker. To avoid this, Jesus forbade the seventy to move from spot to spot.

purse

scrip

shoes

4. What was the purpose of wiping off the dust?

Similar advice was given the twelve when they were sent out. Note that the terminology here and that used in the three places where the sending of the twelve is described differs slightly: Luke 10 speaks of wiping off the dust (v. 11); Matthew says, "shake off the dust of your feet" (10:14); Mark, "shake off the dust under your feet" (6:11); Luke 9, "shake off the very dust from your feet" (v. 5). Barnes states: "The Jews taught uniformly that the dust of the Gentiles was impure, and was to be shaken off. To shake off the dust from the feet, therefore, was a significant act, denoting that they regarded them as impure, profane, and heathenish, and that they declined all further connection with them."—*Notes on the New Testament, Matthew* p. 111. Acts 13:51 records the practice of the act by Paul and Barnabas.

117

5. How will judgment be more tolerable for Tyre and Sidon?
This question is answered in Lesson Nine.

6. What success did the seventy have?
Verse 17 indicates that the mission was a tremendous success. They were especially happy because they had been able to expel demons. This was evidence that the power in the name of Jesus was superior to the forces of evil.

7. When did Satan fall from Heaven?
Perhaps the reference is to the time Satan was cast out of Heaven before the creation of the world. Christ would have witnessed this in His pre-earthly existence. This expulsion is mentioned in Isaiah 14:12ff, and alluded to in Jude 6. Another interpretation, one more in harmony with the context, is offered by McGarvey and Pendleton: "The sense indicates that the words refer to the victories over the unclean spirits just reported by the seventy. In their successes Jesus saw Satan falling from lofty heights with the swiftness of lightning."—*The Fourfold Gospel,* p. 473.

The Parable of the Good Samaritan . . . Luke 10:25-37

1. What precipitated the teaching of this parable?
A young lawyer, expert in Jewish Canon Law, tempted (i.e., tested) Jesus with a question about the way to inherit eternal life. Jesus put the responsibility of answering the question back on the man by asking one of His own: "What is written in the law?" Citing Deuteronomy 6:5 and Leviticus 19:18, the lawyer concluded a man must love God supremely, and his neighbor as himself. Wishing to avoid the responsibility entailed in the latter, the man asked, "Who is my neighbor?" Jesus taught this parable in order to answer that question.

2. Is this a parable or an actual event?
Because Jesus mentioned a specific road, some have concluded this was an event which had recently happened, with which the audience was familiar. However, a characteristic of all parables is that their details are all true to life—they either had happened or could happen. Probably this is a fictional account of an event, the likes of which had happened numerous times on the steep road (the level of the land descends nearly four thousand feet in eighteen or nineteen miles) that descended from Jerusalem to Jericho.

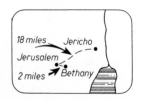

| | | | | | J | F | M | A | M | J | J | A | S | O | N | D | | | | |

3. Who were the priest and Levite?
Nothing specific is revealed about either of them. Priests were responsible for offering sacrifices in the temple, burning incense, conducting the daily services, etc. The Levites were temple ministers who assisted the priests in performing their functions. The following Scriptures describe the work of the Levites: Numbers 8:5-22; 1 Chronicles 23:3-5, 24-32.

4. Who, according to Jesus, is a man's neighbor?
That person is a neighbor who shows compassion toward another. He may be of a different and hated race, have a different skin color, and speak a different language, but if he has a willingness to show neighborliness, he is indeed a true neighbor.

5. What three attitudes are shown in this story?
The philosophy of the thieves was, "What is yours is mine, and I will take it." That of the priest and Levite was, "What is mine is mine, and I will keep it." The Samaritan's philosophy was, "What is mine is yours, and I will share it."

Jesus and Mary and Martha . . . Luke 10:38-42

1. What is known about Mary and Martha?
This is the first reference in the Gospels to these sisters. They are also mentioned in John 11 in connection with the death and raising of their brother, Lazarus. John 12 (Matthew 26; Mark 14) relates how Mary anointed Jesus with very costly ointment. The name Mary is from the Hebrew *Mara*, and means "bitter." Martha means "mistress." Lazarus or Laazar, and is an abbreviated form of Elazar or Eleazar, and literally means "God is helper."

2. Is it right to neglect the physical things of life?
No, nor did Jesus teach that it is. The spiritual, however, must take precedence over the physical; it must be recognized as the better part. Too many, too often, follow Martha's example and become distracted from spiritual things by their interest in the physical. It was against this tendency that Jesus spoke.

WHEN AND WHERE

Leviticus 23:34 gives the date for the beginning of the feast of Tabernacles as the fifteenth day of the seventh month (Tishri; also called Ethanim, 1 Kings 8:2). This time would be comparable to the

On the Jericho Road

Palestinian inn

Mary = "bitter"
Martha = "mistress"
Lazarus = "God is helper"

119

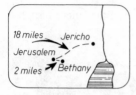

last part of September and the first part of October. The feast lasted for eight days (Leviticus 23:36). Coming as it did at the completion of the harvest, it was a time of thanksgiving to God for His bountiful goodness.

Bethany, mentioned in connection with the last event of this lesson, was a small village about two miles southeast of Jerusalem. Today it is known as El-Azariyeh, a name derived from its famous inhabitant, Lazarus. Locate it on the map that is provided.

PROJECTS AND PLANS

Working together as a class, seek to discover what is being done in your community to help the sightless. Endeavor to make available to them the Word of God in Braille and/or on records.

Read the article entitled, "Feasts and Fasts," by Ella Davis Isaacs, in *The International Standard Bible Encyclopedia*, pp. 1103, 1104.

DISCOURSES, DISCUSSIONS AND DENUNCIATIONS

TOPICS AND TEXTS

Discourse on Prayer . . . Luke 11:1-13
Discussion of the Charge That Jesus Was in League With the Devil . . . Luke 11:14-36
Denunciation of the Pharisees . . . Luke 11:37-54
Disciples Warned Against Fear of Men . . . Luke 12:1-12
The Parable of the Rich Fool . . . Luke 12:13-21
Exhortation to Trust in God . . . Luke 12:22-34
Watchfulness: Parable of the Waiting Servants and the Wise Steward . . . Luke 12:35-59
Discourse on Repentance . . . Luke 13:1-9
Discussion of Healing on the Sabbath and of the Coming Kingdom . . . Luke 13:10-21
Jesus at the Feast of Dedication . . . John 10:22-39

CONTEXT AND CONTINUITY

The preceding lesson ended with Jesus in Bethany at the home of Martha, Mary, and Lazarus. Where Jesus went after that is unknown. Probably He remained in or near Jerusalem, or at least in Judea, until the feast of Dedication.

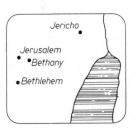

As indicated by the lesson title, much of this time was spent in delivering discourses, participating in discussions, and issuing denunciations. Much of the material handled in this lesson is of a repetitious nature. It is similar to, and sometimes identical with, material taught by Jesus to Galilean audiences. Even the events that precipitated some of His teaching opportunities are like earlier ones. This is as would be expected. Teachers today recognize that repetition is one of the keys to successful teaching, and certainly Jesus, the master teacher, was aware of it. The audiences of Jesus varied greatly; disciples taught in Galilee would seldom be in His audience in Judea. Since there were a number of truths to be taught to as many people as possible, and since there were no moden media to report His teaching to the masses, it was essential that His basic lessons be repeated frequently. In light of these circumstances, it is surprising that there isn't more repeition in the Gospel records.

The following list shows the extensiveness of this repetition. The texts considered in this lesson are on the left; the parallel passages from Jesus' earlier teaching are on the right:

Luke 11:2-4 . . . . . Matthew 6:9-13
Luke 11:9-13 . . . Matthew 7:7-11
Luke 11:14, 15 . Matthew 12:22, 24; Mark 3:22
Luke 11:17-22 . . Matthew 12:25-29; Mark 3:23-27
Luke 11:23 . . . . . Matthew 12:30
Luke 11:24-26 . . Matthew 12:43-45

			J	F	M	A	M	J	J	A	S	O	N	D					

A.D. 28 | A.D. 29 | A.D. 30

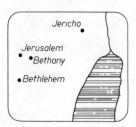

Jericho

Jerusalem
• Bethany

• Bethlehem

Luke 11:29-32 .. Matthew 12:39-42
Luke 11:33 . . . . . Matthew 5:15; Mark 4:21
Luke 11:34, 35 . Matthew 6:22, 23
Luke 12:1 . . . . . . Matthew 16:6; Mark 8:15
Luke 12:2-9 . . . . Matthew 10:26-33
Luke 12:10 . . . . . Matthew 12:31, 32; Mark 3:28-30
Luke 12:11, 12 . Matthew 10:17-20
Luke 12:22-31 .. Matthew 6:25-33
Luke 12:33, 34 . Matthew 6:20, 21
Luke 12:51-53 .. Matthew 10:34-36
Luke 12:54-56 .. Matthew 16:2, 3
Luke 12:58, 59 . Matthew 5:25, 26
Luke 13:18, 19 . Matthew 13:31, 32; Mark 4:30-32
Luke 13:20, 21 . Matthew 13:33

In studying the texts of this lesson, it would be profitable to check preceding lessons where the parallel texts have been discussed.

In addition to the above passages which show similarity to earlier teaching of Jesus, there are several texts which contain material taught at this time and repeated later. These will not be itemized.

Although there is much that is repetitious, there is enough new material to make this lesson both interesting and helpful.

INQUIRIES AND INSIGHTS

Discourse on Prayer . . . Luke 11:1-13

1. What is learned about John the Baptist?
From verse 1 we learn that John recognized the value of prayer and instructed his disciples as to how to pray. Obviously John, like Jesus, was a man of prayer who gained his strength through regular communion with God.

2. What elements of prayer are found in this model?
Two elements are clearly revealed: *adoration* and *petition*. Although not expressed, it is evident from the spirit of the entire prayer that a third element, *thanksgiving*, is included.

3. What is the central teaching of this parable?
The word *importunity* used in verse 8, is the key word of the parable. It is defined: "persistent demand, insistence." "Men must be persistent in their prayer life" is the parable's central teaching.

4. How do verses 9-11 differ from Matthew 7:7-11?
To the two illustrations of Matthew (bread, stone; fish, serpent), Luke adds a third: "If he shall ask an

This prayer is popularly known as the "Lord's Prayer." It is not, however, a prayer which the Lord offered, but one which He taught. It is a model prayer. See John 17 for an example of a prayer offered by Jesus.

egg, will he offer him a scorpion?'' Also, whereas Matthew states, ''How much more shall your Father which is in heaven give good things to them that ask him?'' (7:11), Luke has, ''. . . give the Holy Spirit to them that ask him?'' (11:13).

Discussion of the Charge That Jesus Was in League With the Devil . . . Luke 11:14-36

1. **What does the Bible teach about demons?**
For an answer to this question see Lesson Ten.

2. **How did the Pharisees unwittingly testify for Jesus?**
The Pharisees didn't deny that Jesus was casting out demons. If they had done this the multitude would have known they were lying immediately, for it was apparent that demons were being expelled. Since this course wasn't open to them, they claimed He was in alliance with the devil, and drew upon his powers. This sneer of His enemies, therefore, contains a testimony to Christ's miraculous power.

3. **What arguments did Jesus use to answer the charge against Him?**
Jesus employed the following four arguments: (1) Satan would not cast out Satan (or one of his agents) because this would weaken his cause. (2) Others, the sons of the Pharisees, had claimed to expel demons, and their claims had not been questioned. (It should be noted that Jesus didn't affirm that the sons of the Pharisees had actually had success; this is an *argumentum ad hominem*.) (3) A strong man's goods can't be stolen until the man is bound, nor can demons be cast out unless Satan is powerless to stop it. (4) As a tree is judged by its fruit, so a man must be judged (as to whether or not he is in league with the devil) by his works.

4. **What is the meaning of the parable of the unclean spirit?**
Luke doesn't offer an interpretation of the parable. In a similar passage, Matthew records the following words as concluding the parable: ''Even so shall it be also unto this wicked generation'' (Matthew 12:45). From this statement we learn that the primary meaning of the parable concerned the generation in which Jesus lived. McGarvey and Pendleton state: ''It is simply an assertion that the last state of that generation would be worse than the first. The reference is to the continually increasing wickedness of the Jews, which culminated in the dreadful scenes which preceded the destruction of Jerusalem. They were now like a

The expression ''demon possession'' is not found in the New Testament. Persons are said to ''have a demon or an unclean spirit,'' or to be ''demonised.''

man with one evil spirit; they would then be like a man with seven more demons added, each of which was worse than the original occupant."
—*The Fourfold Gospel* pp. 308, 309.

5. How did Jesus respond to the words of this unknown woman?

The woman pronounced a beatitude upon Mary because she had given birth to Jesus and had nursed Him as a baby. Jesus responded that the one who hears the Word of God and keeps it is the one who is truly blessed. Here, as elsewhere, Jesus made it clear that there was no merit in physical relationship to Him, only in spiritual.

6. What kind of sign did the Jews seek?

Their request was for a sign from Heaven similar to the miracles mentioned in the following texts: Exodus 9:22-24; Joshua 10:12-14; 1 Samuel 7:9, 10; 1 Kings 18:36-39; 2 Kings 1:10; Isaiah 38:8. There was a belief among the Jews that false gods and demons could work signs on earth, but only the true God could work signs from Heaven. It was one of this kind that they wanted to see.

7. What sign did Jesus give them?

Jesus promised them the sign of Jonah. As the prophet had spent three days in the belly of a fish, the Son of man would spend three days in the heart of the earth. See Matthew 12:39, 40, and Matthew 16:4.

8. Why the references to the "queen of the south" and "the men of Nineveh"?

The two Old Testament illustrations have in common the fact that action was taken because of the presence of a great person. With the queen of the south it was Solomon; with the men of Nineveh, Jonah. Greater than these Old Testament men was the Christ, whose presence should have produced favorable action with the men of His generation.

Denunciation of the Pharisees . . . Luke 11:37-54

1. Why did the Pharisees marvel?

In failing to bathe himself before eating, Jesus violated one of the numerous traditions of the elders. It was this apparent disregard for ritual that irritated His host. The Pharisees felt that through mingling with the multitudes one might become ceremonially defiled through body contact with an unclean person. Hence, they felt it necessary to bathe themselves in order to remove this defilement.

Some say Jonah was the first foreign missionary. Read the Old Testament book named for him.

The "Queen of the South" (also called the Queen of Sheba) is also mentioned in 1 Kings 10, 2 Chronicles 9, and Matthew 12:42.

Ceremonial vessel

2. How many woes did Jesus pronounce on the Pharisees and scribes?

Six woes are mentioned in this discourse—three against the Pharisees and three against the scribes. The Pharisees were condemned for their misplaced values, their striving after recognition and praise, and their conduct which caused others to stumble. The lawyers were condemned for burdening others, for their attitude toward the prophets, and for their destruction of the key of knowledge. The basic sin Jesus condemned in each pronouncement was hypocrisy.

3. Who were Abel and Zechariah?

This is that Abel, son of Adam, who was murdered by his brother Cain (Genesis 4:1-8). In a similar passage Matthew called him, "righteous Abel" (23:35). The Zechariah mentioned is probably the priest of 2 Chronicles 24 who was slain at the command of Joash, King of Judah. Some writers identify him with Zechariah the prophet.

Disciples Warned Against Fear of Men . . . Luke 12:1-12

1. Whom should we fear?

Men should not be feared for they can harm only the body. Rather, our fear should be of God who can harm not only the body but the soul as well. God is not to be feared as a tyrant, but respected as our father.

2. How did Jesus show that a man is precious in the sight of God?

As valueless as sparrows may be to men, they are precious to God. Not one falls to the earth without His awareness. Men, who are far more valuable than sparrows, can be sure God is concerned about them. To give an indication of the measure of that concern, Jesus said even the number of hairs on our head is known to God.

> Sparrows in Palestine are small, seed-eating birds, much like our American house sparrow. They are noisy, active, plentiful, and cheap.

3. What is the blasphemy of the Holy Spirit?

Numerous opinions are held concerning the blasphemy against the Holy Spirit (or, as frequently called, "the unpardonable sin"). Some of these are: (1) mere rejection of Jesus Christ (unpardonable because it is unpardoned); (2) the simple act of attributing the work of the Holy Spirit to the devil; (3) perpetual rejection of the Holy Spirit; (4) rejection of God and His religion by those who were once His followers, including the attributing of their former experience to the power of the devil. Before forming an opinion, the following Scriptures should be studied: Hebrews

> For further insight on blasphemy of the Holy Spirit, study Hebrews 6:4-8; 10:26-31; 1 John 5:16.

125

Jesus apparently remained in or near Jerusalem from the time of the feast of Tabernacles until after the feast of Dedication in that year (October through December in A. D. 29).

6:4-8; Hebrews 10:26-31; 1 John 5:16. A combination of positions three and four meets all requirements. Foster, quoting Plummer, offers the following definition: "Constant and consummate opposition to the influence of the Holy Spirit because of a deliberate preference of darkness to the light (which) renders repentance, therefore forgiveness, morally impossible is the blasphemy of the Holy Spirit."—R. C. Foster, *Gospels Syllabus.*

The Parable of the Rich Fool . . . Luke 12:13-21

1. What motivated Jesus to teach this parable?
A man, described as "one of the company," requested that Jesus help him get his share of inheritance from his brother. Rather than assist the man, Jesus took the occasion to speak against the sin of covetousness, a sin of which either one or both of these brothers were guilty. It is impossible to conceive of any words that could better describe the sin, or more vividly portray its outcome.

2. From the rich man's speech what is learned about his character?
The man was an egotist of the first order who seldom thought of others except as to how they might benefit him. In the few sentences which he spoke to himself, he used the word *I* six times, *my* five times, and *thou* and *thine* (when addressing himself) once each.

3. What lesson is taught by this parable?
The key to the parable's interpretation is verse 21: "So is he that layeth up treasure for himself, and is not rich toward God." Unless a man has God, at the Judgment his soul will be as barren as his coffers have been full.

Exhortation to Trust in God . . . Luke 12:22-34

1. How does this passage differ from that of Matthew 6?
The passages are quite similar, differing mainly in terminology and arrangement. Luke 12:32, with its precious promise, has no parallel in Matthew.

2. Was Jesus' warning against forethought or anxiety?
The Greek word, *merimnáo,* translated "Take no thought" in the King James version is better translated "Be not anxious" in later versions. In 1611, when the King James translation was made, the word "thought" meant "anxious thought," and was so used by a number of English authors of that day. After issuing the prohibition against anxiety, Jesus illustrated repeatedly the futility of worry.

Watchfulness: Parable of the Waiting Servants and the Wise Steward . . . Luke 12:35-59

1. How did Jesus teach watchfulness?
By a parable, then an illustration, and another parable, Jesus taught His disciples the virtue of preparedness. The first parable was about servants who watched for their Lord's coming (vv. 36-38). The illustration concerns the uncertainty of the hour a thief may strike (v. 39). The second parable is about a faithful and wise steward who operated his lord's household properly (vv. 42-48).

2. Are there to be degrees of reward and punishment?
Verses 47 and 48 teach that there will be degrees of punishment. Here, as well as elsewhere in the Bible, the criterion for determining the number of stripes a man will get is his opportunity to know his lord's will. Other passages (Matthew 16:27; 1 Corinthians 3:8; 2 Corinthians 9:6; Revelation 22:12) indicate degrees of reward also.

> Degrees of reward? See Matthew 16:27, 1 Corinthians 3:8, 2 Corinthians 9:6, and Revelation 22:12.

3. What fire did Jesus wish to be kindled?
As a natural consequence of Jesus' coming, the fires of discord and contention were brought to earth. Families will continue to be divided over the question, "What think ye of Christ?"

4. What baptism did Jesus have in mind?
Baptism is used here in a figurative sense to represent the suffering and death which Jesus faced in the near future. (Read also Matthew 20:22.)

> Baptism is a transliteration of the Greek baptidzo, which means "to dip, plunge, or immerse." Here the element is sorrow and death. The ordinance of Christian baptism is performed in water (Acts 8:38, 39).

Discourse on Repentance . . . Luke 13:1-9

1. Who were these Galileans?
Nothing is known of them except what is revealed in this text, which is very little. While they offered sacrifices in Jerusalem, they were slain by the command of Pilate.

2. When did this tower fall?
Siloam was a village southeast of Jerusalem on the lower slope of the Mount of Olives. The Pool of Siloam was to the west of the village, on Mount Ophel. The tower was probably in this general vicinity. What specific tower it was and when it fell are unknown. Probably the tragedy had recently occurred and was fresh in the minds of the people.

3. What is repentance?
"It is a change of that stubborn will which is the seat of all rebellion and all sin against God. When

The Greek word for repent is <u>metanäéo</u>, meaning "to change one's mind."

a man is so thoroughly filled with sorrow and mourning and self-reproach on account of his sins that his will is subdued to the will of God, and he says, I will sin no more, I will hereafter submit to the will of my God, this results in a change of his life, and it is repentance—a change of will in regard to sin."—J. W. McGarvey, *Sermons,* p. 100.

4. In the parable of the barren fig tree, what lesson is taught?
Jesus taught there is an end to the patience of God, that His Spirit will not always strive with men, that the opportunity to repent will pass away.

Discussion of Healing on the Sabbath and of the Coming Kingdom . . . Luke 13:10-21

1. What was wrong with this woman?
Luke states she had a "spirit of infirmity" and was "bowed together." Evidently she had some affliction of the spine caused by a demon.

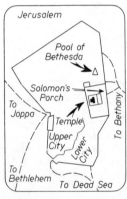

2. To whom did the ruler of the synagogue direct his remarks?
His words were spoken *to* the people, but *for* the benefit of Jesus. Probably cowardice kept him from openly rebuking Jesus.

3. How did Jesus answer the ruler?
Jesus reminded him that on the Sabbath an ox or ass is loosed from its stall and led to a place of watering. Similarly, this woman deserved to be given relief from an eighteen-year-old affliction.

Jesus at the Feast of Dedication . . . John 10:22-39

1. Where was Solomon's Porch?
It was a covered section on the east side of the temple. Josephus says that the wall against which the porch was built was the work of Solomon (*Antiquities* 20:9:7). Since it was winter, Jesus was in this covered section of the temple.

2. Why refer to His former teaching about the good shepherd and his sheep?
By claiming to be the good shepherd (which He did on an earlier occasion), Jesus made claim to the messiahship. Two famous Old Testament prophecies pictured the Messiah as a shepherd (Ezekiel 34:23; Zechariah 13:7) and were so understood by the Jews. These men did not believe Jesus' claim because they were not His sheep.

3. What claim of Jesus greatly angered the Jews?
When Jesus claimed unity with God, it was more

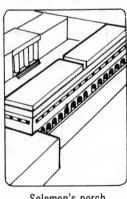

Solomon's porch

than the hostile Jews would tolerate. They therefore picked up rocks to stone Him. (See John 8:59.)

4. How did Jesus answer them?

First He reminded them of His many good works from the Father, and asked them for which of these He was being stoned. Next He quoted the law (actually the quotation is from Psalm 82:6, and was a part of the law in the sense that it was a part of the Old Testament) where judges were called gods because of the dignity of their office. Jesus didn't mean to imply that He was a god in the sense that these Old Testament magistrates were. Rather His argument was that others had used the term "god" of men without being condemned for its use, and therefore He should not be condemned.

WHEN AND WHERE

The feast of Dedication, also called the feast of Lights, was not an Old Testament feast. It came to be observed after the close of the Old Testament Canon. It commemorated the purifying of the temple after its defilement by the Syrians under Antiochus Epiphanes. The feast began on the twenty-fifth of Chisleu, which in A. D. 29 was the same as our December twentieth. It lasted for eight days, the length of time Judas Maccabaeus, the deliverer of the city, took in purifying it. It came to be called the feast of Lights because the city of Jerusalem was brightly illuminated for its observance. The feast can be read about in the following places: 1 Maccabees 4:36-59; 2 Maccabees 10:1-8; *Antiquities* 12:7:6, 7. The events of this lesson occurred in the four- or six-week's period preceding and culminating in this feast.

Notice on the map the location of the Tyropeon Valley and the Pool of Siloam. Familiarize yourself with this area.

PROJECTS AND PLANS

As a project for this lesson memorize Luke 12:16-21, the parable of the rich fool. Perhaps each one who succeeds could quote the passage in an assembly of the church.

Check through the Gospels to see how many different controversies Jesus had concerning the Sabbath Day.

> The feast of Dedication, also called the feast of Lights, was not an Old Testament feast.

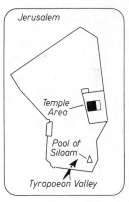

Jerusalem

Temple Area

Pool of Siloam

Tyropoeon Valley

(See Luke 13:4)

JESUS IN PEREA

TOPICS AND TEXTS

Retirement From Jerusalem to Perea . . . John 10:40-42
Discussions in Perea . . . Luke 13:22-35
Healing in a Pharisee's Home on the Sabbath . . . Luke 14:1-24
Sermon on the Cost of Discipleship . . . Luke 14:25-35
Parables of the Lost Sheep, Coin, and Son . . . Luke 15:1-32
Parable of the Unjust Steward . . . Luke 16:1-13
Parable of the Rich Man and Lazarus . . . Luke 16:14-31
Parable of the Unprofitable Servant . . . Luke 17:1-10

The feast of Dedication commemorated the purifying of the temple after its defilement by the Syrians under Antiochus Epiphanes. This happened between the Old Testament and New Testament periods.

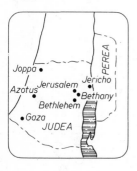

CONTEXT AND CONTINUITY

Sometime after the feast of Dedication, Jesus left Judea and went into Perea. John tells about this departure into the land "beyond Jordan," and of the success Jesus experienced there (10:40-42). However, after mentioning His departure and briefly commenting on His success, John reveals no more of the specifics of this ministry. (He does tell of an interruption of the Perean ministry when Jesus returned for a brief period to Judea. This came about because of the illness and death of Lazarus whom Jesus raised from the dead [John 11:1-54]. This material will be considered in the next lesson.)

We must look to Luke to learn of the events of the first part of the Perean ministry, and to all three Synoptics to learn of its concluding transactions.

Luke's first reference to the Perean ministry centers about a question from one of the multitude regarding the number that will be saved (13:23), and of Jesus' answer. On that same day (13:31) some Pharisees came to Jesus with a warning, which they obviously delighted to give, that He should get out of Perea lest Herod kill Him. Having shown by His answer that He had no fear of that "fox," He then lamented over Jerusalem and its unfortunate plight.

Luke next relates that Jesus was invited into the home of a Pharisee to dine on a Sabbath Day, and that while there He healed a man afflicted with dropsy. He then taught a parable against the seeking of chief seats, and gave an admonition concerning inviting the needy to meals. This was followed by the parable of the great supper or "parable of excuses," as it is frequently called. After this Jesus spoke concerning the cost of true religion and the necessity for counting the cost.

Sometime later (and there are no time references), Jesus taught six very well-known parables. Three of them—the parables of the lost sheep, lost coin, and lost son—are recorded in the fifteenth chapter of Luke. Two others—the parable of the unjust steward and the parable of the rich man and Lazarus—are in the sixteenth chapter. The sixth one—the parable of the unprofitable servant—is in the seventeenth chapter.

At this time, if our harmony is correct, Jesus departed for Judea to raise Lazarus. This event will be considered in the next lesson.

INQUIRIES AND INSIGHTS

Retirement From Jerusalem to Perea . . . John 10:40-42

1. Where did Jesus go at this time?
John says He went "beyond Jordan into the place where John at first baptized" (10:40). Whether this refers to a spot on the Jordan across from Jericho, or to a place farther north near Bethabara (or *Bethany,* according to the most ancient reading of John 1:28), is difficult to say.

2. Did John the Baptist perform miracles?
John 10:41 says he didn't. However, he was able to make predictions about the Christ which were later fulfilled. This ability served as a credential to substantiate his message.

3. What did John say about Jesus?
The wording in this text indicates John had much to say about the Christ. For some examples of his predictions check the following texts: Matthew 3:7-12; Mark 1:7, 8; Luke 3:7-18; John 1:29-34.

Discussions in Perea . . . Luke 13:22-35

1. What is a strait gate?
Jesus used this figure to illustrate the difficulty of getting into the kingdom of Heaven. The word *strait* must not be confused with *straight.* The former means "pent up, narrow, difficult to be entered," whereas the latter simply means "not crooked." Jesus said men should *strive* to enter. The Greek word used here is taken from the Grecian games where men strove, or literally "agonized," to win the victory. Similarly, men should put forth every effort to be saved.

2. What lesson is taught in verse 26?
Many seem to think that because their community is "Christian," this qualifies every one of its inhabitants for eternal bliss in Heaven. This verse serves as a warning against this position. It is not enough that men have eaten and drunk in His presence, or that He has taught in their streets. Salvation is an individual matter which requires personal dedication to the Christ.

> The territory on the east side of the Jordan River, opposite Judea and Samaria, is referred to in the Bible as "beyond Jordan." Josephus and others used the term <u>Perea</u>.

131

> ### GENTILES ACCEPTABLE IN CHRIST'S KINGDOM
>
> "And they shall come from the east, and from the west, and from the north, and from the south, and shall sit down in the kingdom of God" (Luke 13:29).

See page 237.

3. Why is verse 29 precious to Gentiles?

This verse, like others in the Gospels, makes it clear that the ultimate plan of Jesus was for the conversion of all of the peoples of the world, Gentiles as well as Jews. (Read Mark 7:27 and John 10:16.)

4. Why call Herod a "fox"?

This Herod was Antipas, son of Herod the Great and Malthace, and brother of Archelaus. He was the murderer of John the Baptist. Jesus called him a "fox" because he was like one in his slyness, destructiveness, and treacherousness.

5. Did all Jewish prophets die in Jerusalem?

No, nor did Jesus mean for the statement to be taken literally. John the Baptist, for one, had not died there, and the people certainly were aware of this. Jesus meant that it was usually true that the Holy City itself was the scene of the martyring of God's prophets. He thus implied it would be the scene of His own death.

Healing in a Pharisee's Home on the Sabbath . . . Luke 14:1-24

1. Why was the man with dropsy present?

The statement in verse 1 that "they watched him" indicates the sick man was there by invitation of the Pharisees for the purpose of serving as a trap for Jesus. The less courageous might have avoided such a trap, but not Jesus. With characteristic boldness, He took command of the situation, healed the sick man, and let him go.

2. What is dropsy?

"Dropsy, in modern medical language called edema, is a condition in which the tissues retain too much fluid. It may be caused by heart disease, kidney disease, or local infection, and may terminate fatally."—*Pictorial Bible Dictionary*, p. 221.

3. What lesson is taught by the parable in verses 7-11?

The parable condemns social pride, the desire for recognition, the seeking after places of importance. Barnes comments: "His chief design here was, no doubt, to reprove the pride and ambition of the Pharisees; but, in doing it, he teaches us that religion does not violate the courtesies of life. It does not teach us to be rude, forward, pert, assuming, and despising the proprieties of refined intercourse. It teaches humility and kindness, and a desire to make all happy, and a willingness to occupy our appropriate situation and rank in life;

and this is true politeness, for true politeness is a desire to make all others happy, and a readiness to do whatever is necessary to make them so."
—*Notes on the New Testament, Luke,* p. 95.

4. Must the poor always be invited to dinners in preference to friends and relatives?
Jesus advocated proper motivation. Guests should not be invited so they can reciprocate or so that we can impress them. They should be invited simply out of love whether they be our friends, our relatives, or the poor and the maimed.

5. What lesson is taught by the Parable of the Great Supper?
The first guests to be invited represented the Jewish leaders. Since they refused to attend the great supper, others, representing the publicans, sinners, and Gentiles, were invited and accepted. The parable was a warning to the Pharisees, Sadducees, and scribes about what was happening to them in their relationship to God.

Sermon on the Cost of Discipleship . . . Luke 14:25-35

1. In what sense must a man hate his own relatives in order to be a disciple of Jesus?
The key here is the expression *his own life also.* Jesus didn't advocate that a man hate himself in order to be a Christian; nor did He say that one must literally hate his relatives. Although not a correct translation, the rendering, "love less," better expresses Jesus' true meaning.

2. How did Jesus teach that it is necessary to count the cost of discipleship?
By the use of two illustrations, Jesus taught this valuable lesson. The first was about a man planning to build a tower without adequate funds. The second concerned a king desirous of going to war but unwilling to do so because of an insufficient number of soldiers.

Parables of the Lost Sheep, Coin, and Son . . . Luke 15:1-32

1. What do these three parables have in common?
In each something was lost, later found, causing rejoicing.

2. Is it wise to leave ninety-nine sheep in the wilderness to seek after one lost one?
We aren't to suppose the shepherd left them in a desolate and dangerous spot, but in their usual

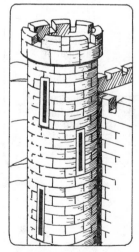

Towers were frequently built for defense. They were high to allow long-distance sighting of enemies, and strong so as to be difficult to capture.

133

Drachmas

STEPS OF THE
PRODIGAL

Demand
Departure
Dissipation
Destitution
Degradation

Reflection
Resolution
Return
Restoration
Rejoicing

place of pasture; perhaps in a fold. Possibly while folding them he discovered the absence of the lost one. A shepherd who would desert ninety-nine sheep, and expose them to all kinds of danger in order to save one, would be foolish. That is not the picture Jesus had in mind.

3. What was the value of the money that was lost?
The Greek says ten drachmas. A silver drachma was equivalent to a Roman denarius. It represented a day's wages in Christ's time.

4. Who is to be the more condemned, the younger or elder brother?
The elder brother represented the Jewish leaders who supposedly stayed in fellowship with God. The younger son represented the publicans and sinners with whom Jesus ate. The attitude of the elder brother, expressed in his failure to do anything to help win back his brother, and his unhappiness upon his return, mark him as the greater sinner.

Parable of the Unjust Steward . . . Luke 16:1-13

1. What lesson did Jesus teach by this parable?
Barclay calls this parable "A Bad Man's Good Example," which is a fitting title. The lesson Jesus intended is not that we should be like this rascal steward. The applications of the parable begin in verse 8 and continue through verse 13. There are five of them: (1) The sons of this world are, for their own generation, wiser than the sons of the light; (2) Use the things of the world to make friends, so that a correct and eternal friendship with its natural blessings will be produced; (3) Faithfulness in little things is indicative of a man's fitness for responsibility in great things; (4) Faithfulness with that which is another's will qualify one to handle properly his own things; (5) It is impossible to serve two masters.

2. Does Jesus approve of cheating?
All cheating is morally wrong and is condemned in the Bible. We must remember that parables contain a basic truth. The actions of the characters of a parable may be good or bad; we are not to imitate their actions, but learn and practice the central truth which is taught.

Parable of the Rich Man and Lazarus . . . Luke 16:14-31

1. What lesson does this parable teach?
It teaches that beyond this life there is another

existence. In it men will be conscious, will remember their former life, will be capable of experiencing pain or blessedness, and will be blessed or cursed according to what they did on earth. Dives, as the rich man is called (the word is the Latin term for *rich man),* obviously abused his wealth, and had contempt for the poor. However, according to Trench, the real sin of the man was unbelief, and the abuse and contempt were only the forms which his unbelief took.—*Notes on the Parables of Our Lord,* p. 162.

> Is this a parable, or an actual event? Although the main character is named, it is probably just a parable. Like all parables, it is true to life.

2. Where is Abraham's bosom?

Hades (the unseen world) is composed of two sections, Paradise (Luke 23:43) and Tartarus (2 Peter 2:4). These are divided by a great gulf which makes access from one to the other impossible (Luke 16:26). To these places the souls of men are taken at death. There they remain until the day of the resurrection. At that time the souls of those in Paradise will be joined to their bodies, which will be raised from their graves (Revelation 20:13), and will pass through the Judgment into glory. Those in Tartarus likewise will be united with their bodies (John 5:28, 29). They will then be judged and condemned to Hell. Verse 23 does not speak of Hell *(Gehenna),* but of Hades, or more specifically, of that section of Hades called *Tartarus.* Abraham's bosom is another name for Paradise. The Jews could desire no better happiness than that of reclining on Abraham's bosom. The following chart helps explain the relationship of the various abodes of man, present and future.

Present World		Unseen World		Future World
CHURCH ↑---↓ SINFUL WORLD	D E A T H	PARADISE GULF TARTARUS	J U D G M E N T	HEAVEN HELL

3. Would Dives' brothers have believed Lazarus had he returned to them from the dead?

The parable indicates not (v. 31). Even if Jesus

hadn't given an answer to the question, our own thinking would drive us to the same conclusion. If the poor outcast beggar, Lazarus, returned to the home of the five rich men and informed them that their brother's soul was in a place of torment, and that he himself had just returned from a place of happiness, they would not only have laughed at him, but undoubtedly would have punished him for spreading such a malicious falsehood.

Parable of the Unprofitable Servant . . . Luke 17:1-10

1. Why is it "impossible but that offences will come"?
Jesus meant that it is to be expected. The world is such that opportunities for stumbling will come.

2. What is the meaning of Jesus' statement concerning the mustard seed?
"It has been supposed by some . . . that he meant to say, If you have the smallest or feeblest faith that is genuine, you can do all things. The mustard-seed produced the largest of all herbs. It has been supposed by others, therefore, to mean, if you have increasing, expanding, enlarged faith, growing and strengthening from small beginnings, you can perform the most difficult undertaking. . . . This is probably the true meaning." *Barnes, Notes on the New Testament, Matthew,* p. 180.

> The teaching of salvation by merit is not in harmony with this parable, nor with any other Bible teaching.

3. What does the parable in verses 7-10 teach?
It teaches that after man has done everything possible to serve God, he has done no more than is required of him, and must still consider himself an unprofitable servant. The doctrine of *supererogation* is destroyed by this passage. Supererogation is a Roman Catholic belief that saints may do works over and above those commanded by God. These good works are "stockpiled" and may be used by others.

WHEN AND WHERE

The feast of Dedication was held December 20-27 in A.D. 29. It was sometime after this feast that Jesus departed into Perea from Judea. The time of this lesson was likely January, A. D. 30.

There are a number of questions relating to the chronology of Jesus' life, from the time of His departure from Galilee to go up to Jerusalem for the feast of Tabernacles (John 7:10—Lesson Thirteen), until His arrival in Bethany at the final Passover (John 12:1—Lesson Nineteen). The chronology for this period used in these lessons is as follows:

1. Jesus left Galilee to go to Jerusalem for the feast of Tabernacles (October, A. D. 29—Luke 9:51; John 7:10; perhaps Matthew 19:1);

2. He left Jerusalem and went to Perea (January, A. D. 30—John 10:40);

3. He returned to Judea, to Bethany, to raise Lazarus (latter part of January, A. D. 30—John 11:15);

4. He left Jerusalem on His way back to Perea and stopped for awhile at the city of Ephraim (John 11:54);

5. He left Ephraim and passed through parts of Samaria and Galilee on His way to Perea (February, A. D. 30—Luke 17:11);

6. He ministered in Perea (latter part of February and March, A. D. 30);

7. He passed through Jericho and came to Bethany (end of March, A. D. 30—Matthew 20:29; Mark 10:46).

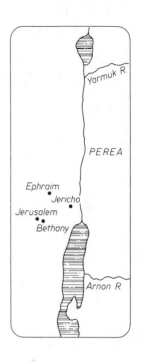

The events of this lesson, as well as those of the following two, transpired in that section of Palestine known as Perea. This name is not found in the Bible. Josephus and others used it to designate the territory on the east side of the Jordan, opposite Judea and Samaria. In the Gospels this area is called the land "beyond Jordan" (Matthew 4:25; Mark 3:7, 8). A check of the map which is provided will show that its western border was the Jordan River, and that its eastern border was rather undefined. To the north it reached as far as the Jarmuk River, and to the south as far as the Arnon, a distance of some sixty miles. During the time of Jesus, Perea, as well as Galilee, was under the rule of Herod Antipas. It was in the southern part of Perea, at Machaerus, that John the Baptist was imprisoned by him. Josephus states that Gadara was its capital *(Wars,* 4:7:3). From other sources it is learned that its population, which was rather dense, was a mixture of Jew and Gentile.

PROJECTS AND PLANS

The parable of the prodigal son is one of the best-loved stories in the world. It would be exciting and constructive to work together as a class to dramatize this story. Perhaps it could be enacted before the entire church assembly. Investigate the possibilites.

One of the events of the next lesson is the healing of the ten lepers. In preparation read the article, "Leper, Leprosy," in *The International Standard Bible Encyclopedia,* Vol. 3, pp. 1867, 1868. Also, seek some information concerning present-day leprosaria and modern methods of treating this ancient disease.

IMPORTANT TRIP TO BETHANY

TOPICS AND TEXTS

The Raising of Lazarus . . . John 11:1-44
Plots to Kill Jesus . . . John 11:45-54
The Healing of the Ten Lepers . . . Luke 17:11-19
Sermon on the Time of the Coming of the Kingdom . . . Luke 17:20-37
Parable of the Unjust Judge . . . Luke 18:1-8
Parable of the Pharisee and Publican . . . Luke 18:9-14

CONTEXT AND CONTINUITY

All miracles share the common feature that they supersede the natural laws of the universe. It is that quality which makes an event a miracle. So, there is a sense in which it is incorrect to say that one miracle ranks above another. However, because of the finality of death, miracles involving the restoration of life are considered the greatest of wonders. This is well-illustrated in Jesus' ministry by the three instances when life was restored to the dead. After He raised the widow of Nain's son, the record says: "And there came a fear on all: and they glorified God, saying, That a great prophet is risen up among us; and, That God hath visited his people. And this rumor of him went forth throughout all Judea, and throughout all the region round about" (Luke 7:16, 17). Similarly, after the raising of Jairus' daughter, the footnote is: "They were astonished with a great astonishment" (Mark 5:42).

The third such miracle was the raising of Lazarus of Bethany, brother of Martha and Mary, and both friend and disciple of Jesus. That Lazarus had been dead and in a grave four days makes the miracle more impressive. Also, the marvelous declarations of faith by his sisters preceding the raising, and the reaction of the hostile Jews following it add to its impact. Probably at the time of the miracle His disciples viewed the raising of Lazarus as the very greatest act of a ministry that had been filled with wonder upon wonder. Years later, they likely considered it to be the most stupendous of all the acts He performed, excluding, of course, His own resurrection.

The miracle so irritated the hostile Jews that "from that day forth they took counsel together for to put him to death" (John 11:53). Realizing that His time was not yet come, He "walked no more openly among the Jews; but went thence unto a country near to the wilderness, into a city called Ephraim, and there continued with his disciples" (John 11:54). How long He remained there is unknown. When He departed, He went northward about forty miles, passed along the borders of Samaria and Galilee, turned eastward, and

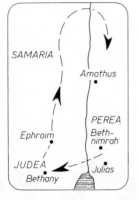

SAMARIA

Amathus

PEREA

Ephraim

Beth-
nimrah

JUDEA

Julias

Bethany

			J	F	M	A	M	J	J	A	S	O	N	D				

A.D. 29   A.D. 30   A.D. 31

crossed the Jordan back into Perea. There in an unnamed village, He healed ten lepers (one of whom was a Samaritan), and sent them to the priests that they might be officially pronounced clean.

Following these episodes, a Pharisee asked Jesus about the time of the coming of the kingdom of God. This provoked a sermon on that general theme. This incident was followed by the teaching of two parables, one concerning an unjust judge, the other about a Pharisee and a publican. With these parables the present lesson is concluded.

INQUIRIES AND INSIGHTS

The Raising of Lazarus . . . John 11:1-44

1. When did Mary anoint Jesus?

This anointing had not yet occurred. It is mentioned here parenthetically to identify the Mary in this incident. "It was that very Mary," John is saying, "who anointed Jesus in preparation for His burial." The actual event is described in John 12:2-8, Matthew 26:6-13, and Mark 14:3-9.

2. How was Lazarus' sickness not unto death?

Although Lazarus actually died and spent four days in a tomb, the death was not final. It must have seemed to him as if he had just been aroused from a long sleep.

3. Why did Jesus wait two days before going to Bethany?

There were perhaps three reasons: (1) By so acting He created greater suspense and, therefore, greater expectancy among His disciples. (2) It was a means of testing the faith of Martha and Mary. (3) It allowed for the death and four-day entombment of Lazarus before Jesus' arrival which added to the conclusiveness of the miracle.

4. What is the meaning of Jesus' reference to the twelve hours of the day?

Jesus' disciples were concerned about His plan to return to Judea where the strength of His enemies was concentrated. But Jesus was not afraid, for He knew that He was walking in the day, and His enemies couldn't destroy Him. It was true that the evening shadows were beginning to fall, that the time of His death was approaching, but it was also true that there was adequate time to perform this stupendous miracle and enhance His claims.

5. Why speak of death as a sleep?

Jesus used the word *sleep* figuratively. One writer states that the word is so used thirteen times in the

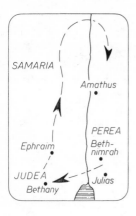

New Testament. Check the following passages: Luke 8:52; Acts 7:60; 1 Corinthians 15:6, 18, 51; 1 Thessalonians 4:13-15; 2 Peter 3:4. For an answer to this question see Lesson Ten, "Raising of Jairus' Daughter."

6. How account for Martha's and Mary's great faith?
In their home and in their synagogue these Jewish girls had been instructed in the Old Testament. Such instruction had doubtless nurtured within them a firm faith in Jehovah and His Word. Like the majority of Jews (the Sadducees being an exception), they believed in a general resurrection. Jesus, by His teaching, had confirmed this faith. Having heard His teaching and having witnessed His power, they were prepared to believe that God would give Him whatever He asked (v. 22).

7. Why did Jesus weep?
The Jews who were present ascribed it to His love for Lazarus, and in this they apparently were correct. While realizing He apossessed the power to restore life to Lazarus, Jesus was human enough to share the burden of sorrow which was Martha's and Mary's. Albert Barnes makes the four following observations: (1) "The most tender personal friendship is not inconsistent with the most pure religion." (2) "It is right, it is natural, it is indispensable for the Christian to sympathize with others in their affliction." (3) "Sorrow at the death of friends is not improper." (4) "We have here an instance of the tenderness of the character of Jesus."—*Notes on the New Testament, John*, p. 300.

John 11:35 is the shortest verse in the Bible: "Jesus wept."

8. Why did Jesus pray before performing the miracle?
There were at least three reasons: (1) It was Jesus' custom to pray on every important occasion of His life (baptism, transfiguration, crucifixion, feeding the 5000, calling the twelve, etc.). (2) His words expressed the close communion which He maintained with the Father at all times. (3) It was a means of instilling faith in the hearts of those who heard Him.

9. How many people did Jesus raise from the dead?
We do not know. Three instances are recorded, but there may have been others.

10. What were the burial customs of the Jews?
Edersheim devotes four pages to this topic, and it would be profitable to read his material.—*The*

Tomb

				A.D. 29				A.D. 30											A.D. 31	

J F M A M J J A S O N D

Life and Times of Jesus the Messiah, Vol. 2, pp. 316-320. The question is also discussed briefly in Lesson Nine in connection with the raising of the widow of Nain's son.

Plots to Kill Jesus . . . John 11:45-54

1. What were the effects of the raising of Lazarus?

There were the usual effects. This miracle produced faith in some who witnessed it; in others it hardened their hearts. Some of the latter went directly to the Pharisees and "told them what things Jesus had done" (v. 46).

2. What motivated the chief priests and Pharisees?

Their ulterior motive is revealed in verse 48: "If we let him thus alone, all men will believe on him: and the Romans shall come and take away both our place and nation." Why belief in Jesus by the Jews would incite the Romans is not explained. Inasmuch as Jesus had repeatedly made it clear that He had no political aspirations, no satisfactory explanation can be given. The charge was a means of keeping in line as many as possible of the Jews who, naturally, wanted to keep such self-rule as they enjoyed. The real concern of the chief priests and Pharisees was that they not lose their place of leadership. This selfish concern motivated them.

3. How account for the prediction made by Caiaphas?

Caiaphas was high priest from A. D. 18 to 36. He was the son-in-law of Annas who held the office before him (A. D. 7-15), and who still retained the title (Luke 3:2). His prediction must be considered from two viewpoints. Caiaphas probably meant no more than that it was better that Jesus should die than that the whole nation should perish in an uprising against Rome (the reason for which is not clear; see answer above). The deeper meaning—that mentioned in verse 51—applies to the atonement which Jesus accomplished for the nation and for "the children of God that were scattered abroad" (v. 52). Obviously Caiaphas didn't intend this latter meaning. John, who relates it, explains that Caiaphas made the prediction functioning in his role as high priest.

4. Was Jesus afraid to face His enemies?

Jesus' withdrawal from the Jerusalem area where His enemies were concentrated was not motivated by fear, but by wisdom. He was aware that

> Caiaphas was high priest A.D. 18-36.

> "Therefore doth my Father love me, because I lay down my life, that I might take it again. No man taketh it from me, but I lay it down of myself. I have power to lay it down, and I have power to take it again. This commandment have I received of my Father" (John 10:17, 18).

141

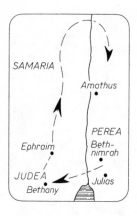

His time was not yet come, that there was yet a ministry to be accomplished, that there were other areas that needed His message. He therefore withdrew to fulfill this part of the purpose of His coming and to await the proper time. No one was going to take His life from Him prematurely; He was going to lay it down of His own accord at the right time (John 10:18).

The Healing of the Ten Lepers . . . Luke 17:11-19

1. Why were the ten lepers together?

As lepers they were excluded from society in general (Leviticus 13:45, 46). It was natural, therefore, that they should band together for fellowship, protection, and other mutual interests. Notice that the animosity between Jew and Samaritan was removed from the hearts of these men, for Jew and Samaritan traveled side by side. Affliction or tragedy often brings together people who otherwise would be worlds apart.

2. Did all the lepers have faith?

Yes, and this is clearly revealed in their plea, "Jesus, Master, have mercy on us." Unfortunately, only one of them possessed the grace of gratitude. The others were no doubt thankful, but failed to express it. Faith and gratitude are two separate qualities. The former should produce the latter, but obviously it doesn't always do so to the extent it should.

3. Why send them to the priests?

Priests under the law of Moses functioned as health officers as well as religious mediators. To them was given the responsibility of determining when a person was leprous and when he was cleansed. (See Leviticus 13 and 14.) Jesus was merely complying with this teaching.

Sermon on the Time of the Coming of the Kingdom . . . Luke 17:20-37

1. Why doesn't the kingdom of God come with observation?

Jesus' point is that the kingdom of God is not basically external. The Jews were seeking an earthly kingdom to be ruled over by a powerful Messiah. "This," Jesus said, "is not how the kingdom is to be."

2. How is the kingdom of God within people?

The principles which Christ taught must be taken into the heart of a man in order to be effective; mere external allegiance is not sufficient. Christ knows that by controlling the inner man the outer

Leprosy is also known as Hansen's disease. There are two types: lepromatous and tuberculoid. The former probably is the type mentioned more frequently in the Bible.

man will be controlled also. Although the kingdom of God has certain outward manifestations, it essentially is one of the spirit rather than of the flesh.

3. To what did Jesus compare His second coming?

Jesus used three illustrations to describe His second coming:
(1) It will be like lightning which shoots instantly from one section of the sky to another, not giving warning as to where it will start or stop. (2) It will be similar to the destruction which came in the days of Noah (everything was progressing normally, and then the end came). (3) It will happen with the swiftness with which destruction came to Sodom (with the exception of Lot's family, the city's inhabitants had no warning about what was going to happen). From these illustrations we learn that no signs (none that can be interpreted) will precede His coming. When things are normal, when people are not expecting it, Jesus will return.

The "coming again" of Jesus is mentioned more than 300 times in the New Testament. Check John 14:1-3, Acts 1:11, 1 Thessalonians 4:13-18, 2 Thessalonians 1:7-10, Hebrews 9:28, and 2 Peter 3:1-18.

4. To what did Jesus refer in verse 31?

This is a difficult verse to understand. Jesus' probable meaning is: "When that day comes, don't think about your earthly goods; you won't have time to assemble them, nor future need of them."

5. What can be learned from verses 34-36 about the situation which will prevail when He returns?

These verses make it clear that when Jesus returns not everyone will be a Christian. Although some will be taken, others will be left. Jesus' illustrations indicate that for every one taken, one will be left. A literal interpretation of these words would have 50 percent saved and 50 percent lost. Such a legalistic interpretation would do an injustice to this figurative language.

6. What is meant by the reference to the body and eagles?

Lamar states: "The true application is clearly indicated by the question of the disciples, 'Where, Lord?' showing that in *their* opinion this great and awful event was to occur at some particular place. For their answer he puts them to considering where do the *eagles* gather together? At any one point? At any certain *place* that may be named and designated beforehand? No; but wheresoever the body is. That is, anywhere and everywhere over the whole world, where the dead body is,

143

thither the eagles or vultures collect. In like manner, this second coming of the Lord will be to humanity—to all nations, and wheresoever human beings are, there the angels will be, in order to 'gather together his elect from the four winds, *from one end of heaven to the other.'* "— *New Testament Commentary, Vol. II, Luke,* pp. 222, 223.

Parable of the Unjust Judge . . . Luke 18:1-8

1. What does this parable teach?

It teaches that we should be persistent in our prayer life, that we should cry unto God day and night, that we should pray without ceasing.

"Pray without ceasing" (1 Thessalonians 5:17).

2. What danger should be avoided in interpreting it?

This is a parable, not an allegory. Spiritual parallels should not be sought for all of the details. By this practice God would be represented as an unjust deity who could be influenced by the persistence of people, whether their cause was right or wrong. Barclay has observed: "It does not *liken* God to an unjust judge; it *contrasts* God to such a person. In this parable Jesus was saying, 'If, in the end, an unjust and rapacious judge can be wearied into giving a widow woman justice, *how much more* will God, who is a loving Father, give His children what they need?' "—*The Daily Study Bible, Luke,* p. 231.

3. What is the answer to Jesus' question in verse eight?

This is a rhetorical question. He didn't expect the disciples who heard Him to speak up with a "Yes" or "No" answer, nor does He expect us to do so. We would like to believe that at His coming some men will possess faith which will manifest itself in prayer and in other ways.

Parable of the Pharisee and Publican . . . Luke 18:9-14

1. What does this parable teach?

The key to its interpretation is found in verses 9 and 14. The parable was directed against the Pharisees and others like them who glory in self-righteousness. God is not in the least impressed by our supposed greatness or goodness. He must be approached with humility as well as faith if one's prayer is to be acceptable.

"Parable, derived from the Greek verb *paraballo*, composed of the preposition *para*, meaning "beside," and the verb *ballo*, "to cast." A parable is thus a comparison of two objects for the purpose of teaching" (Pictorial Bible Dictionary, page 621).

2. What was wrong with the Pharisee's prayer?

Remove the name of God from its beginning, and it is impossible to identify it as a prayer. It sounds more like a recitation of an egotist before his bedroom mirror. It contains not one word of adoration of God, not a single expression of gratitude for His previous blessings, not a trace of a request for future guidance. It's an excellent model of what a prayer should not be.

3. Why did God honor the publican's prayer? God always answers the prayers of those who come to Him with genuine faith and sincerity. Such was the attitude of this publican. Therefore he "went down to his house justified."

WHEN AND WHERE

Between the raising of Lazarus and Jesus' final Passover, a considerable amount of time appears to have elapsed. In A.D. 30 the Passover was held during the eight-day period of April 6-13 (the fourteenth to twenty-first of Nisan). The events of this lesson probably occurred in the latter part of January and February of that year.

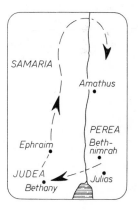

From Bethany, fifteen furlongs (one and seven-eighths miles) southeast of Jerusalem, Jesus and His company withdrew to Ephraim, a city "near to the wilderness" (John 11:54). Apparently this is the same city which Joshua called Ophrah (Joshua 18:23). It is also mentioned in 2 Chronicles 13:19 where it is called Ephrain. It has been identified with a village now called Et-Taiyibeh, about sixteen miles northeast of Jerusalem and five miles east of Bethel. This is the only reference to it in the New Testament. After some time, Jesus left there, went northward, and crossed into Perea where He remained until the time of the Passover. Locate Ephraim on the map.

PROJECTS AND PLANS

Working together as a class, itemize the qualities that would be desirable in a just judge. Contrast this ideal judge with the unjust one of the parable.

In the following lesson the teaching of Jesus concerning divorce will be considered. In preparation for that lesson investigate the laws of your state in regard to divorce. How well is God's Word honored in respect to this important phase of life? What can be done to bring the laws of the state into harmony with the law of God?

FROM PEREA TO JERUSALEM

TOPICS AND TEXTS

CONTEXT AND CONTINUITY

Within the texts covered by this lesson are the accounts of two men who experienced interesting conversations with Jesus. One of the men is unnamed; the other is called Zaccheus. The unnamed man is described with three words: he was young, rich, and a ruler (probably referring to his role in a local synagogue). Zaccheus (whose name means "pure") also was a man of means, one who earned his livelihood as a tax collector. The young ruler probably enjoyed a great deal of popularity in his home area; many folks no doubt thought of him as a model young man. The tax collector, on the other hand, was quite unpopular with his fellow Jews, who considered him a traitor because of his collaboration with the Romans. Both men had in common a desire to see Jesus, and to learn from Him the way of salvation.

With great enthusiasm the young ruler came running to Jesus and inquired what one must do to inherit eternal life. When Jesus responded with a clear, concise answer based upon the law of Moses, the young man went away sorrowful. He failed in his quest because of a reluctance to do what the Lord required.

Although we are not told that Zaccheus asked about salvation, his actions and his speech reveal that it was his interest in this topic which brought him to Christ. Sensing this, the Master invited himself into the home of this chief tax collector. The exact words that Jesus said to Zaccheus are not recorded. It is clear, however, that the transaction led Zaccheus to repent of his wrong doing and reform his life. Therefore, unlike the rich young ruler who sorrowfully departed from Jesus, Zac-

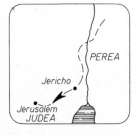

cheus heard Jesus announce: "This day is salvation come to this house."

Jesus' encounters with the rich young ruler and Zaccheus are but two of ten events to be covered in this lesson. Chronologically, the first event of this lesson is the one which deals with the teaching of Jesus about divorce. This teaching was precipitated by a question asked by some Pharisees. Immediately after this impromptu lesson, a number of little children were brought to Him, and He blessed them by laying His hands upon them. The next incident involves the rich young ruler. Then followed a discussion between Jesus and His disciples concerning the perils of riches. From this account comes the well-known saying of Jesus: "It is easier for a camel to go through the eye of a needle, than for a rich man to enter into the kingdom of God" (Matthew 19:24). This discussion led to another, introduced by Peter, concerning rewards for Jesus' disciples.

Next, Jesus taught a parable entitled "The Laborers in the Vineyard." Then Jesus took the twelve apart and prophesied about His forthcoming death and resurrection. The records of both Matthew and Mark specifically state that Jesus did this teaching as the group made their way toward Jerusalem (Matthew 20:17; Mark 10:32).

Then it was that Salome came to Jesus with her sons, James and John, requesting for them the chief places in His kingdom. Although Jesus refused the request, the fact that it was made aroused indignation among the other apostles. Jesus responded by denouncing all such honor-seeking.

Coming to Jericho, Jesus was confronted by two blind men who successfully besought Him to restore their sight. The encounter with Zaccheus which followed has already been discussed.

This lesson concludes with a study of the parable of the pounds. Luke writes: "And when he had thus spoken, he went before, ascending up to Jerusalem" (19:28). Thus is concluded Jesus' Perean ministry. With the next lesson we begin a study of His last public ministry in Jerusalem.

INQUIRIES AND INSIGHTS

Jesus in Perea: Teaching Concerning Divorce . . . Matthew 19:1-12, Mark 10:1-12

1. When did this event occur?
Matthew says it took place after Jesus departed from Galilee (19:1). He does not, however, specify which departure from Galilee he means. It may be that Matthew condensed his account at

147

this point and that this reference is to Jesus' departure from Galilee at the time of the feast of Tabernacles (see Lesson Thirteen). If so, it is a reference to the same departure mentioned in Luke 9:51 and John 7:10. In favor of this view is the fact that the event described in Matthew 19:1-12 is the first event mentioned by Matthew since that time. Another possibility is that Matthew merely refers to the fact that Jesus passed into the borders of Galilee as He went from Ephraim (John 11:54) back into Perea (Luke 17:11). These two views are not at odds. Matthew's meaning isn't clear.

2. What was the motive of the Pharisees?

Mark says their question was put to Him, "tempting him" (10:2). They knew what Moses taught about divorce. Perhaps they also were aware of what Jesus had said on the topic earlier (Matthew 5:31, 32). Their motive was to get Him to contradict either Moses or himself. He did neither.

> Other New Testament passages dealing with divorce: Matthew 5:31, 32; Luke 16:18; 1 Corinthians 7:27.

3. From where was Jesus quoting?

Genesis 1:27; 5:2 and 2:24.

4. Where can the Mosaic teaching regarding divorce be found?

Deuteronomy 24:1-4.

> Old Testament on divorce: Deuteronomy 24:1-4; Ezra 10; Jeremiah 3:1.

5. Does God ever permit divorce and remarriage?

During the Mosaic dispensation God permitted divorce on a number of grounds. This, Jesus said, was because of the Jews' hardness of heart. Those who were divorced could re-marry with God's sanction. However, under the Christian dispensation, there is only one basis for divorce recognized by God—fornication. (See Matthew 5:32 and 19:9.) If one of the marriage partners is unfaithful to his or her wedding vows, and commits adultery, the innocent mate is entitled to a divorce which carries with it the privilege of re-marriage.

6. Why the conclusion of the disciples?

Matthew records the words of the disciples: "If the case of the man be so with his wife, it is not good to marry" (19:10). It was their feeling that such strict regulations made the institution of marriage less desirable than the unmarried state. In reality, His teaching has made marriage *more* desirable, as well as more permanent.

> Notice the beautiful passage regarding marriage in Ephesians 5:22-33.

7. Why the reference to eunuchs?

Jesus meant that marriage is not for everyone. Some by their personal nature, some by choice, and some as a result of the cruelty of men do not marry.

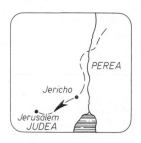

Jesus and the Little Children ... Matthew 19:13-15; Mark 10:13-16; Luke 18:15-17

1. Why bring the children to Jesus?
Jesus was recognized as a great religious teacher. It was natural, therefore, that parents would want Him to hold their little ones, place His hands on them, pray for them, and in these ways bless them. That the motive of these parents was pure is indicated by the fact that Jesus offered them no word of reprimand.

2. Why did the disciples turn back the parents and their children?
They apparently acted out of consideration for their Master. They knew He was engaged in teaching and healing and was therefore, in their opinion, too busy to be bothered with little children.

3. What is the meaning of the expression "of such is the kingdom of heaven"?
Like children, men of God's kingdom must have faith and be humble and unambitious.

For teaching regarding responsibilities of children, see Ephesians 6:1-3 and Colossians 3:20.

The Rich Young Ruler ... Matthew 19:16-22; Mark 10:17-22; Luke 18:18-23

1. What other event in Jesus' life is similar to this one?
The event recorded in Luke 10:25-37 involving "a certain lawyer" who came to Jesus inquiring about eternal life is similar. Since Luke records both of them it is clear that they are separate events.

2. What sort of person was the rich young ruler?
That he was a shallow thinker is apparent in the casual way he used the word "good." His claim to have kept all the commandments from his youth should be taken with the proverbial grain of salt. He probably thought he was telling the truth, but his self-evaluation was obviously too exalted. Still he likely was a model young man who was highly respected by his associates. Mark tells us there was something about him that caused Jesus to love him (10:21).

3. In rebuking the man for using the term "good," did Jesus deny His own divinity?
Certainly not. Jesus' purpose was to shock the young man out of his state of thoughtlessness and cause him to consider the full import of his words. ✱

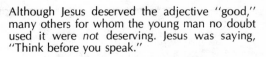
Although Jesus deserved the adjective "good," many others for whom the young man no doubt used it were *not* deserving. Jesus was saying, "Think before you speak."

4. Why did Jesus cite these specific commandments?

Slight differences exist between the Synoptic accounts. All three quote the fifth through the ninth commandments, but their arrangement is different. Nor do they agree with the order in Exodus 20 and Deuteronomy 5. In addition to these five, Matthew adds, "Thou shalt love thy neighbor as thyself," and Mark has, "Defraud not." Luke records only five. Notice that all of these commandments deal with man's relationship to man, rather than man's relationship to God. It would have been superfluous to tell the man to believe in, worship, and serve the one true God (the first four commands of the Decalogue), for these things he already did. His deficiencies were centered in his relationships with his fellowman. Jesus, realizing this, insisted he share his riches with those in need.

Of the Ten Commandments (Exodus 20:1-17; Deuteronomy 5:6-21), four deal with man's relationship to God; the last six concern man's relationship to man.

5. Why did the man depart from Jesus?

When Jesus insisted that he sell all he had and give the money to the poor, it was more than the man was willing to do. Although he desired salvation, he was not willing to part with his possessions to attain it.

Discussion of the Peril of Riches and the Reward of the Disciples . . . Matthew 19:23-30; Mark 10:23-31; Luke 18:24-30

1. What did Jesus mean by His reference to a camel and a needle?

It is a hyperbole, a purposeful exaggeration used to show the difficulty of those who "trust in riches" being saved. Actually it was a proverb then in common use among the Jews, and still known and used by some in that area of the world. Attempts to identify the eye of the needle with a small gate, or to change the word "camel" to "cable" are foolish and miss the point of the illustration.

2. Why is it difficult for the rich to be saved?

A tendency of the rich is to trust in their riches and thereby become proud and arrogant. Also, it is sometimes true that riches are obtained in sinful ways and used to promote evil causes. Of course these things may be overcome. To men such a victory may seem impossible, but not so to God.

3. What is the reward of those who faithfully follow Jesus?

Jesus said that in the regeneration the apostles would sit on twelve thrones, judging the twelve tribes of Israel. He added that everyone who had forsaken things on His behalf would be greatly blessed both here and in the eternal state. The word "regeneration" appears only here in Matthew 19:28 and in Titus 3:5. It literally means "the new birth," and is so used by Titus. In Matthew it refers to the future state and to the restoration of things which shall occur at that time. The promise to the apostles about the twelve thrones is figurative. The meaning is that they will occupy places of power and authority, not that they will literally sit on thrones. Similarly, disciples shouldn't expect a hundredfold of wives, children, parents, etc. The meaning is that the things given His followers (peace, joy, etc.) are worth a hundred times the things which are sacrificed.

Parable of Laborers in the Vineyard . . . Matthew 20:1-16

1. What is the central teaching of this parable?

Salvation is a gift bestowed by God. It is not man's prerogative to dictate who can be saved, or upon what terms. In spite of human opposition, God will keep His promise and take to Heaven all who fulfill His requirements.

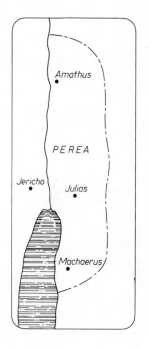

2. What system of time did Matthew use?

Jewish time. By this system the third hour was 9:00 a.m., the sixth hour, 12:00 noon, etc.

3. Was the householder unfair?

Those who labored all day felt He was. Although they had contracted for a penny a day, when they saw the latecomers being paid that amount they anticipated more. Out of their disappointment and frustration, they spoke against the householder.

The "penny" (denarius) was usual day's wages for a laborer.

Another Prediction of the Death of Jesus . . . Matthew 20:17-19; Mark 10:32-34; Luke 18:31-34

1. Why were the disciples at this time afraid?

Obviously they were amazed that Jesus should so soon return to Jerusalem after having encountered harsh opposition from the religious leaders there. Fear under such circumstances is natural.

2. Why did the apostles have such difficulty in accepting predictions of Jesus' death and resurrection?

Luke answers this question: "And they understood none of these things: and this saying was hid from them, neither knew they the things which were spoken" (18:34). They *refused* to believe that any tragedy could befall their Master.

Rebuke of James and John for Asking the Chief Honors . . . Matthew 20:20-28; Mark 10:35-45

1. Who made the request?

Matthew says it was the mother of Zebedee's children. Mark ascribes the act to James and John themselves. Perhaps Salome came with her sons and initiated the conversation with her request for them. Thereafter they, as well as she, became engaged in the discussion.

2. Exactly what did James and John want?

Shortly before this time Jesus had spoken of the twelve thrones upon which the apostles were to sit (Matthew 19:28). Possibly this promise inspired James and John to make their request for the most important of the twelve seats. To sit on the right or left of a sovereign indicated his special favor and hence additional authority.

> James and John played important roles in the early church. James met an early death at the hands of Herod Agrippa I. John lived to an old age.

3. What is the meaning of Jesus' answer?

Jesus explained that the two didn't understand the full import of their request. Then, by the use of two figures, made it clear that the leaders in His kingdom could expect suffering and death rather than greatness and power. The figurative use of a cup to represent sorrow can be found in the Old Testament (Isaiah 51:17; Jeremiah 49:12). Jesus had previously used the figure of baptism to represent immersion in sorrow (Luke 12:50).

4. Are there to be chief places in the kingdom?

Yes, for Jesus said such places are for those for whom they were prepared by His Father.

5. How did Jesus resolve the difficulty among His apostles?

He reminded them that in His kingdom greatness is gained through ministering, and the chief place through serving. He cited His own life as an example of what theirs should be.

Healing of the Blind Men at Jericho . . . Matthew 20:29-34; Mark 10:46-52; Luke 18:35-43

1. What textual differences are there?

There are two significant differences: (1) There is a difference concerning where the miracle occurred. Matthew says it was "as they departed from Jericho" (20:29), and with this Mark agrees. Luke, however, locates the miracle "as he was

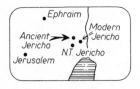

come nigh unto Jericho" (18:35). The texts can be reconciled by remembering there were three Jerichos—the old one which had been destroyed by Joshua, and two others which were later erected. The miracle probably was performed between two of these as Jesus left one and came near another. (2) There is a difference concerning the number of men healed. Matthew mentions two but Mark and Luke, one. Mark gives the man's name, Bartimeus. Probably this one is mentioned because he was the more outstanding of the two and served as the spokesman for them.

2. Why did Jesus honor their request?
Mark quotes the words of Jesus: "Go thy way; thy faith hath made thee whole" (10:52). Jesus honored their request because of their faith in Him.

Jesus and Zaccheus . . . Luke 19:1-10

1. What position did Zaccheus hold?
He is called "chief among the publicans" in the King James Version (Luke 19:2). The Greek word, *architelonāse* is not used elsewhere in the New Testament. Its exact meaning is unknown. Zaccheus was some type of official who had authority over other tax gatherers.

2. What kind of tree did he climb?
It is called a sycamore tree (spelled sycomore in the KJV) but should not be confused with the American sycamore (buttonwood). It was a type of fig-mulberry with fruit like the fig and leaves like the mulberry.

3. Had Zaccheus been an evil man?
Certainly Zaccheus wasn't a righteous man. But, on the other hand, we have no reason to assume he was an exceptionally vile person. He was a sinner who was in need of repentance. He admitted that he was guilty of defrauding men. The indicative mood is used in the Greek, making the words of Zaccheus: "If I have taken any thing . . . (and I admit I have), I restore . . . fourfold."

4. What was Jesus' motive in coming to the earth?
Luke 19:10 answers the question. Notice that this statement, as profound as it is, is composed of sixteen one-syllable English words.

The Parable of the Pounds . . . Luke 19:11-28

1. Why did Jesus teach this parable?
Luke gives two reasons: (1) He was nigh to Jerusalem; (2) they (His disciples) thought the

Modern Jericho

Sycamore tree

"For the Son of man is come to seek and to save that which was lost" (Luke 19:10).

The "pound" here is the Hebrew minah (Gk.: mna), equal to 50 shekels in Attic weight, 100 in Old Testament weight.

153

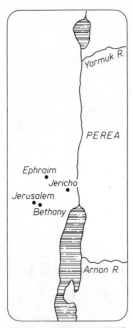

Palm tree

kingdom of God should immediately appear. The two are connected. Because they were approaching Jerusalem the disciples believed the time was near when He would establish the earthly kingdom which they anticipated.

2. What lesson does it teach?
The Son of man must be separated from His followers. During His absence they must faithfully use what has been entrusted to them in His service. It also teaches that unfaithfulness and opposition will be punished at His return.

3. How will those who have, be given more?
It is a principle of life that the ones who demonstrate the ability to manage small affairs will be entrusted with greater ones.

WHEN AND WHERE
The events of this lesson immediately preceded Jesus' arrival at Bethany, at which time the triumphal entry took place. Accepting that this event occurred on Sunday, April 2, we conclude that the transactions of this lesson took place during the month of March, A. D. 30.

Jesus journeyed through Perea, crossed the Jordan either at the Damieh Ford or the Pilgrim's Ford, spent some time in Jericho, and ascended to Bethany near Jerusalem. Jericho, called the "city of palm trees" (Deuteronomy 34:3), is probably the oldest city in the world. It is best remembered in connection with the espionage of the spies sent by Joshua (Joshua 2) and its unusual conquest (Joshua 6). The Jericho of Jesus' day was a magnificent Roman-type city, containing pools, villas, a hippodrome, a theater, and a great civic center. Modern Jericho has a population of about 40,000.

PROJECTS AND PLANS
Have a class discussion concerning specific rich men who used, or are using, their wealth for noble causes.

To better understand the triumphal entry of Jesus, read one or both of the following selections: *The Life and Times of Jesus the Messiah*, Vol. 2, pages 363-373; *The Life of Our Lord Upon the Earth*, pages 429-436.

Lesson Nineteen

THE TRIUMPHAL ENTRY

TOPICS AND TEXTS

The Arrival at Bethany . . . John 11:55—12:1, 9-11
The Anointing of Jesus by Mary . . . Matthew 26:6-13; Mark 14:3-9; John 12:2-8
The Triumphal Entry . . . Matthew 21:1-11; Mark 11:1-11; Luke 19:29-44; John 12:12-19
Cursing the Fig Tree: Second Cleansing of the Temple . . . Matthew 21:18, 19, 12-17; Mark 11:12-18; Luke 19:45-48

CONTEXT AND CONTINUITY

We would like to believe that it was a beautiful spring day when the multitude assembled on the Mount of Olives and Jesus, using a borrowed animal, rode in triumph into the Holy City. Unfortunately it is not possible to determine the weather conditions of a time so long removed, and our only sources of information about the events of that day didn't see fit to give us a weather report. They did, however, relate some facts, directly and indirectly, which help us understand this important event in Jesus' life.

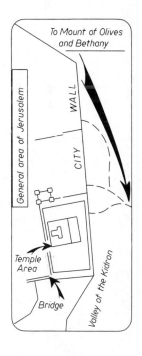

John informs us that Jesus' arrival at Bethany occurred six days before the Passover (12:1). That would make it Friday, March 31. Though it is only a conjecture, we are probably correct in saying that the Sabbath Day was spent in worship and rest, and that the supper mentioned by John (12:2) took place sometime that evening. At this supper, possibly given jointly by numerous grateful friends of Lazarus, Mary aroused the indignation of Judas and others by using costly ointment to anoint the body of Jesus. The supper appears to have been a large affair with numerous guests, many of whom came uninvited to see Lazarus, who had been brought back to life. They were also curious to see the One who had restored his life (John 12:9). How the remainder of that night was spent by Jesus, we do not know. Perhaps it was spent in prayer; perhaps in sleep, preparing for the ordeals which were ahead of Him.

Sometime on Sunday, possibly near mid-morning, Jesus sent two of His disciples to secure a colt for His triumphal entry into Jerusalem. Apparently the reason for getting the animal was kept even from the apostles. Probably they knew no more than that the Lord had need (Matthew 21:3). Obviously their curiosity was aroused. They could sense that something was in the air, but they were unable to determine the nature of the event.

Groups of pilgrims, who had observed the Sabbath by resting, came pouring into Jerusalem from Galilee, Perea, and the Decapolis. Many of them paused on the Mount of Olives to greet and be greeted by Jesus and His companions. Others, in-

155

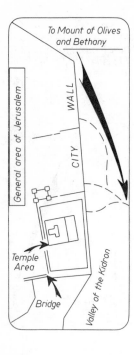

To Mount of Olives and Bethany

General area of Jerusalem

CITY WALL

Temple Area

Bridge

Valley of the Kidron

cluding early arrivals and local disciples who had learned of Jesus' whereabouts, went toward Bethany, and were soon caught up in the excitement of the occasion.

By early afternoon the enthusiasm had reached such a point that it could no longer be contained. Nor did Jesus have any desire to restrain it, for this was to be His day. In triumph like a victorious king He mounted the colt and began His descent into the fickle city that would first joyously accept, then cruelly reject, Him within the span of one week.

When the multitude learned it was Jesus' intention to enter triumphantly into Jerusalem, they took their garments and small branches from nearby trees and placed them in the pathway before the Lord. From somewhere the cry, "Hosanna," went up. This served as the spark to ignite the whole multitude into vociferous praise. "Hosanna to the Son of David," "Blessed is he that cometh in the name of the Lord," "Hosanna in the highest," "Hosanna," "Blessed be the kingdom of our father David," "Blessed be the King that cometh in the name of the Lord," "Peace in heaven and glory in the highest," "Blessed is the King of Israel," are the various words uttered by the multitude.

It was indeed a joyous occasion, a time for laughter and shouting and praise. Yet, in the midst of the happiness, Jesus paused when He had gone partway down the western slope of the mount. There He gazed out over Jerusalem, and wept for the city. Although there seemed to be every reason for the Holy City to survive and prosper, Jesus knew it was soon to be destroyed.

After the descent from the mount, which required considerable time with such a large multitude on hand, Jesus went into the city and "looked round about upon all things." Then, in the evening He returned to Bethany (Mark 11:11).

On Monday morning Jesus and His apostles returned to Jerusalem. On their way He saw a fig tree in foliage. Since He was hungry, He paused as though to gather some fruit, but found none on the tree. He therefore pronounced a curse on the tree: "Let no fruit grow on thee henceforward for ever" (Matthew 21:19), and then continued His journey. Arriving in Jerusalem, He went directly into the temple. In righteous indignation He cast out the sellers and buyers, overthrew the tables of the money changers and the seats of the dove merchants, and would not even permit any to carry vessels through the outer court. Naturally His action irritated the religious leaders, and they reaffirmed among themselves their intent to kill Him (Mark 11:18).

Jesus then healed some blind and lame people (Matthew 21:14), and subsequently had a discussion with the chief priests and scribes (Matthew 21:15, 16). Then, "when even was come, he went out of the city" (Mark 11:19) to Bethany (Matthew 21:17), His headquarters during this last week.

INQUIRIES AND INSIGHTS

The Arrival at Bethany ... John 11:55—12:1, 9-11

1. What was the feast of the Passover?

The Passover was one of three annual Jewish feasts which every able male was expected to attend (Exodus 23:14-17; Deuteronomy 16:16). It was held on the fourteenth of Nisan, the first month of the Jewish religious year. On the following day, the feast of Unleavened Bread began and continued for seven more days. The two feasts thus formed a double festival which historically and religiously was the most important of all the Jewish feasts. The Passover dated from the time of the exodus (Exodus 12), and was instituted by Jehovah himself. The title was derived from the Lord's "passing over" (i. e., sparing of) the homes of the obedient Hebrews, when He slew the firstborn of both man and beast in all of Egypt.

> The Biblical record of the first Passover is in Exodus 12.

2. What purification was required prior to observing the Passover?

The purification mentioned by John was that required by God in Leviticus 22:1-9. Uncleanness could be caused in numerous ways: by being a leper, having a running issue, touching a corpse, etc. Those who were unclean and could be purified, if they wanted to participate in the Passover, would go up to Jerusalem earlier than other pilgrims in order to take care of this matter.

3. Why did some believe Jesus wouldn't attend the feast?

Many felt Jesus would avoid the Passover to prevent an open clash with His enemies. Two months before this, at the time of the raising of Lazarus, the hostility of the religious leaders at Jerusalem was so intense His disciples felt it was foolhardy to leave Perea and return to Judea (John 11:8, 16). During this two-month interval the opposition had become even more pronounced.

> This is the fourth Passover during the ministry of Jesus. The others are mentioned in John 2:23, John 5:1, and John 6:4.

4. Why did Jesus go to Bethany?

Like all other pilgrims to Jerusalem, Jesus was in need of some place to live during the Passover.

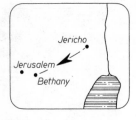

There was a friendship between Him and Lazarus' family that made their home in Bethany the logical place to serve as His headquarters during the last hectic week of His life.

5. Why the concern about Lazarus?

The raising of Lazarus was considered the most stupendous act which Jesus had yet performed. Because of it His fame had increased, and this in turn had produced additional hostility. Disciples who had heard about the miracle took advantage of their proximity to Bethany, and went out to see this one who had been brought back to life. When the chief priests realized what was happening, they determined that Lazarus, as well as Jesus, must be put to death. They knew that as long as Lazarus lived there would be conclusive evidence of the power of Jesus.

The Anointing of Jesus by Mary ... Matthew 26:6-13; Mark 14:3-9; John 12:2-8

1. When did this event occur?

John implies that the supper took place soon after Jesus' arrival at Bethany (12:1, 2). This, he says, was six days before the Passover, hence on Friday, or possibly Saturday. Edersheim says the supper was held on the Sabbath, and calls it "the special festive meal of the Sabbath."—*The Life and Times of Jesus the Messiah,* Vol. 2, p. 358. Matthew and Mark, however, place it at a later time. Both have it following statements that the Passover was only two days away (Matthew 26:2; Mark 14:1). This apparent discrepancy has caused some writers to conclude there were two anointings during Christ's last week (Lightfoot, Clericus, Clarke, McKnight, Whitby). This seems unlikely. Probably John has the correct chronological placement. If so, we would conclude that Matthew and Mark inject the event (with Jesus' statement that Mary's anointing was in preparation for His burial) parenthetically to further prepare their readers for Christ's forthcoming death.

2. Where did this anointing take place?

Matthew and Mark locate it in the house of Simon the leper at Bethany. His identity is unknown. One tradition has him as the father of Lazarus; another as the husband of Mary. There is no evidence to support either view. Simon was probably a former leper who had been healed by Jesus, and who was a friend of Lazarus and his sisters.

3. Could this be the same event as that in Luke 7:36-50?

The one outstanding similarity of the two events is

that in both, the name of the host was Simon. The differences make it clear that there were two anointings: one happened in Galilee in the house of Simon *the Pharisee;* the other in Bethany in the house of Simon *the leper.* One was performed by a sinful, but repentant, woman of the street, whose sins were forgiven; the other by Mary, a faithful disciple whose conduct was commended.

4. What is spikenard?
Spikenard is a rose-red, fragrant ointment made from the dried roots and woolly stems of the spikenard plant. It was imported into Palestine from northern India. Because of this it was extremely costly.

5. What is an alabaster box?
Alabaster is a carbonate of lime which is found in stalagmitic formations of varying shades and colors. Tenny states that such boxes are still used to transport spikenard because they preserve so well its fragrance.—*Pictorial Bible Dictionary,* p. 668.

6. Who first made the objection about the waste of money?
Neither Matthew nor Mark is specific about the source of the objection. John, however, says it was Judas Iscariot, Simon's son. He also reveals Judas' motive: "This he said, not that he cared for the poor" (the pretense which he had made); "but because he was a thief, and had the bag, and bare what was put therein" (John 12:6). At some earlier time Judas, who was highly respected by the other apostles, had begun to steal some of the money which interested followers gave Jesus to help finance His campaign. It pained Judas that the spikenard wasn't sold and the money given into his keeping.

7. In what sense was the anointing done for His burial?
Although Jesus said the anointing was for His burial, it should not be concluded that Mary understood this purpose. Even the apostles weren't able to grasp that He was going to die. Jesus, however, understood and accepted the anointing as a preparation for His forthcoming burial. It was customary that bodies be anointed prior to being placed in a sepulchre.

8. What promise did Jesus make about Mary's action?
Matthew 26:13 answers this question. We can be sure that in keeping with Jesus' words, wherever

Spikenard

Judas, the treasurer of Jesus' group, was a thief.

"Verily I say unto you, Wheresoever this gospel shall be preached in the whole world, there shall also this, that this woman hath done, be told for a memorial of her" (Matthew 26:13).

159

the good news has gone, the gracious act of Mary has been related.

The Triumphal Entry . . . Matthew 21:1-11; Mark 11:1-11; Luke 19:29-44; John 12:12-19

1. How did Jesus know about the ass and her colt?
Whether there was prearrangement, or whether this was an act of foreknowledge, we are not told.

Jesus' triumphal entry had been foretold by the Old Testament prophets. (See Isaiah 62:11 and Zechariah 9:9.)

2. Where is the cited prophecy to be found?
In Zechariah 9:9. It should be borne in mind that the prediction was made because the Holy Spirit knew Jesus would so act, rather than that Jesus acted as He did because of the prophecy.

3. On which animal did Jesus ride?
Only Matthew mentions that both the ass and her colt were brought. The other three writers mention only the colt. It is quite obvious that He rode on the colt. Apparently both were brought because the colt would be more manageable with its mother present.

4. Why did the disciples spread garments and branches before Jesus?
Such was often done by the ancients to honor conquerors and princes. It was, therefore, an appropriate gesture for the King of kings and Lord of lords.

5. What is the meaning of "Hosanna"?
It is a Syriac word which means "Save now" or "Save, I beseech thee." As used on this occasion, it was a joyful acclamation as well as a prayer.

Hosanna means "Save now," or "Save, I beseech thee."

6. How was the triumphal entry accepted by the religious leaders?
Naturally they were irritated by the whole affair. Luke relates how some of the Pharisees turned upon Jesus, demanding that He rebuke His disciples because of the magnificent words of praise uttered on His behalf (19:39). Matthew mentions that some children took up the refrain in the temple, much to the displeasure of the chief priests and scribes (21:15). John presents the conclusion of certain Pharisees: "Perceive ye how ye prevail nothing? behold, the world is gone after him" (12:19).

7. How was Jesus identified by His disciples?
In their exclamations of praise the disciples applied the families Messianic title, "son of David," to Jesus. After the procession had entered the city,

the people inquired concerning the identity of the one being honored. The disciples then responded: "This is Jesus the prophet of Nazareth of Galilee" (Matthew 21:11).

8. What did Jesus do after He entered the city?
From Matthew and Luke it appears that He cleansed the temple on the same day of His triumphal entry. Mark, however, places the event on the following day, i.e., Monday. Most harmonists favor Mark's arrangement since he alone makes specific reference to the conduct of Jesus after entering Jerusalem on Sunday. (See Mark 11:11.)

9. Why did Jesus weep over Jerusalem?
Concerning His motive, Foster has written: "The verb is very strong, indicating 'wailing and sobbing.' Jesus was not misled by the praise and enthusiasm of the crowd. He realized that the nation was about to reject Him and crucify Him. Yet His thoughts were not about His death, but the terrible fate of the city. Instead of the shouts and songs of the people, He could hear the groans and shrieks of the dying as the Romans destroyed the city."—*Gospels Syllabus*. This destruction occurred in A. D. 70.

10. What does the expression "the time of thy visitation" mean?
It refers to the coming of Jesus to earth. Many of the Jews, especially the leaders, did not appreciate His visit. The *New International Version* renders this: "You did not recognize the time of God's coming to you" (Luke 19:44). A similar expression is found in Luke 7:16.

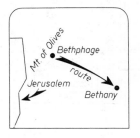

Cursing the Fig Tree: Second Cleansing of the Temple ... Matthew 21:18, 19, 12-17; Mark 11:12-18; Luke 19:45-48

1. Which of these events occurred first?
Although Matthew has the cleansing of the temple before the cursing of the fig tree, he apparently has inverted the events. Mark's seems to be the correct sequence. He places the cleansing later on the same day of the cursing. Neither Luke nor John helps with this question. John doesn't mention either event, and Luke has nothing about the cursing of the tree.

2. What was Jesus' motive in cursing the tree?
Jesus knew the tree had no fruit on it, for He realized that "the time of figs was not yet" (Mark 11:13). However, since the tree had the foliage

161

Fig tree

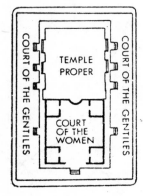

usually associated with the time of figs, it was "guilty" of claiming to have something it didn't. Jesus used the tree to teach a valuable lesson to His disciples. It would be foolish to claim that the same Jesus who knew about the presence of a coin in a fish's mouth (Matthew 17:24-27) was ignorant about the condition of a tree.

3. When did the disciples become aware that the fig tree had withered and died?
Matthew doesn't specify the time when the disciples saw the tree's condition, but merely states their reaction when they saw it. Mark has it on the following day (Tuesday), when Jesus and His disciples were again on their way to Jerusalem from Bethany.

4. How many times did Jesus cleanse the temple?
Twice: once at the beginning of His ministry, as recorded by John (2:13-22); and this time, at the conclusion of His ministry, as recorded by the Synoptics. Although the same basic procedure was used in both instances there are slight differences in the two events.

5. What miracles did Jesus perform at this time?
Matthew says He healed the blind and the lame who came to Him in the temple. Luke mentions that He spent His time in teaching. Here, as throughout His ministry, the two—teaching and healing—complemented each other.

6. Why did the chief priests and scribes become "sore displeased"?
They did so because of the growing influence of Jesus. They resented the fact that ever-increasing multitudes followed Him.

WHEN AND WHERE
It is difficult to determine the exact sequence of events in this lesson. However, the following seems to harmonize best with the texts:

Friday, March 31, A. D. 30. . . Arrival of Jesus at Bethany;

Saturday, April 1, A. D. 30 . . . Day spent in rest and worship; in the evening, the supper at the house of Simon, at which Mary anointed Jesus;

Sunday, April 2, A. D. 30 . . . Triumphal entry and weeping over

Jerusalem; retirement to Bethany;

Monday, April 3, A. D. 30 . . . Cursing of fig tree, second cleansing of the temple; retirement to Bethany.

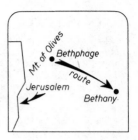

Bethany, sometimes called "the Judean home of Jesus," was located approximately two miles southeast of Jerusalem, on the eastern slope of the Mount of Olives. Nearby, apparently to the northwest, was the village of Bethphage where Jesus obtained the colt for His triumphal entry. Somewhere in the vicinity of this village He cursed the fruitless fig tree. From Bethany, a footpath to Jerusalem passes this site. This was probably the route taken by Jesus on His triumphal entry. Because of its steepness, this route usually was avoided by those coming out of Jerusalem. Instead of it, a longer, more southerly route was used. Probably Jesus followed the custom of using one route into the city and the other on His way back to Bethany. This accounts for how the fig tree could be cursed one day and its withered condition not be discovered until the next. Locate Bethany and Bethphage on the map which is provided.

PROJECTS AND PLANS

Using four-columned paper, do a "word harmony" of the triumphal entry. Follow this example:

Matthew	Mark	Luke	John
And	And	And	
		it came to pass	
when they	when they	when he	
drew nigh	came nigh	was come nigh	
unto Jerusalem,	to Jerusalem,		
and were come			
to Bethphage,	unto Bethphage	to Bethphage	
	and Bethany,	and Bethany,	
unto	at	at	
		the mount	
		called	
the mount of	the mount of	the mount of	
Olives	Olives	Olives	

In two of the events of the next lesson, money plays an important role. To prepare for this lesson, secure a good Bible dictionary and read the material concerning *money* in New Testament days.

QUESTIONS AND PARABLES

TOPICS AND TEXTS

Discussion About the Withered Fig Tree . . . Matthew 21:20-22; Mark 11:19-26; Luke 21:37, 38

The Authority of Jesus Challenged by His Enemies . . . Matthew 21:23-27; Mark 11:27-33; Luke 20:1-8

The Parable of the Two Sons . . . Matthew 21:28-32

The Parable of the Vineyard . . . Matthew 21:33-46; Mark 12:1-12; Luke 20:9-19

The Parable of the Wedding Garment . . . Matthew 22:1-14

The Question of Tribute to Caesar . . . Matthew 22:15-22; Mark 12:13-17; Luke 20:20-26

The Question of the Resurrection . . . Matthew 22:23-33; Mark 12:18-27; Luke 20:27-40

The Question of the Greatest Commandment . . . Matthew 22:34-40; Mark 12:28-34

The Question About the Son of David . . . Matthew 22:41-46; Mark 12:35-37; Luke 20:41-44

Denunciation of the Scribes and Pharisees . . . Matthew 23:1-39; Mark 12:38-40; Luke 20:45-47

The Widow's Mites . . . Mark 12:41-44; Luke 21:1-4

CONTEXT AND CONTINUITY

Tuesday of what has come to be known as "passion week" was one of the tremendous days in Jesus' life. Viewed as to the number of known events in which He became engaged, it qualifies as His busiest day, surpassing even the one on which He taught the seaside parables (Lesson Nine; see also "Context and Continuity" section of Lesson Ten). In Matthew's Gospel, four entire chapters and portions of two others are devoted to it. In addition to Matthew's material, much of which is presented by Mark and Luke also, two other events are known to have transpired: the incident involving the widow's mites (recorded by Mark and Luke), and the sermon on the significance of life and death (presented by John). In fact this single day was so filled with activities that two lessons, this one and the next, are devoted to it.

As far as the record is concerned, the day began for Jesus as He and His apostles traveled the same road from Bethany to Jerusalem which they had used the previous morning. When they arrived at the fig tree which Jesus had cursed on Monday, Peter called attention to its withered condition. This led Jesus to teach a lesson about the power of faith and prayer.

Entering Jerusalem, He was confronted by some of the chief priests and rulers who challenged Him concerning His authority. After this encounter He taught three parables: one about *two sons,* another about a *vineyard,* and a third about a *wedding garment.* Next He was approached by

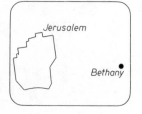

Jerusalem

Bethany

some of the Pharisees' disciples and Herodians who questioned Him about paying tribute to Caesar. This was followed by a question from the Sadducees about the state of the resurrected. Then a question about the greatest commandment was asked by a lawyer, a Pharisee, whose motive was to tempt rather than to learn. After this Jesus turned on the Pharisees with questions of His own concerning the ancestry of the Messiah. These many questions have earned for the day the title, "the great day of questioning", as it frequently is called by Bible scholars.

Addressing the multitude, Jesus denounced the scribes and Pharisees as hypocrites and blind guides, and then lamented over the city of Jerusalem.

Mark and Luke tell how Jesus, when he was near the treasury, watched people cast in money. Seeing a widow throw in two coins of little value, He commended her because she gave all that she had.

Next John tells how certain Greeks desired to see Jesus, how they contacted Philip, and how he and Andrew took them to the Master. Then it was that Jesus delivered a sermon pertaining to the significance of life and death.

Wailing Wall

Departing from the temple He went eastward toward Bethany. As He left the temple, the disciples commented about the large stones of which it was made, and also about its beauty. Jesus then predicted: "There shall not be left here one stone upon another, that shall not be thrown down" (Matthew 24:2). Crossing the Brook Kedron, He and His disciples began to ascend the Mount of Olives. When partway up the mount, Peter, James, John, and Andrew asked Him with concern, "When shall these things be?" Jesus responded by speaking regarding the destruction of Jerusalem, His second coming, and the end of the world.

Then Jesus taught two more parables (the *ten virgins,* and the *talents),* and lectured concerning the final judgment. Later He went on to Bethany where, probably after sunset (hence the Jewish Wednesday), He gave the fifth prediction of His death. That same evening Judas slipped away from the rest of the apostles, returned to Jerusalem, sought out the chief priests, and made his infamous bargain for betrayal. Thus was concluded Tuesday's activities.

The present lesson deals with the events up to and including the one involving the widow's mites. Lesson Twenty-One will deal with the remaining incidents of the day.

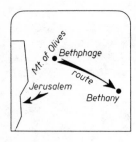

INQUIRIES AND INSIGHTS

Discussion About the Withered Fig Tree . . . Matthew 21:20-22; Mark 11:19-26; Luke 21:37, 38

1. What lessons did Jesus teach from the fig tree?
The principal lesson was that men should have faith in God through which they would be able to accomplish great things. Specific emphasis was made by Jesus upon the necessity of faith as the basis of successful prayer.

2. What additional teaching regarding prayer does Mark introduce?
Mark records that Jesus spoke concerning the necessity of forgiving others in developing an effective prayer life.

The Authority of Jesus Challenged by His Enemies . . . Matthew 21:23-27; Mark 11:27-33; Luke 20:1-8

1. What two questions did the rulers ask Jesus?
They asked about His authority and its source. He could have answered, "I have the authority of the Messiah and act by the power of God." He didn't answer this way because He knew His antagonists wouldn't accept such answers. Instead He asked a question of His own.

2. What of Jesus' answer?
A dilemma is an embarrassing situation requiring a choice between equally undesirable alternatives. It was just such a situation which Jesus created for His enemies with His question: "The baptism of John, whence was it? from heaven, or of men?" (Matthew 21:25). Although He agreed to answer their question if they answered His, He knew they wouldn't attempt an answer. They would not risk the repercussions of either of the two possible answers.

The Parable of the Two Sons . . . Matthew 21:28-32

1. Whom did Jesus represent by the two sons?
The son who refused but later did his father's will represented the publicans and sinners; the other boy represented the Jewish religious leaders.

2. What lesson does the parable teach?
The parable was directed against the religious leaders who claimed to be, but in reality were not doing God's will. Because these men had refused

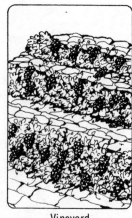

Vineyard

both the message of John and of Jesus, the publicans and sinners, who were heeding the message, were going into the kingdom before them.

The Parable of the Vineyard . . . Matthew 21:33-46; Mark 12:1-12; Luke 20:9-19

1. What lesson does this parable teach?

The Jewish nation, although founded and specially blessed by God, continually refused to accept the message of His servants, the prophets. The Jews' final act of rebellion (at that time, yet to come) was their rejection and murder of His own Son. Yet, in spite of their rejection, Christ would still be the head of the corner of the building which God was going to erect. The result of their failure to accept Him was that the kingdom of God would be taken from them and ·given to others.

2. What did Jesus mean about the stone?

Jesus no doubt had in mind Isaiah 8:14, 15. Christ is the stone, and those who come in contact with Him with an evil motive shall be broken, even as those who run into a protruding cornerstone may be injured. Or ,it may be that He, as the stone, will fall upon the evildoer as the huge stones of punishment executed Jewish lawbreakers.

The Parable of the Wedding Garment . . . Matthew 22:1-14

1. What is the central teaching of this parable?

Apparently Jesus had a double purpose in mind in teaching this parable. First, it was directed against the Jews who had shamefully rejected and abused God's servants (some were pictured as refusing an invitation to the "marriage" of His Son). The second purpose is indicated in verse 14: "For many are called, but few are chosen." Not everyone who accepts God's invitation will receive the reward which He offers. Some will find themselves in a place where there will be weeping and gnashing of teeth.

2. Why should a guest be punished for not having a wedding garment?

When the guest was confronted by the king concerning his lack of proper attire, "he was speechless." This indicates he was without excuse. We conclude that one of two things was true: (1) The king provided garments but this guest refused to wear one; (2) The man had had adequate time and possessed the means for securing the kind of garment that he knew was required. In either case the man was personally responsible.

Cornerstone

Jesus as the "cornerstone": Psalm 118:22; Acts 4:11; Ephesians 2:20-22; 1 Peter 2:6-8; 1 Corinthians 3:11.

								F	S	S	M	T	W							

The Question of Tribute to Caesar ... Matthew 22:15-22; Mark 12:13-17; Luke 20:20-26

1. Who asked this question?

Mark says the antagonists were Pharisees and Herodians. Matthew agrees but specifies that the men with the Herodians were disciples of the Pharisees (apparently younger, less-prominent men) who had been sent by their leaders. Luke has the most picturesque description: "They . . . sent forth spies, which should feign themselves just men" (20:20).

2. Who were the Herodians?

They were Jews who supported the dynasty of Herod and therefore the rule of Rome. They are mentioned in connection with only two events in the New Testament: one in Mark 3:6 (see Lesson Seven), and this one. In both instances they are associated with the Pharisees in opposing Jesus. This association is strange inasmuch as their feelings about the Roman Empire would be opposite.

> The only source of information about the Herodians is the Gospels.

3. What coin was brought to Jesus?

The King James Version says it was a penny, which unfortunately creates a misconception. Readers are apt to associate this Bible penny with the present-day American cent. The Greek name for the coin is *dānarion,* called "denarius" in more recent translations of the Bible. It represented a day's pay in the Roman world.

4. Did Jesus avoid answering the question of His enemies?

Not at all! Instead He established a principle that is as valid today as when it was first given. Although it is not always easy to determine what things are Caesar's and what things are God's, such difficulty does not negate the principle.

The Question of the Resurrection ... Matthew 22:23-33; Mark 12:18-27; Luke 20:27-40

1. Who were the Sadducees?

The Sadducees were members of a politico-religious party that had its origin in the intertestamental period. The name probably was derived from Zadok, high priest during the time of David, from whom all succeeding high priests claimed to descend (2 Samuel 8:17). Our chief sources of information about them are the New Testament (where they are mentioned by name about a dozen times), and Josephus (whose information is not wholly reliable since he was a member of the opposition party, the Pharisees).

> The Sadducees, priestly and aristocratic, were never as numerous as their rivals, the Pharisees.

Jesus had fewer conflicts with, and many less words of condemnation for, the Sadducees than the Pharisees. Thomson suggests the following reason for this difference: "As His position, both doctrinal and practical, was much nearer that of the Pharisees, it was necessary that He should clearly mark Himself off from them. There was not the same danger of His position being confused with that of the Sadducees." *The International Standard Bible Encyclopedia,* Vol. IV, p. 2661.

Most of the Sadducees were priests who prided themselves on their aristocratic standing. Doctrinally they are better remembered for what they did *not* believe. They denied the resurrection of the body, personal immortality, and retribution in a future life; they disbelieved in angels and spirits (Acts 23:8); they rejected the traditions of the elders, holding only to the Old Testament Scriptures (some say only to the Pentateuch); they refused to accept divine interposition in the government of the world. After the destruction of the temple, the Sadducean party disappeared.

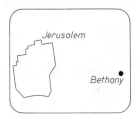

Jerusalem

Bethany

2. To which Mosaic law did the Sadducees refer?

The reference was to levirate marriage, commanded by Moses in Deuteronomy 25:5-10. The practice is mentioned in Genesis 38:8-10 and Ruth 4:5. Its purpose was to avert the extinction of name and family, and to provide a way for a man's inheritance to be handed down.

The Old Testament teaching regarding levirate marriage is found in Deuteronomy 25:5-10.

3. Of what two things did Jesus say the Sadducees were ignorant?

One, they were ignorant of the Old Testament Scriptures which teach a future existence (see Exodus 3:6, 15). Two, they didn't understand the power of God which can change the form of man's existence in the future life so that marriage will no longer be practicable.

4. How does the Old Testament reference prove the resurrection?

Although Abraham, Isaac, and Jacob had been dead many years when God appeared to Moses (Exodus 3), He spoke then as still being their God. They were not extinct or annihilated, but continued to live.

The Question of the Greatest Commandment . . . Matthew 22:34-40; Mark 12:28-34

1. What was the motive of the lawyer in asking this question?

Matthew says he did it, "tempting him," which

Lawyers were those well-versed in the oral and written law. They were responsible for deciding questions concerning the law and for teaching younger men. (See Luke 7:30; 10:25; 11:45ff; 14:3; Titus 3:13.) Lawyers are also called "scribes" (Matthew 5:20; 12:38; Mark 7:5; Luke 5:21, 30; John 8:3) and "doctors of the law" (Luke 5:17; Acts 5:34) in the New Testament.

> "Thou shalt love the Lord thy God with all thine heart, and with all thy soul, and with all thy might" (Deuteronomy 6:5). "Thou shalt love thy neighbor as thyself" (Leviticus 19:18).

doesn't speak very well of the scribe. However, unlike some of his associates who could say nothing good concerning Jesus, this lawyer at least conceded that the Master spoke truth (Mark 12:28, 32, 33). Jesus' comment to the man, "Thou art not far from the kingdom of God" (Mark 12:34), makes us wonder if he ever found and entered the kingdom.

2. Where in the Scriptures are the two commandments that Jesus cited?
Deuteronomy 6:5 and Leviticus 19:18.

3. In what way are they the two greatest commandments?
Albert Barnes comments: "It [love for God] is the first and greatest of all; *first,* not in *order of time,* but of *importance; greatest* in dignity, in excellence, in extent, and duration. It is the fountain of all others." The second, love for one's neighbor, is like the first in its "importance, dignity, purity, and usefulness."—*Notes on the New Testament, Matthew,* p. 237.

The Question About the Son of David . . . Matthew 22:41-46; Mark 12:35-37; Luke 20:41-44

1. Why could the Pharisees so quickly answer Jesus' first question?
As students of the Old Testament they were thoroughly familiar with the numerous passages that predicted that the Messiah would be a descendant of David: 2 Samuel 7:8-17; Psalm 132:10, 11; Isaiah 9:6, 7; 11:1-10; Jeremiah 23:5-8. Therefore without hesitation they answered Him.

> Jesus, Son of David: Matthew 1:1; 12:23; 15:22; 21:19; Mark 10:48; John 7:42; Romans 1:3; 2 Timothy 2:8; Revelation 5:5.

2. What is the force of Jesus' argument?
Jesus quoted from Psalm 110 where David, under inspiration, spoke of the Messiah as his own Lord. The passage says: "The Lord (God the Father) said unto my Lord (the Messiah), Sit thou at my right hand, until I make thine enemies thy footstool." It is not difficult for us to understand the verse, for we recognize that although the Messiah is the Son of David, He is also the Son of God. This fact wasn't clear to the Pharisees. They were unable to see how David's son could also be his Lord, and therefore they could not answer the question.

3. When did the questioning of Jesus cease?
The last question put to Him on this great day of questions was the one about the greatest commandment (Matthew 22:34-40; Mark 12:28-34). We should not suppose that all questions then

| | | | | | | | | F | S | S | M | T | W | | | | | | | | |

ceased forever, for the record proves otherwise. Rather, the verse expresses the fact that all hostile questioning stopped. His marvelous answers to His enemies' questions, coupled with the brilliant questions which He put to them (Matthew 21:23-27; 22:41-46), completely dumbfounded them. They therefore ceased asking Him publicly questions to ensnare Him in His speech.

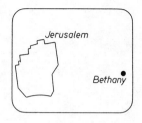

Denunciation of the Scribes and Pharisees . . . Matthew 23:1-39; Mark 12:38-40; Luke 20:45-47

1. Who were the scribes?
The scribes were learned men, mostly Pharisees, who devoted their time to the study, interpretation, and expounding of the law. There are a number of references to them in the Gospels, where they are usually associated with the Pharisees in either attacking or receiving the rebuke of Jesus.

2. Who were the Pharisees?
The word *Pharisees* means "the separatists" or "the separated ones." It describes the most prominent sect of the Jews in Jesus' day. (Josephus says there were as many as six thousand of them at the height of their power.) They are repeatedly mentioned in the Gospels where they are represented as the enemies of Jesus. Their origin is somewhat uncertain, but they apparently date to the time of the Maccabees. The first appearance of the name Pharisee was in 35 B. C. As is evident from the present texts, Jesus reserved His harshest rebukes for them, calling them fools, hypocrites, blind, children of Hell, serpents, and comparing them to platters clean on the outside but dirty on the inside, and to whitewashed sepulchres. Of course not all Pharisees were such, for numbered among them were such men as Nicodemus, Gamaliel, and Saul. The vast majority, however, had forgotten the real purpose of religion, and contented themselves with outward manifestations of piety, while being void of its real presence and fruits. They were noted for their legalism and nationalism, and for such doctrines as special divine providence, immortality of the soul, and future reward for the righteous and punishment for the wicked. They strongly believed in the coming of the Messiah, but refused to accept Jesus as Christ.

> Josephus says there were as many as 6,000 Pharisees at the height of their power. They are mentioned dozens of times in the New Testament.

3. For what things did Jesus condemn the scribes and Pharisees?
He condemned them specifically because they: (1) bound burdens on others that they wouldn't

bear; (2) performed various hypocritical acts in order to receive the praise of men; (3) blocked the entrance to the kingdom of God; (4) took advantage of widows; (5) harmed those who were proselyted to the faith; (6) established false standards of evaluation; (7) emphasized the wrong values; (8) harmed the servants of God.

4. What were phylacteries?

They were small slips of parchment or vellum on which were written certain portions of the Old Testament (Exodus 13:3-16; Deuteronomy 6:4-9; 11:13-21), enclosed in a leather case, and worn, especially at prayer time, as amulets or charms. There were two types: one which was worn on the forehead, called a frontlet; the other on the left arm, reaching from the elbow to the top of the middle finger. The practice originated from a literal interpretation of the above passages.

5. In what sense should one not be called "rabbi" or "father"?

Jesus' warning was against the wearing of religious titles to indicate a superior rank, or to call attention to one's supposed importance. The word rabbi means teacher. When a man is so called because of his specific contribution to life and to God's kingdom, there is no violation of Jesus' principle. Similarly Paul humbly spoke of himself as a father of the Corinthians (1 Corinthians 4:15). This was not that they might honor him unduly, but merely that they might remember that through him they had been won to Christ.

> The word proselyte is only found three other times in the New Testament, all in the book of Acts (2:10; 6:5; 13:43). It refers to a person of Gentile origin who had accepted the Jewish religion.

6. What is a proselyte?

A proselyte is one who has changed from one opinion, religious belief, sect, or the like, to another; a convert. The word appears only four times in the New Testament (Matthew 23:15; Acts 2:10; 6:5; 13:43). In the three Acts passages the reference is to Gentiles who had accepted the Jewish faith. The Matthew passage may either refer to the same, or to fellow Jews, proselyted by the Pharisees to their sect; probably the former.

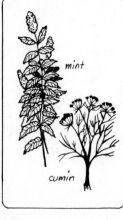

mint

cumin

7. What are mint, anise, and cummin?

They are herbs which have a fine aromatic quality. They were of little value, but were tithed by the Pharisees who prided themselves upon their exactness in little details, while neglecting the more important matters of the law.

8. Who were Abel and Zechariah?

This question is answered in Lesson Fifteen.

The Widow's Mites ... Mark 12:41-44; Luke 21:1-4

Mite

1. What treasury was this?

In the temple, in the court of the women, were thirteen containers with trumpet-shaped mouths into which offerings could be dropped. The money thus received was used for the service of the temple.

2. How much money did the woman contribute?

The mite (leptón) was the least valuable of all coins used by the Jews. It was worth one-fourth or one-fifth of a cent. The first such coins were cast by the Maccabees with Hebrew inscriptions. Later the Herods and the Romans minted similar coins with Greek legends. Probably two of the former ones were given by the widow since the latter ones would be considered unlawful for temple use.

3. Why did Jesus commend her action?

It was her motive and her sacrifice, rather than her money, that brought forth words of praise from the Master. She gave to God because she loved Him, and she gave all that she had.

WHEN AND WHERE

The events of this and the next lesson took place on Tuesday of Jesus' last week. It was the twelfth of Nisan, or April 4, in A. D. 30.

Check the diagram of the temple which is provided. Notice especially the court of the women where the incident involving the widow's mites transpired. Also examine the court of the Gentiles where Jesus did much of His teaching and preaching while in the temple.

PROJECTS AND PLANS

Using the New Testament and such helps as are available, prepare a paper on the subject "Christian Stewardship." Perhaps the class will find time to read and discuss the papers.

Read the article, "Eschatology of the New Testament," by Geerhardus Vos, in *The International Standard Bible Encyclopedia*, Vol. 2, pp. 979-993.

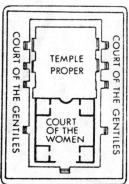

FINAL WORDS ABOUT LAST THINGS

TOPICS AND TEXTS

Sermon on Significance of Life and Death . . . John 12:20-50
Prediction of the Fall of Jerusalem and the Second Coming . . . Matthew 24:1-51; Mark 13:1-37; Luke 21:5-36
Parable of the Ten Virgins . . . Matthew 25:1-13
Parable of the Talents . . . Matthew 25:14-30
Discussion of the Final Judgment . . . Matthew 25:31-46
Fifth Prediction of Jesus' Death . . . Matthew 26:1-5; Mark 14:1, 2; Luke 22:1, 2
The Plot of Judas to Betray Jesus . . . Matthew 26:14-16; Mark 14:10, 11; Luke 22:3-6

Eschatology is the study of last things. It deals with such topics as death, the resurrection, the return of Christ, the end of the world, divine judgment, and the future life.

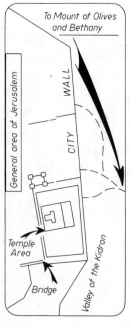

To Mount of Olives and Bethany

General area of Jerusalem

WALL

CITY

Temple Area

Bridge

Valley of the Kidron

CONTEXT AND CONTINUITY

Eschatology, "the study of last things," has always held a certain fascination for the student of the Bible. Such interest is not surprising, for those who accept the Bible as the Word of God want to understand what He says about the end times. The prophecies of the Old Testament, fulfilled in the New, give ample evidence of the power of God to disclose future events. Consequently they give initiative to present-day Bible students to seek in it for an understanding of that which is yet to be fulfilled.

Christian eschatology deals with the subjects of death, the resurrection, the second coming of Christ, the end of the world, divine judgment, and the future state. This present lesson is concerned with a number of these topics. The passage with which we begin this lesson, John 12:20-50, is about life and death. The next topic, based on Matthew 24 and the parallel texts in Mark 13 and Luke 21, is concerned with the destruction of Jerusalem, Jesus' second coming, and the end of the world. Matthew 25, the next passage for discussion, contains two more of Jesus' parables (there is also one at the conclusion of Matthew 24 and Mark 13): the *ten virgins* and the *talents*. Both prophesy His return and the Judgment that follows. This chapter also contains Jesus' description of the separation which will take place at the Judgment. Men will be classed as sheep or goats (i.e., acceptable or unacceptable) according to the treatment they have given to His followers (e.g., food for the hungry, clothes for the naked, etc.). The sheep will be given eternal life, but the goats "shall go away into everlasting punishment" (Matthew 25:46).

In addition to this material, all of which has eschatalogical significance, our present lesson also includes a study of the fifth prediction of Jesus' death, and the bargain of Judas with the chief priests and captains to betray Jesus for thirty pieces of silver (Luke 22:4).

INQUIRIES AND INSIGHTS

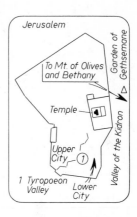

Sermon on Significance of Life and Death . . . John 12:20-50

1. Who were these Greeks?
They were proselytes to the Jewish religion who had come to Jerusalem to worship at the Passover. They probably made their contact with Philip because he had a Greek name. Notice that it was John, whose Gospel originally went to Gentiles, who records this event.

2. Was Jesus' sermon directed toward the Greeks?
John says, "Jesus answered *them*," but the pronoun probably refers to the apostles, Andrew and Philip, rather than the Greeks. Some question whether Jesus met and talked with these men at all, but to fail to do so would be out of character for the Son of God. Also, since much of the sermon seems particularly appropriate for Greek hearers, we conclude that these inquirers, as well as others, heard Jesus' message.

3. What frequently quoted statements did Jesus make in this sermon?
Verses 24 and 32 contain such statements.

4. According to the record, how many times did God speak on behalf of His Son?
"Three times the Father's voice was heard from the sky; *first,* when Christ was buried in Jordan, a type of his own burial; *second,* when Moses and Elias talked with him on the holy mount about his death; *third,* when he had his struggle of soul in view of death portrayed here and triumphed. These facts show the tender, agonizing interest the Father felt in the suffering of the Son."—B. W. Johnson, *The New Testament Commentary, John,* p. 194.

> God spoke three times in recognition of His Son: (1) His baptism—Matthew 3:17; (2) His transfiguration—Matthew 17:5; (3) Near the end of His life—John 12:28.

5. How was the prince of the world cast out?
Jesus, by His death and resurrection, vanquished Satan. As a result of Jesus' actions, men may have the forgiveness of their sins and the promise of eternal life. (Read Hebrews 2:14.)

6. Who blinded the eyes of the Jews?
Although the text says that God blinded their eyes, it obviously means that He permitted the blinding, not that He directly caused it. That men are responsible for their own actions is the teaching of the entire Bible.

7. In what sense did He not come to judge the world?

The primary purpose of His coming was to *save* men. That is why He came as the Lamb of God. Later He will return as the Lion of Judah to execute judgment upon the world.

Prediction of the Fall of Jerusalem and the Second Coming ... Matthew 24:1-51; Mark 13:1-37; Luke 21:5-36

1. How many questions did the disciples ask at this time?

Some believe that they asked only two—the first about the destruction of Jerusalem, and the second about Jesus' coming and the end of the world (a question with two parts). However, since it is unlikely that the disciples would have equated Jesus' coming with the end of the world, it appears that they asked three, not two, questions. (See Matthew 24:3.) It may be that Jesus, realizing that His return was directly connected with the world's end, treated the latter two questions as one. The relationship of these two events (the second coming and the end of the world) is a point of contention among millennialists.

> "And as he sat upon the mount of Olives, the disciples came unto him privately, saying, Tell us, when shall these things be? and what shall be the sign of thy coming, and of the end of the world?" (Matthew 24:3).

2. In what order did Jesus answer the questions?

There is such an intermingling of His answers that it is unwise to be dogmatic here. It seems that Jesus spoke first in a general way concerning the end of the world, then specifically about the destruction of Jerusalem, and next about His second coming. After this He gave summary statements about the last two topics. The following is a suggested order:

	Matthew 24	Mark 13	Luke 21
General statements about the end of the world ...	4-14	5-13	8-19
Destruction of Jerusalem	15-22, 32-35	14-20, 28-31	20-24, 29-33
Second Coming	23-31, 36-51	21-27, 32-37	25-28, 34-36

3. What was Jesus' purpose in delivering this discourse?

Jesus did not intend for His followers to become sign-watchers who would spend their time and energy trying to interpret the events of history. Rather, it was to assure them that the events He described were going to happen, that God was aware of them, and that they, not knowing how the future would unfold, should remain in a state

| | | | | | | | | F | S | S | M | T | W | | | | | | | | |

of readiness for all eventualities. Such readiness can be accomplished by maintaining a proper relationship with God and man at all times.

4. Has the Gospel been preached in all the world?

Jesus said that the gospel of the kingdom would "be preached in all the world for a witness unto all nations" before the end would come (Matthew 24:14; see also Mark 13:10). This requirement has been met. It would be difficult to find any nation that has never had a witness of the gospel. (See Colossians 1:23, where Paul indicates that in a general sense this requirement had been fulfilled in his lifetime.)

5. Did Jesus teach the necessity of faithfulness as an essential of salvation?

Yes, in several places, one of which is Matthew 24:13: "He that shall endure unto the end, the same shall be saved." (See also Mark 13:13.)

6. What was "the abomination of desolation"?

Luke 21:20 connects the phrase with the encompassing of Jerusalem by armies—obviously the Roman armies that sacked and destroyed the city in A.D. 70. Daniel was the first to mention the abominable desecrating of the temple, which occurred when the city was destroyed (Daniel 8:13; 9:26, 27; 11:31; 12:11), and which made it desolate.

7. In what way will Jesus' coming be like lightning?

"This is not designed to denote the *quarter* from which he would come, but the *manner*. He does not mean to affirm that the Son of man will come from the east, but that he will come in a rapid and unexpected manner, like the lightning." *Notes on the New Testament, Matthew,* p. 258.

8. What is meant by the reference to the carcass and the eagles?

First it must be determined whether the reference is to the time of Jerusalem's destruction or to the time of Christ's return. If we are correct in assuming the latter, then the meaning must be that as eagles or vultures are drawn to a dead body, so God's judgment will be brought upon a world grown putrid with sin and wickedness. On the other hand, if the passage refers to the time of the destruction of the Holy City, then Jerusalem is represented by the dead carcass, and the eagles are the Roman armies.

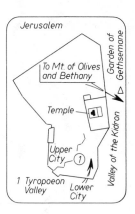

Jerusalem

To Mt. of Olives and Bethany

Garden of Gethsemane

Temple

Valley of the Kidron

Upper City ①

1 Tyropoeon Valley

Lower City

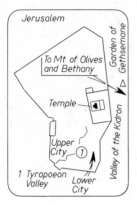

Jerusalem

Garden of Gethsemane

To Mt. of Olives and Bethany

Temple

Upper City ①

1 Tyropoeon Valley

Lower City

Valley of the Kidron

9. What is the sign of the Son of man?

The sign of the Son of man is His coming in the clouds. There is not to be some unusual occurrence that will serve as a warning to men so that they can have time to prepare before He arrives. When His sign appears it will be too late to get ready. When the phenomena mentioned in Matthew 24:29 (Mark 13:24; Luke 21:25, 26) occur there will be no time left to repent of evil and get right with God. Then "the tribes of the earth [will] mourn" (Matthew 24:30), not repent.

10. How is the coming of Jesus comparable to the coming of the flood in Noah's day?

The people of Noah's day didn't believe their world was going to be destroyed. They went on living normal lives, eating, drinking, and marrying. At a time when they thought not, the flood came and "took them all away" (Matthew 24:39). Similarly, at a time when men do not anticipate it, when everything is progressing in a normal fashion, Jesus will return to claim His own.

11. How is Jesus' coming similar to a thief's unlawful entry?

They are comparable in that it is impossible to determine when either may take place. Constant preparation is the lesson that is being taught.

12. Who is the faithful and wise servant, and who is the evil one?

In this parable all Christians are represented as servants, placed by their lord over his household. The wise servants are those who constantly anticipate their lord's return and therefore keep the household operating properly. The evil servants represent Christians who feel the Lord's return has been delayed, and begin to neglect their duties and do wickedly toward others.

Parable of the Ten Virgins . . . Matthew 25:1-13

1. What were the marriage customs in Jesus' day?

The marriage ceremony often took place in the outdoors, on the banks of a stream. After the ceremony there followed a feast at the bride's home. It lasted seven days if she was a virgin, and three, if a widow. Then the bride was escorted, in the evening time, to the home of the bridegroom, or to some other place provided for the occasion. The couple was accompanied by friends, and this procession was met by yet other friends. These were female friends of the bridegroom who came to welcome him and his new companion. The

Oil lamp

group entered the selected place, and a time of feasting and festivity began. Many of these customs still prevail in the East.

2. What is the principal teaching of this parable?

The main truth concerns the necessity of constant preparedness for the coming of the Son of man. All of the virgins represent Christians, but five were excluded from the wedding celebration because of their foolish failure to be ready when the bridegroom came. It is not enough to accept the invitation of Christ; one must develop Christian character and be in daily expectation of His return.

3. Was it wrong for the virgins to sleep?

No, this is merely "scenery" in the parable. Since it would be natural for young women to rest and await the coming of a wedding party, Jesus mentioned this fact. Nor should any significance be attached to the *number* of the virgins.

Parable of the Talents . . . Matthew 25:14-30

1. What is the lesson of this parable?

Through this parable Jesus taught the necessity of using our talents as we await the coming of our Lord from the "far country" into which He has gone. It does not teach that we must have great success in the use of our talents. (The one-talent man would not have been condemned if he had given his money into the hands of the exchangers.) Rather it teaches that we must not be negligent in employing all we have for the Master. The three men were judged on the basis of faithfulness, not success. When we use what we have for the Master, He will bless as He sees fit.

2. Of what value was a talent?

A talent was a weight measurement. When applied to money a talent could be either of gold or silver. Since Jesus didn't specify which kind of talent, it is impossible to determine the value involved in this parable. But, whether of gold or silver, a talent represented a large sum of money.

3. How does this parable connect with the preceding one?

In Matthew 24 and 25 there is a trilogy of parables. These should be studied together since they are part of the same discourse. All three are concerned with the conduct of Christians during the absence of the Lord. The first, that of the servant who was placed in charge of a household (Mat-

Coins

thew 24:45-51; Mark 13:34-37), presents the responsibility of a Christian to his fellow Christians. The second, the parable of the ten virgins, presents the responsibility of an individual Christian to himself to keep his lamp trimmed and his oil supply adequate. The third, the talents, shows the universal responsibility of each Christian. It makes clear that he must be out using his talents faithfully and to the best of his ability, for in this way they will be increased.

4. To what other parable is this one similar?
This parable is similar to the parable of the pounds, taught by Jesus in Jericho, and recorded in Luke 19:11-27.

Compare Luke 19:11-27.

Discussion of the Final Judgment ... Matthew 25:31-46

1. Is this a judgment of nations or individuals?
Matthew 25:32 might be construed as teaching a judgment of nations. However, the remainder of the passage, as well as the rest of the Bible, make it evident that the final judgment is upon the individual citizens of the nations, and not upon the nations taken as a whole.

"When the Son of man shall come in his glory, and all the holy angels with him, then shall he sit upon the throne of his glory: and before him shall be gathered all nations: and he shall separate them one from another, as a shepherd divideth his sheep from the goats" (Matthew 25:31, 32).

2. What basis of judgment is mentioned in this passage?
Rewards and punishments are meted out in proportion to the individual's benevolent acts performed upon Jesus' "brethren." It should not be concluded that this is the only standard of judgment, that all who are charitable toward Jesus' followers will be saved. Such a position violates other Scriptural teaching. This passage stresses the need for Christian benevolence. It should be interpreted in the light of all other Bible teaching.

3. Is the purpose of the Judgment to determine one's innocence or guilt?
No, a trial isn't needed to determine that. Such is already known to God, and becomes known to the individual immediately after his death. Judgment Day is yet in the future. It is a point in time toward which all of history is moving. Sinners will have all of their evil exposed, but Christians will not come into this kind of judgment. Christ will be there to claim His own—those whose sins He has forgiven and whose guilt He has removed.

4. What does this passage teach about Heaven and Hell?
It tells that the duration of both will be the same. There will be "everlasting punishment" for the

cursed and "life eternal" for the blessed. In the Greek of this passage the word translated "everlasting," and the word translated "eternal" is the same word, *aiónion*. It appears sixty-six times in the New Testament. It expresses absolute eternity, i. e., something that always exists. (See Matthew 18:8 and Hebrews 5:9.)

Fifth Prediction of Jesus' Death ... Matthew 26:1-5; Mark 14:1, 2; Luke 22:1, 2

1. When was this prediction made?
It was made two days before the Passover (Matthew 26:2). This places it sometime on Tuesday evening, probably after 6:00 p.m., hence on the Jewish Wednesday.

2. Why the meeting of the religious leaders at this particular time?
They had seen Jesus' extreme popularity in the triumphal entry, and this irritated them. Then, having failed to conquer Him in their verbal encounters, they determined that One so popular and powerful must be put to death as soon as it was feasible to do it.

3. Why were they reluctant to put Him to death during the feast?
The leaders realized that He was very popular with the multitude, and that many accepted Him as the Messiah. Therefore, to attempt to kill Him when so many of His followers were in Jerusalem would be foolhardy.

The Plot of Judas to Betray Jesus ... Matthew 26:14-16; Mark 14:10, 11; Luke 22:3-6

1. What is known about Judas Iscariot?
Nothing is known about his birth and early life. His name indicates he was from Kerioth, a small town in the southern part of Judah (Joshua 15:25). After he was selected to be an apostle, he was further honored by being made treasurer of the group (John 12:6; 13:29). His true character was revealed when Jesus was anointed by Mary of Bethany (John 12:2-8). In connection with this incident John informs us that Judas was a thief. His wickedness, however, wasn't known by the apostles until after his act of betrayal (John 13:21-30). Having sold the Lord for thirty pieces of silver, he became remorseful and returned the money to the chief priests and elders (Matthew 27:3-10). His life ended in suicide by hanging (Matthew 27:5).

2. What was Judas' motive in betraying Jesus?
The Bible doesn't answer this question. It was a

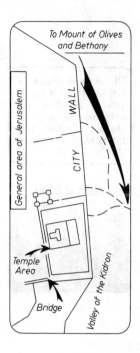

Judas **Iscariot** means Judas **of Kerioth**.

> "If the ox shall push a manservant or a maidservant; he shall give unto their master thirty shekels of silver, and the ox shall be stoned" (Exodus 21:32).

Mount of Olives

personal choice over which Judas had complete control. He didn't have to betray Jesus simply because there were Old Testament predictions of the betrayal. Rather, the predictions are there because God knew that Judas would so act (*knowing it should not be equated with causing it*).

3. How much was Judas paid?

Neither Mark nor Luke mentions the amount. Matthew says it was thirty pieces of silver. The coins were probably shekels—Jewish silver coins. The shekel, the drachma, and the denarius were of similar value—worth a day's wages. According to the law, thirty pieces of silver was the price of a slave (Exodus 21:32). This price was probably agreed upon by the chief priests as one more means of showing their contempt of Jesus.

WHEN AND WHERE

The only reference to time in this lesson is in Matthew 26:2 (Mark 14:1) where the fifth prediction of Jesus' death is said to have been made two days before the Passover. This apparently refers to Tuesday evening (Jewish Wednesday) since the Passover Feast was eaten on Thursday evening (Jewish Friday). Jesus' encounter with the Greeks, as well as His discourse on eschatology, evidently occurred late on Tuesday afternoon, the latter as He and His apostles returned to Bethany for the evening. Judas' plot with the chief priests and captains happened later that same night.

While Jesus "sat upon the mount of Olives" He taught the material recorded in Matthew 24 and 25 and in the parallel passages, Mark 13 and Luke 21. This mount, which lies to the east of Jerusalem, is somewhat over one mile in length. It rises 250 feet above Mount Moriah, the hill on which the temple had been erected. Separating these two hills is the Valley of Jehoshaphat (the Valley of the Kedron). From the Mount of Olives one has an excellent view of the temple and the eastern part of Jerusalem. At some spot on this hillside Jesus delivered His discourse, possibly gesturing toward the temple and the city as He spoke concerning their future.

PROJECTS AND PLANS

In this lesson we studied the fifth prediction of Jesus' death. When were the other four made; where are they recorded; and what specifically did Jesus say in each prediction?

To prepare for the next lesson, read chapters 9 and 10 in book 5 of *The Life and Times of Jesus the Messiah,* Vol. 2, pp. 479-512.

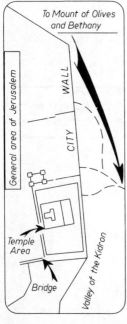

General area of Jerusalem

To Mount of Olives and Bethany

CITY WALL

Temple Area

Bridge

Valley of the Kidron

THE EVE OF THE TRAGIC DAY

TOPICS AND TEXTS

Preparation for the Passover Meal . . . Matthew 26:17-19; Mark 14:12-16; Luke 22:7-13
The Passover Meal . . . Matthew 26:20; Mark 14:17; Luke 22:14-16, 24-30
The Disciples' Feet Washed by Jesus . . . John 13:1-20
Judas Pointed Out as the Traitor . . . Matthew 26:21-25; Mark 14:18-21; Luke 22:21-23; John 13:21-30
The Disciples Warned (Peter's Denial Foretold) . . . Matthew 26:31-35; Mark 14:27-31; Luke 22:31-38; John 13:31-38
The Lord's Supper Instituted (1 Corinthians 11:23-26) . . . Matthew 26:26-29; Mark 14:22-25; Luke 22:17-20
Jesus' Farewell Discourse . . . John 14:1-31
The Parable of the Vine . . . John 15:1-27
Further Solemn Instruction . . . John 16:1-33
The Prayer of Jesus . . . John 17:1-26
The Agony in the Garden . . . Matthew 26:30, 36-46; Mark 14:26, 32-42; Luke 22:39-46; John 18:1

CONTEXT AND CONTINUITY

According to the traditional view, Jesus rested on the Wednesday of passion week. Perhaps the day was spent in fellowship with His apostles and communion with His Father. On Thursday He sent Peter and John to make preparation for the Passover meal (Luke 22:8). That evening after sunset (Jewish Friday) He assembled with His apostles in an upper room and ate the Passover meal. He then washed His apostles' feet, indicated His knowledge of the plot of Judas to betray Him, foretold the denial of the other apostles, and instituted the Lord's Supper. It was on this occasion that He delivered His farewell address (John 14), taught the parable of the vine and the branches (John 15), gave further instruction to the apostles (John 16), and offered His high priestly prayer (John 17). Later that night He went into the Garden of Gethsemane where He prayed earnestly to God and where, still later, He was arrested by a band of men who had been led to the garden by Judas Iscariot.

As indicated, this is the traditional view. Of course, not all accept it. Samuel J. Andrews, in *The Life of Our Lord Upon the Earth,* devotes twenty-five pages to a "discussion of the disputed points connected with the Lord's last paschal supper." Two main points are dealt with: the time of the observance of the supper by Jesus and His apostles, and the manner in which they kept it. It would be profitable to read this material (pages 450-503).

Some contend that Jesus didn't observe the regular paschal supper on Thursday evening but substituted for it a memorial supper, or farewell sup-

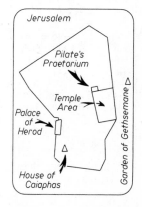

Jerusalem

Pilate's Praetorium

Temple Area

Palace of Herod

Garden of Gethsemane

House of Caiaphas

March, A.D. 30 | April ↓

							F	S	S	M	T	W	T	F						

per, at an earlier time. According to this view, He died as the Lamb of God on the day the Passover lamb was slain (Thursday). The following Scriptures seem to oppose this view, and reinforce the position advocated in this book: Matthew 26:17; Mark 14:12, 14; Luke 22:7, 11, 15.

The last complete day of our Lord's earthly life should be of interest to every disciple.

INQUIRIES AND INSIGHTS

Preparation for the Passover Meal ... Matthew 26:17-19; Mark 14:12-16; Luke 22:7-13

1. What was the feast of Unleavened Bread?

This feast began on the fifteenth of Nisan, the day following the Passover, and continued for seven days, ending on the twenty-first. The two feasts formed a double festival which were viewed by the Jews as one. Luke explains that the two names were used interchangeably (22:1). During these eight days no bread made with yeast or leaven could be eaten or allowed in the house. On the evening following Nisan 13, the Jews searched their houses with lights for any leaven that might be there. The day of the week referred to by these texts, the day that preparation for the Passover was made, was Nisan 14 (Thursday), as indicated in Mark 14:12. (See Exodus 12:6.)

> See Exodus 12:6 and Leviticus 23:4-8 for information concerning the feast of the Passover and the feast of Unleavened Bread.

2. Why the secrecy in securing the place for the supper?

Probably the reason was to keep Judas from knowing the spot in advance. Thus he was prevented from bringing soldiers to interrupt prematurely the fellowship of Jesus and the apostles. The detail about following a man bearing a pitcher is mentioned only by Mark and Luke.

3. What did the apostles do to prepare for the supper?

In addition to obtaining the place, provisions had to be secured. Possibly the owner of the building where they met took care of this matter, but if not, then Peter and John probably had this responsibility. We would assume it also fell to them to slay the paschal lamb, which would have been done within the temple.

> ## CALENDARS
>
> | Jewish | Gregorian |
> |---|---|
> | Nisan | —Mar.-Apr. |
> | Iyyar | —Apr.-May |
> | Sivan | —May-June |
> | Tammuz | —June-July |
> | Ab | —July-Aug. |
> | Elul | —Aug.-Sept. |
> | Tishri | —Sept.-Oct. |
> | Heshvan | —Oct.-Nov. |
> | Kislev | —Nov.-Dec. |
> | Tebeth | —Dec.-Jan. |
> | Shebat | —Jan.-Feb. |
> | Adar | —Feb.-Mar. |
> | Adar Sheni* | |
>
> *Nothing comparable; intercalary month

The Passover Meal ... Matthew 26:20; Mark 14:17; Luke 22:14-16, 24-30

1. When was the Passover meal eaten?

The Passover lamb was to be slain "in the evening" of the fourteenth of Nisan (also called Abib), "at the going down of the sun" (Exodus 12:6;

							F	S	S	M	T	W	T	F						

Deuteronomy 16:6). The Hebrew actually has "between the evenings," and was understood as referring to the period from 3:00 to 6:00 p.m. Later that same evening the supper was eaten. All of the paschal lamb was to be consumed during the night. If any remained it was to be burned (Exodus 12:10).

2. Of what did the meal consist?
These items would be found at a Passover meal: wine, drunk in four cups as part of the ceremony, cakes of unleavened bread, bitter herbs of perhaps five kinds, and the Passover lamb.

> Ingredients of a Passover meal: wine, cakes of unleavened bread, bitter herbs, Passover lamb.

3. How were the people divided for eating the Passover?
The Israelites would gather into households or families of not less than ten, nor more than twenty, and eat the paschal meal.

4. Why the strife among the apostles?
Luke, who alone tells of this strife, says it was caused by a desire to see who was greatest. Luke 22:27 seems to indicate it had something to do with the seating arrangement at the meal. Similar strife had arisen previously (Luke 9:46-50, Matthew 20:20-28). This argument helps explain Jesus' action in washing the apostles' feet.

> "If the household be too little for the lamb, let him and his neighbor next unto his house take it according to the number of the souls; every man according to his eating shall make your count for the lamb" (Exodus 12:4).

5. What kingdom did Jesus appoint for His apostles?
The reference is to Heaven. Jesus said the apostles would "sit on thrones judging the twelve tribes of Israel," which indicates special honor among the redeemed. This passage, as well as others, teaches degrees of reward in the future life. Essential to this doctrine is the requirement that all of the redeemed be content with their rewards.

The Disciples' Feet Washed by Jesus . . . John 13:1-20

1. Is the supper of John 13 the same as the Passover meal of the Synoptics?
Some feel it isn't, but the following points favor the view: (1) At this supper (in John and the Synoptics) Judas is designated as the one who should betray Jesus. (2) Peter's denial is foretold in both; (3) Luke's record of the strife at the supper explains the need for the washing of feet described by John.

2. Why did John omit the institution of the Lord's Supper?
Probably because the event had been told by

185

three inspired writers, and their records had been widely circulated, and were generally known. The supper should be inserted after verse 30 or 32.

3. Is the translation, "supper being ended," correct?
No, it should say, "when supper was made (or begun)." The washing of feet didn't occur after the meal, but near its beginning.

4. What was Jesus' purpose in this act?
It was His means of teaching the apostles humility. If He, their Master and Lord, was willing to perform this menial task, one usually reserved for slaves, they should be willing to do the same.

5. Why Peter's reluctance?
Probably Jesus approached Peter first, and he, not understanding His motive, refused. When Jesus emphasized the importance of being washed, Peter desired to have not only his feet but his hands and head washed also. The reversal of attitude was characteristic of impetuous Peter.

6. Should foot-washing be practiced as an ordinance of the church?
It was not so understood, commanded, or practiced by the apostles, and certainly they would have understood Jesus' purpose. His words, "I have given you *an example*," should be noted. Not until the fourth century was foot-washing practiced as an ordinance of the church. First Timothy 5:10 mentions the practice, but not as an ordinance. It is a reference to a lowly service performed by widows for other saints. To ritualize an act of humility tends to destroy its true meaning.

Judas Pointed Out as the Traitor ... Matthew 26:21-25; Mark 14:18-21; Luke 22:21-23; John 13:21-30

1. Did the other apostles suspect that Judas was the guilty one?
No, his hypocrisy had been successful. At Jesus' words, "One of you shall betray me," none of the apostles said, "He means Judas; I have known it all along." Instead, each man sincerely asked, "Lord, is it I?" Luke states, "They began to inquire among themselves, which of them it was that should do this thing" (Luke 22:23). Although they discussed the subject, they were unable to conclude who it was. John shows that even when Jesus said to Judas, "That thou doest, do quickly," still he wasn't suspected of being the guilty one (13:27-30).

2. Did Jesus reveal that Judas was the traitor?

Although Jesus said, "He that dippeth his hand with me in the dish, the same shall betray me" (Matthew 26:23; see John 13:26 for slightly different wording), the other apostles didn't realize He meant Judas. No doubt many were dipping at the same time, making it impossible for all except Judas to know whom He meant. To the traitor, however, a glance, and a quick handing of the morsel revealed that the Lord knew his identity. This was the last warning Jesus gave Judas. After this he went out into the blackness of night to perform his heinous deed.

3. What was the seating arrangement at the supper?

Edersheim offers the following arrangement (illustrated at right) which seems true to the texts: Each man reclined on a single divan, with his head (A) nearest the table, and his feet (B) away from it. It was customary to lie on one's left side. The chief person would take a middle divan, and next to him would be the chief places. On this occasion (if the diagram is correct) they were occupied by John, on His right, and Judas, on His left. Peter, according to this theory, was in the lowest place, a spot he no doubt chose after Jesus' rebuke of the apostles because of their strife.

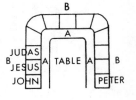

The Disciples Warned (Peter's Denial Foretold) . . . Matthew 26:31-35; Mark 14:27-31; Luke 22:31-38; John 13:31-38

1. When were these warnings given?

Actually, we are studying several warnings given by Jesus, evidently within a brief period during this evening. Some, apparently, were spoken before He left the scene of the paschal supper (Luke 22:39). Others were given after the departure from the upper room (Matthew 26:30).

2. How would the apostles be offended in Jesus?

The Greek word, *skandalídzo,* means to put a stumbling block in the way, to cause to stumble. The arrest of Jesus would be such a stumbling block to them. Their reaction would be that of shame, and by their conduct they would deny Him.

3. Did Jesus say the cock would crow once or twice?

Only Mark says twice. We assume that his are the specific words of Jesus, and that the other three writers make only a general reference to His warn-

187

Winnowing basket

ing to Peter. The meaning is clear—before cockcrowing, Peter would deny Jesus three times.

4. What did Satan desire to do to Peter?

Luke tells of Jesus' warning to Peter that the devil wanted to sift him as wheat. In other words, just as grain is shaken to rid it of chaff, so Satan wanted to set trials and temptations before Peter which would agitate him and shake out of him his faith. The words of Christ recorded in Luke 22:32 must have been very comforting to Peter after his denial.

5. Why buy a sword?

The instructions in Luke 22:36 were not for their present situation, but for the future. As His ambassadors they would soon be going into areas infested with wild beasts and robbers. To protect themselves from these dangers, they would need swords. Unfortunately the apostles misunderstood Jesus (see verse 38). That He was not advocating the use of arms for His defense is clear from the scene in Gethsemane where He forbade Peter's use of a sword (John 18:10, 11).

6. What is a distinguishing characteristic of Jesus' disciples?

John, who had much to say about Love, records Jesus' statement that one clear indication of discipleship is love of the brethren (John 13:35).

7. Where was Jesus going?

Jesus was going to die, after which He would be resurrected and would return to His Father in Heaven. His disciples would have to be separated from Him, remain in the world, do His will, and anticipate a reunion with Him in the future.

The Lord's Supper Instituted (1 Corinthians 11:23-26) . . . Matthew 26:26-29; Mark 14:22-25; Luke 22:17-20

1. Was Judas present during the institution of the Lord's Supper?

Luke indicates that he was. Matthew and Mark, on the other hand, tell about Jesus' encounter with Judas before relating the information concerning the Lord's Supper. It is impossible to know which is correct. Each Gospel writer had his own plan for writing Jesus' life. That plan, though always presenting the truth, was not always chronological.

2. What items were used?

Unleavened bread and "fruit of the vine." The Greek word for *wine* is not used in the Bible for the liquid portion of the Lord's Supper.

3. How was the bread His body, and the fruit of the vine His blood?
The bread *represented* His body, and the cup, His blood. They were *emblems* or *symbols* of His body and blood.

> Read 1 Corinthians 11:23-26.

4. What connection is there between the shedding of His blood and the remission of sins?
Only Matthew records the words of Jesus, "for the remission of sins" (26:28). This phrase was not understood by the apostles at the time it was uttered. Later it came to have great significance as it helped to clarify the true purpose of Jesus' death. (See Leviticus 17:11 and Hebrews 9 and 10.)

> "Forasmuch as ye know that ye were not redeemed with corruptible things, as silver and gold, from your vain conversation received by tradition from your fathers; but with the precious blood of Christ, as of a lamb without blemish and without spot" (1 Peter 1:18, 19).

5. Does the Greek word, *diatháka* (pronounced dee-uh-*thay*-kay), mean *covenant* or *testament*?
The primary meaning of the word was "testament" or "will." The term is used, however, in the Septuagint to translate the Hebrew word for covenant (a pact or agreement between two parties). Among the Jews, blood was used in making covenants (Exodus 24:6-8). And of course blood must be shed (i.e., one, the testator, must die) to bring into force a testament. Therefore either term could be used here. Jesus' blood sealed the agreement (covenant), which He made with His followers, and His death brought into effect the new will (testament) through which He saves and rules men.

Jesus' Farewell Discourse . . . John 14:1-31

1. What kind of mansions will there be in Heaven?
The word rendered "mansions," *monā,* (pronounced moe-*nay)* doesn't imply a palatial home as many speakers have made it to do. In fact, a good rendering would be: "In my Father's house there is ample room for all who will come."

> Heaven is described in figurative language in Revelation 21.

2. What is the significance of Jesus' claim to be "the way, the truth, and the life"?
Because Jesus made this stupendous claim, He must be recognized as divine or as a deceived person or as a deceiver. No other options are open.

3. How does one see the Father by seeing the Son?
The two are so perfectly united that to see the actions of the Son is equivalent to seeing the actions of the Father.

189

4. What greater works can Christians do than Jesus did?

Jesus referred to the evangelizing of the world. No matter how marvelous a miracle may be, none can compare to the saving of a lost soul. Jesus gave this greatest of all work to His followers.

5. Whom did Jesus say He was sending?

Jesus promised that the Holy Spirit would come to be with and bless His followers. In this text He is called "the Comforter" (Greek, *Paráklātos,* a term peculiar to John's Gospel), "the Spirit of truth," and "the Holy Spirit." He is "another Comforter," separate and distinct from the Father and the Son. Yet, so perfect is the unity of the three that the coming of the Holy Spirit involves the coming of the Father and Son also (verses 18, 23).

The Parable of the Vine . . . John 15:1-27

1. What is the main teaching of this parable?

The parable teaches us "Christ's relationships. (1) Toward the Father—Husbandman and Vine. (2) Toward man—Vine and branches. (3) Toward good works—Vine, branches and fruit. (4) The negative condition, or *lack* of relationship—the Vine, the dissevered branches, the fire."—*The Fourfold Gospel,* p. 668.

2. How had Jesus chosen them?

Not as disciples. This choice they had to make for themselves. This reference is to their selection as apostles (Luke 6:13). Discipleship was, and is, open to all men.

3. What did Jesus mean: "They have no cloak for their sin" (v. 22)?

The Jewish leaders had rejected Christ and His message although He had substantiated His claims in many ways. In the judgment they will have no excuse or cloak behind which to hide. Nor will present-day man, who has available in the Bible an accurate record of Jesus' life.

Further Solemn Instruction . . . John 16:1-33

1. What did Jesus mean: "None of you asketh me, Whither goest thou" (v. 5)?

John 13:36 and 14:5 show that both Peter and Thomas had asked concerning where He was going. Perhaps He meant that the apostles' *motive* in asking had been incorrect.

2. Of what did Jesus say the Holy Spirit would reprove the world?

Sin, righteousness, and judgment. Having

The Holy Spirit reproves the world in respect of sin, righteousness, and judgment.

March, A.D. 30 | April

specified these, He then assigned reasons the world would be so reproved.

3. How did Jesus speak in proverbs?

A better rendering would be "figures." Much that He had said in this speech had been veiled somewhat in figures which required study to understand. The time was coming when there would be no more enigmas or sayings difficult to comprehend. His reference was to the time following the coming of the Holy Spirit who would testify of Jesus.

The Prayer of Jesus . . . John 17:1-26

1. What notes of interest are there about this prayer?

John says that Jesus "lifted up his eyes to heaven" (v. 1) as He began His longest recorded prayer. That it was a public prayer is evident from verse 1. It is correctly called the Lord's prayer since He himself prayed it, and should be distinguished from the model prayer (Matthew 6:9-13; Luke 11:1-4) which He taught His disciples to pray. In this prayer He prayed for himself (vv. 1-8), for His disciples (vv. 9-19), and for the church (vv. 20-26).

2. How is it eternal life to know God and Christ?

Such knowledge is the source of eternal life; it is the means by which it can be obtained.

3. How did Jesus have glory with the Father before the world was?

Prior to His incarnation, Jesus existed as the *Logos,* or *Word* of God. In that state He shared in the glory of the Father. (See John 1:1-18, and Lesson One where the passage is discussed.)

4. How were the apostles to be sanctified?

The word sanctification can either express moral purity, or refer to being set apart to a holy cause. Both definitions are applicable in this text. Jesus' prayer for His apostles was that through the truth of God (His Word being truth), they might progress in their spirituality. In becoming less attached to the world, and more to God, they would be more fully consecrated to the holy task which was before them.

5. How analyze Jesus' prayer for unity?

Verse 21 contains Jesus' *plea:* "That they all may be one"; His *plan* for bringing about this state: "As thou, Father, art in me, and I in thee, that they

"Neither pray I for these alone, but for them also which shall believe on me through their word; that they all may be one; as thou, Father, art in me, and I in thee, that they also may be one in us: that the world may believe that thou hast sent me" (John 17:20, 21).

191

also may be one in us"; and His *purpose:* "That the world may believe that thou hast sent me."

The Agony in the Garden ... Matthew 26:30, 36-46; Mark 14:26, 32-42; Luke 22:39-46; John 18:1

Olive press

1. What does *Gethsemane* mean?
It is the Greek form of a Hebrew word which means "oil press." Located on the Mount of Olives (Matthew 26:30), it was apparently an olive orchard with a press. It was situated outside the city, was secluded, and was ideal for Jesus' purpose.

2. Why take the three with Him?
We don't know. Apparently there was the desire for fellowship during this great hour of suffering. If so, it was not well-provided by these three who suffered from exhaustion, and slept when Jesus wanted them to watch with Him.

3. What did Jesus mean by "the cup"?
The cup is a common Biblical figure to express human emotion—both joy and sorrow (Psalms 11:6; 23:5; 75:8; Matthew 20:22, 23; John 18:11; Revelation 14:10). Here it refers to Jesus' death on Calvary, which He would like to have avoided if redemption could have been accomplished in any other way.

4. Why did the apostles go to sleep?
It was late and they were exhausted from the strain of the week's activities. Sitting on the ground, wrapped perhaps in their outer garment, and under the bright Passover moon, they were unable to ward off sleep. Matthew and Mark mention that their "eyes were heavy" (Matthew 26:43; Mark 14:40), and Luke states that they were "sleeping for sorrow" (22:45).

5. Did Jesus literally sweat drops of blood?
Only Luke mentions this (22:44), and he alone tells about the ministrations of the angel from God (22:43). Perhaps nothing more is meant than that His sweat resembled drops of blood by their size and profusion. It may be that there was a literal mixing of His blood with His perspiration.

6. Why tell them to sleep on, then immediately tell them to arise?
Although Matthew and Mark have these statements in connecting verses, there was a gap of time between the two utterances. How long they were permitted to sleep before the arrival of Judas

and the multitude is unknown, but it couldn't have been long.

WHEN AND WHERE

From Mark 14:12 and Luke 22:7 it is clear that the day Jesus sent Peter and John to prepare for the Passover was Nisan 14, the Thursday of Passover week. The law specified this was the day the Passover was to be slain (Exodus 12:6), and it was on the day "when the passover must be killed" (Luke 22:7) that they were sent. That evening after sunset (Jewish Friday), the meal was eaten, and the other events of this lesson transpired. The time of entering Gethsemane is not definite. Some scholars place it as early as 8:00 p.m.; others, as late as midnight. We would suggest sometime between 10:00 p.m. and 12:00, but there is little evidence to support this or any other exact time.

Some writers (Canon Cook, Alfred Edersheim) feel that the upper room in which the Passover meal was eaten was in the house of John Mark. This house was used by the early church (Acts 12:12), and may well have been the one used by Jesus. The mention by Mark alone (14:51, 52) of a young man who followed Jesus after His arrest, and who was naked except for a linen cloth, fits well with this theory. Probably that young man was Mark himself. When Jesus and the others left his house, Mark may have arisen from bed, put on a linen cloth, and followed them to Gethsemane. The sindon, or linen vestment, worn by the young man was an expensive item.

As previously stated, Gethsemane was on the Mount of Olives. Locate the garden on the map which is provided.

> The upper room used for the Passover meal may have been in John Mark's house. His house was used by the early church (see Acts 12:12).

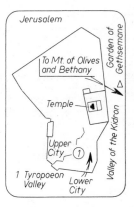

PROJECTS AND PLANS

Prepare and eat a Passover-type supper at one of your class meetings. The items needed can be secured at a Jewish store. Ask your preacher to assist in this endeavor.

Use your concordance to find, and then read the various Old Testament passages that pertain to the office of high priest.

ARRESTED AND TRIED

TOPICS AND TEXTS

The Arrest . . . Matthew 26:47-56; Mark 14:43-52; Luke 22:47-53; John 18:2-12

The Trial Before Annas . . . John 18:12-14, 19-23

The Trial Before Caiaphas . . . Matthew 26:57, 59-68; Mark 14:53, 55-65; Luke 22:54, 63-65; John 18:24

The Denials of Peter . . . Matthew 26:58, 69-75; Mark 14:54, 66-72; Luke 22:54-62; John 18:15-18, 25-27

The Final Condemnation by the Sanhedrin . . . Matthew 27:1; Mark 15:1; Luke 22:66-71

The Death of Judas (Acts 1:18, 19) . . . Matthew 27:3-10

The First Trial Before Pilate . . . Matthew 27:2, 11-14; Mark 15:2-5; Luke 23:1-5; John 18:28-38

Jesus Before Herod . . . Luke 23:6-12

The Second Trial Before Pilate . . . Matthew 27:15-26; Mark 15:6-15; Luke 23:13-25; John 18:39—19:16

CONTEXT AND CONTINUITY

Jesus appeared before the following four men in His six trials: Annas, Caiaphas, Pilate, and Herod. A word about each is in order.

Annas, before whom Jesus first appeared (John 18:13), served as high priest from A. D. 7 to 15. He was appointed to the office by Quirinius, governor of Syria, and deposed by Valerius Gratus. After his removal he continued to wield great influence among both the Jews and the Romans, managing to elevate to the high priesthood five of his sons, as well as Caiaphas, his son-in-law. Long after his deposition he was still referred to as high priest (Luke 3:2; Acts 4:6). He was the son of a man named Seth, was of Sadducean aristocracy, and was extremely wealthy. In the list of important priests in Acts 4:6 his name appears first, preceding even that of Caiaphas, the actual high priest.

After Jesus appeared before Annas, He was sent bound to Caiaphas (John 18:24), who, along with other scribes and elders, examined, condemned, and then abused Him (Matthew 26:57-68). Caiaphas (also called Joseph), as indicated above, was the son-in-law of Annas. His term of office was from A. D. 18 to 36. At that date he was deposed by Vitellius, the legate of Syria. As the reigning high priest during the trials of Jesus, he took a leading part in His condemnation (Matthew 26:3, 4; 26:65; John 11:49, 50).

Very little is known about Pontius Pilate, the Roman procurator before whom Jesus was tried. We know nothing concerning his birth or early years, and most of that which concerns the years after his involvement with Jesus is legendary. His procuratorship lasted for ten years, from A. D. 27 to 37, after which he also was removed from of-

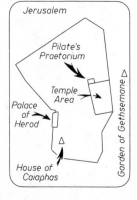

Jerusalem

Pilate's Praetorium

Temple Area

Palace of Herod

Garden of Gethsemane

House of Caiaphas

				12:00 p.m.	1:00 a.m.	2:00	3:00	4:00	5:00	6:00	7:00	8:00	9:00	10:00		

April 7,   A.D. 30   Friday

fice by Vitellius. As procurator he was the personal servant of the emperor, and directly responsible to him. In addition to the references to him in the Gospels, he is three times mentioned in Acts (3:13; 4:27; 13:28). A very interesting discussion of his character is offered by J. Macartney Wilson in *The International Standard Bible Encyclopedia*, Vol. 4, p. 2398.

The Herod to whom Pilate sent Jesus was Herod Antipas, son of Herod the Great and Malthace, a Samaritan woman. At his father's death he was given the territories of Galilee and Perea. He ruled over these as a tetrarch from 4 B. C. to A. D. 39. This is the Herod who imprisoned, and later decapitated, John the Baptist (see Lesson Ten). He was superstitious (Matthew 14:1, 2), foxlike (Luke 13:32), and wholly immoral. His only actual contact with Jesus was this incident, although for a long time he had wanted to see Him.

These men, into whose hands Jesus passed, have become universally infamous because of their part in the crucifixion of God's Son.

Pontius was his family name. It indicates that he descended from the Roman family of Pontii. Pilate probably comes from the word pilatus. It means "one armed with a pilum or javelin."

See page 237.

INQUIRIES AND INSIGHTS

The Arrest . . . Matthew 26:47-56; Mark 14:43-52; Luke 22:47-53; John 18:2-12

1. Who were included in the multitude which came to arrest Jesus?
According to Luke, the crowd was composed of chief priests, captains of the temple, and elders (22:52). John describes the group as "a band of men and officers from the chief priests and Pharisees" (18:3; see also v. 12). Matthew and Mark speak only of "a great multitude."

2. Why was the kiss necessary?
Apparently Judas had agreed to give this sign to the members of the throng that came for Jesus to assure that the correct person was arrested.

3. Which apostle used his sword in Jesus' defense?
All of the Gospels relate this incident, but only John identifies Peter as the one who performed the deed. John also tells the name of the wounded man, Malchus (18:10). Luke alone records that Jesus restored the man's ear (22:51).

4. How many is a legion?
A legion was a division of the Roman army consisting of more than 6,000 men. Jesus said He could call forth more than 72,000 angels to protect and assist Him (Matthew 26:53).

					12:00 p.m.	1:00 a.m.	2:00	3:00	4:00	5:00	6:00	7:00	8:00	9:00	10:00		

Friday

Josephus: "Now the report goes that this eldest Ananus proved a most fortunate man; for he had five sons who had all performed the office of a high priest to God, and who had himself enjoyed that dignity a long time formerly, which had never happened to any other of our high priests" (Antiquities of the Jews, 20:9:1).

The Trial Before Annas . . . John 18:12-14, 19-23

1. Why take Jesus first to Annas?

That Jesus was taken first to Annas, rather than the ruling high priest, Caiaphas, testifies to the great influence of the man. It also illustrates the regard in which he was held by his son-in-law, Caiaphas, and/or others. Only John mentions this trial, which apparently was no more than a preliminary hearing.

2. When did Caiaphas offer the advice mentioned in John 18:14?

It was given at a council meeting of chief priests and Pharisees immediately after the raising of Lazarus (John 11:50). (See Lesson Seventeen.)

3. What questions did Annas ask?

He asked concerning Jesus' disciples and doctrine. Probably he wanted to know the number and power of His disciples so that he could use the information against Him in the Roman court. If it could be established that He was the leader of a large band of men, the charge of sedition could be laid against Him. The question concerning His doctrine was asked in the hope that He would confess to teaching things contrary to either the Mosaic law or the Roman government.

4. How did Jesus answer?

His answers were indirect. He admitted that He taught "the world," i.e., all who would hear Him, and pointed out that His teaching had been done openly. His answers irritated one of the officers of the temple, who slapped Him on His cheek with an open hand, and rebuked Him for speaking as He did to the high priest.

The Trial Before Caiaphas . . . Matthew 26:57, 59-68; Mark 14:53, 55-65; Luke 22:54, 63-65; John 18:24

1. What does the Old Testament teach about the office of high priest?

The office of high priest was to be hereditary (Exodus 29:9-30; Numbers 25:12, 13). It began with Aaron, passed to his son, Eleazar (Numbers 20:28), and in turn to his son, Phinehas (Numbers 25:11). During the Old Testament period and the era between the testaments, there were several changes in the direct line of descent, but the office was still considered hereditary. With the coming to power of Herod the Great, this was altered, for Herod set up and deposed high priests at his pleasure. The Romans, after they gained control of

Palestine, followed the same practice. Because of the frequent changes both Annas and Caiaphas are called high priests (Luke 3:2), when in reality only one man could hold the office officially at any one time.

2. Who besides Caiaphas sat in on this trial?
Scribes, elders, chief priests, and "all the council" are specifically mentioned. The council, or Sanhedrin, was the highest court of the Jews. It was composed of seventy men (elders, chief priests, scribes) plus the high priest.

3. Why the difficulty in finding false witnesses?
At first no false witnesses whose testimony had even the semblance of reasonableness came forward. Finally the two mentioned in the texts appeared with their twisted interpretation of Jesus' words about destroying and rebuilding the temple. Mark says the testimony of the two didn't agree (14:56-59).

4. Had Jesus said He would destroy the temple?
No. What He had said was, "Destroy this temple, and in three days I will raise it up" (John 2:19), but the reference wasn't to the temple in Jerusalem, but to His own body. Notice He didn't say, "*I* will destroy this temple," but, "(You) destroy this temple, and *I will raise it up*." This was just the opposite of the interpretation given by the false witnesses.

5. How was Jesus guilty of blasphemy?
To blaspheme is to claim the attributes, or speak profanely, of God. In this instance the former is meant. Jesus, in answer to Caiaphas' question concerning His identity, affirmed that He was the Christ, the Son of God ("Son of the Blessed," according to Mark). The Sanhedrin was correct in its evaluation of the seriousness of Jesus' claim. If what He claimed isn't true, He was guilty of blasphemy.

6. Why did Caiaphas rend his clothes?
To rend one's clothes was a token of grief or indignation. It consisted of tearing a particular portion of one's garment, near the neck, reserved for the purpose. The Old Testament forbade a high priest to rend his clothes (Leviticus 10:6; 21:10). Evidently this was interpreted as prohibiting the act while he performed certain of his high-priestly duties.

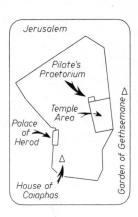

Jerusalem

Pilate's Praetorium

Temple Area

Palace of Herod

House of Caiaphas

Garden of Gethsemane

				12:00 p.m.	1:00 a.m.	2:00	3:00	4:00	5:00	6:00	7:00	8:00	9:00	10:00		

April 7,   A.D. 30   Friday

7. Who participated in abusing Jesus?

Mark says some of the servants struck Him with the palms of their hands (14:65). Others spat upon Him, blindfolded Him, buffeted and ridiculed Him, but their identity isn't given. Perhaps they were members of the Sanhedrin who stooped to such low and vile tactics to show their utter contempt of Jesus.

8. What interesting addition is given by Luke?

Luke declares: "And many other things blasphemously spake they against him" (22:65). Those who falsely accused Him of blasphemy were guilty of that very sin.

The Denials of Peter . . . Matthew 26:58, 69-75; Mark 14:54, 66-72; Luke 22:54-62; John 18:15-18, 25-27

1. Are there differences in the accounts of the denials of Peter?

Yes, there are such differences as might be expected in four independent accounts. The apparent discrepancies can be harmonized with but little effort. The chief difficulty concerns the identity of the persons who made the charges against Peter which led to his second and third denials. In the second denial the questioner is called by Matthew "another maid," by Mark "the (same) maid," by Luke "a man," and by John "they." Probably not one, but several accusers simultaneously attacked Peter. A similar problem exists with the third denial.

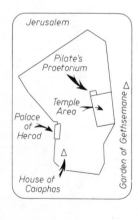

Jerusalem

Pilate's Praetorium

Temple Area

Palace of Herod

House of Caiaphas

Garden of Gethsemane △

2. Where did the denials take place?

The Synoptics locate the three denials in the court of Caiaphas. A possible interpretation of John's account would have the first denial in the court of Annas, but such an interpretation isn't necessary. Some believe the court of Annas is the same as that of Caiaphas (the two sharing the same palace). This view eliminates any possible problem.

3. How did Peter gain entrance to the high priest's palace?

John indicates that it was through his (John's) efforts that Peter got inside (18:15, 16).

4. Did Peter use profanity?

The King James translation of Matthew 26:74 has, "Then began he to curse and to swear," (similar words are in Mark 14:71). Based on this translation, some writers affirm that Peter lost his temper and resorted to the use of the vile language he had known and used as a fisherman. This is a case of an inaccurate and misleading translation. Both Greek words mean "to take an oath," or "to affirm an oath."

The Final Condemnation by the Sanhedrin ...
Matthew 27:1; Mark 15:1; Luke 22:66-71

1. Why was this meeting necessary?

At the earlier trial before Caiaphas when "all the council" had been present, Jesus was condemned as being guilty of blasphemy. That trial, however, had been held at night, and consequently was illegal. Therefore this meeting was necessary to legalize that decision.

2. Was Jesus asked the same question at this trial as at the former one?

Probably so. (See Matthew 26:63, 64 [trial before Caiaphas], and Luke 22:66-71 [trial before the Sanhedrin].)

> The Sanhedrin was the highest Jewish tribunal during the Greek and Roman periods. Its origin is unknown. There is no historical evidence that it existed before the Greek period. It was composed of seventy members plus the president, who was the high priest.

The Death of Judas (Acts 1:18, 19) ... Matthew 27:3-10

1. How did Judas repent himself?

He didn't repent toward God and seek forgiveness, but was overwhelmed with disappointment, sorrow, and remorse. Had he truly repented, he would have changed his life. Instead he added another crime to his record—the taking of his own life.

2. Where did he throw the money?

Matthew says "in the temple" without specifying what part. It could have been in the treasury, in the area where the Sanhedrin usually met, or in some other spot. Having found the chief priests and elders, offered them the money and been refused, he cast down the pieces of silver and departed.

3. What is a potter's field?

It is a field which has been stripped of all its good soil for the making of pottery. The term has come to mean: "A piece of ground that is reserved as a burial place for strangers and the friendless poor."

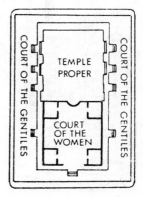

4. Why was the field called "the field of blood"?

Two reasons are given: 1. It was bought with blood money (Matthew); 2. Judas' swollen body fell and burst asunder on the land (Acts 1:18, 19). The priests used Judas' money to buy the field in which he hanged himself, and set it aside as a place to bury strangers. Thereafter some spoke of

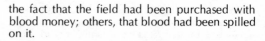
"And I said unto them, If ye think good, give me my price; and if not, forbear. So they weighed for my price thirty pieces of silver. And the Lord said unto me, Cast it unto the potter: a goodly price that I was prized at of them. And I took the thirty pieces of silver, and cast them to the potter in the house of the Lord" (Zechariah 11:12, 13).

Pilate's hall—?

the fact that the field had been purchased with blood money; others, that blood had been spilled on it.

5. What prophecy was fulfilled in the buying of the field?
A prophecy in Zechariah 11:12, 13. Matthew supposedly attributes the prophecy to Jeremiah, but this is obviously a scribal error.

The First Trial Before Pilate ... Matthew 27:2, 11-14; Mark 15:2-5; Luke 23:1-5; John 18:28-38

1. Why did Pilate ask Jesus if He were the King of the Jews?
Luke says one of the charges made against Jesus by the Sanhedrin was that He claimed to be "Christ a King" (23:2). It was logical that Pilate, concerned about the political situation, should inquire about this claim.

2. Of what other crimes was He accused?
He further was accused of perverting the nation, of forbidding to give tribute to Caesar, and of stirring up the people (Luke 23:2, 5). Mark says they "accused him of many things" (15:3).

3. Why did Jesus refuse to answer the accusations of the Jewish leaders?
He realized it would be futile to do so. There was a majesty in His silence which said far more than any words He might utter. Matthew relates that "the governor marvelled greatly" (Matthew 27:14).

4. Why did the Jews refuse to enter Pilate's judgment hall?
John says they refused to do so that they might not be defiled, but might eat the Passover (18:28). This verse has contributed to the view that Jesus and His apostles didn't eat the regular Passover meal, but a substitute one a day earlier (see "Context and Continuity," Lesson Twenty-two). The expression, "eat the passover," evidently doesn't refer to eating the paschal lamb, but to participating in the feast of Unleavened Bread which followed the Passover.

5. Why did Pilate ask the question, "What is truth?"
Whether he asked in sincerity or in derision can't be determined. From what is known of the character of Pilate, as well as from his failure to await an answer, it appears that he asked the question as a sneer, and not to gain information.

6. What was Pilate's judgment of Jesus?

Having heard the charges and examined the prisoner, Pilate gave his evaluation: "I find no fault in this man" (Luke 23:4).

Jesus Before Herod . . . Luke 23:6-12

1. Why did Pilate send Jesus to Herod?

Luke, who alone tells of this trial, says it was done because Jesus "belonged unto Herod's jurisdiction" (23:7). It is apparent that Pilate was not happy about having to judge Jesus, and may have done this to escape the responsibility, and/or to reconcile his differences with Herod.

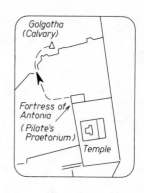

2. Why had Herod been desirous of seeing Jesus?

Herod was curious. He had heard much about Jesus, and wanted to see Him and evaluate Him personally. It was this same curiosity that had caused Herod to listen to the preaching of John the Baptist (Mark 6:20). Luke says that Herod questioned Jesus with many words, but Jesus answered him nothing. Herod had heard that Jesus was capable of performing miracles, and desired to see one. It is no surprise that Jesus refused to work a miracle simply for this evil ruler's amusement.

See page 237.

3. What charges were made against Jesus at this time?

They are not included in the record, but probably similar ones to those made in the trial before Pilate. Luke says they "vehemently accused him" (23:10).

4. What did Herod do to Jesus?

With the aid of his men of war he "set him at nought, and mocked him, and arrayed him in a gorgeous robe, and sent him again to Pilate" (Luke 23:11). The men of war were his soldiers, or perhaps his personal bodyguard. To "set at nought" means to treat with contempt and ridicule. The mocking probably consisted of laughing at His claim to be a king. The "shining robe" aided in this mockery.

5. What caused Pilate and Herod to become friends?

The cause of their enmity isn't known. Perhaps it had something to do with "the Galileans, whose blood Pilate had mingled with their sacrifices" (Luke 13:1). The respect which Pilate showed to Herod in sending him Jesus was the cause of the reconciliation.

April 7,	A.D. 30							12:00 p.m.	1:00 a.m.	2:00	3:00	4:00	5:00	6:00	7:00	8:00	9:00	10:00		

Friday

The Second Trial Before Pilate ... Matthew 27:15-26; Mark 15:6-15; Luke 23:13-25; John 18:39—19:16

1. Who was Barabbas?

Barabbas (son of Abbas) was "a notable prisoner" (Matthew 27:16), who was guilty of insurrection, murder, and robbery (Mark 15:7; Luke 23:19; John 18:40).

2. What of the origin of the custom of releasing a prisoner?

Nothing definite is known about the origin of this custom, nor are there any traces of it in later Jewish writings. It was probably begun by the Jews, and continued by the Roman governors.

3. What is known about Pilate's wife?

Only her name, Claudia Procula (or Procla), is known. Whether her dream was natural or supernatural is not revealed. The early church fathers generally regarded it as supernatural, which seems to fit better with Matthew's account.

4. Is the scourging of John's Gospel the same as that in Matthew and Mark?

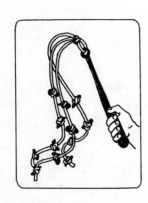

The scourgings are probably the same. Scourging was a terrible punishment, often sufficient in itself for execution. Scourges were made of thongs, in the end of which were placed pieces of metal or bone. The person to be beaten was stripped and tied to a low post so that the skin of his back would be stretched. The Jews limited the number of stripes to forty (2 Corinthians 11:24), but among the Romans the number was left to the whim of the commanding officer. John's placement of this event is thought to be correct. It seems that Pilate hoped the scourging would satisfy the mob, then he would escape the responsibility of passing the death sentence.

5. Why was the sin of those who delivered up Jesus the greater?

Pilate's involvement in the trial came about because of the office he held, not because of personal choice. Judges are necessary and right, and their office is ordained of God (Romans 13). The greater condemnation belonged to those who sought the death of Jesus.

6. What was the purpose of the hand-washing of Pilate?

It was a symbolic act to indicate he wasn't guilty of the death of Jesus. In response the Jews cried out that they would take the responsibility (Matthew 27:25). Later there was resentment on the part of the Jewish leaders because the apostles placed the blame for Jesus' death on them (Acts 5:28). Of course Pilate's act didn't free him.

WHEN AND WHERE

The time of Jesus' arrest is unknown. It had to be at an early enough hour to allow the trial before Annas and part of the trial before Caiaphas to be completed before "cock crowing." When that occurred is subject to question. It is known that the third watch of the night (12:00—3:00 a.m.) was called "cock crowing," and perhaps Jesus' reference was to this time (Matthew 26:34). If we assume that the cock which Peter heard crew about 3:00 a.m., then the arrest will have to be placed at about 1:00 a.m. to allow adequate time for the above mentioned trials.

As a rule Roman courts didn't open until sunrise (about 6:00 a.m.). Since there is no reason to suppose that an exception was made in this case, we place the beginning of Jesus' trial before Pilate at, or shortly after, 6:00 a.m. This would allow three hours for the trials before Pilate and Herod; then the crucifixion at about 9:00 (Mark 15:25).

From the Garden of Gethsemane on the Mount of Olives, Jesus was taken to the palace of Annas, thought to have been located on the southern half of the summit of Mount Zion. This house possibly was shared by both Annas and Caiaphas. From here Jesus was taken to Caiaphas' home (if the two had separate residences) and/or then to the Praetorium, a Roman castle northwest of the temple area. It had been built by Herod the Great and was called the Tower of Antonia. In some palace near this tower, perhaps the palace of the Maccabeans, Herod was residing. To this place Jesus was sent and later returned to the Praetorium. Locate these places on the map which is provided.

PROJECTS AND PLANS

Thoroughly investigate the trials of Jesus and make a list of all the unjust and illegal procedures employed.

Using only your Bible, try to discover the correct order of the seven sayings of Jesus on the cross. They are found in the following Scriptures: Matthew 27:35-50; Mark 15:24-37; Luke 23:33-46; John 19:18-30. After you have made your arrangement, compare it with the one offered in Lesson Twenty-four.

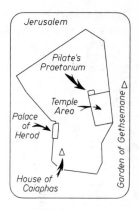

Jerusalem

Pilate's Praetorium

Temple Area

Palace of Herod

House of Caiaphas

Garden of Gethsemane

SUFFERING AND DEATH

TOPICS AND TEXTS

The Torture by the Roman Soldiers . . . Matthew 27:27-30; Mark 15:16-19
The Way to Golgotha . . . Matthew 27:31-34; Mark 15:20-23; Luke 23:26-33; John 19:16, 17
The Death of Christ . . . Matthew 27:35-50; Mark 15:24-37; Luke 23:33-46; John 19:18-30
Miracles Accompanying the Death of Christ . . . Matthew 27:51-56; Mark 15:38-41; Luke 23:45, 47-49
The Burial . . . Matthew 27:57-60; Mark 15:42-46; Luke 23:50-54; John 19:31-42
The Watch at the Tomb . . . Matthew 27:61-66; Mark 15:47; Luke 23:55, 56

CONTEXT AND CONTINUITY

"There they crucified him." With these four words Luke describes the death of Jesus (23:33). How few and simple his words, and yet how deep and unexplorable. Were ever so many volumes contained in so few words? They speak of suffering, shame, and sacrifice; of treachery and trouble, of deceit and death. Whole epics about God, glory, and forgiveness; about hope, love, life, and salvation are contained in them.

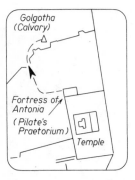

Golgotha (Calvary)

Fortress of Antonia (Pilate's Praetorium)

Temple

There. The place of Jesus' crucifixion is called "Golgotha" in the Hebrew, and "Calvary" in the Latin. Both words mean "skull." The location of this "place of a skull" (Matthew 27:33) is a matter of dispute, but evidence favors "Gordon's Calvary." Named for its discoverer, it is located a few hundred feet northeast of the old Damascus Gate. In its favor is its location outside the old city walls, a Scriptural requirement (John 19:20; Hebrews 13:12). Also favoring it is the fact that it's a hill with cave formations so positioned in its side as to give it the appearance of a skull.

They. Who is to be included in the word? Or, a better question is, "Who is to be excluded?" The Jewish leaders were guilty. It was they who rejected Him, plotted His death, and insisted on His crucifixion. The Jewish people in general must share in the guilt. When Jesus came unto His own, they that were His own received Him not (John 1:11). Instead they agreed that the responsibility for His blood should be put on them and their children (Matthew 27:25). So also must Pilate, the Roman governor, bear the blame. Possessing the power to release Him, he chose rather to appease the Jews, and "delivered Jesus to their will" (Luke 23:25). Nor is Herod's record spotless. If he had chosen to speak one good word on Jesus' behalf, it might have given Pilate the strength to do what he knew to be right. The soldiers who participated in the punishment and death of Christ must also be blamed. Although it may be argued that they were merely carrying out their duty, the mistreatment they gave Him indicates a certain enjoyment on their part (Mark 15:16-20). Nor does the responsibility cease with those who perpetrated the crime, for all mankind must share in the guilt. His death was caused by our sin. "Christ died for us" (Romans 5:8). "He was wounded for our transgressions" (Isaiah 53:5).

Crucified. Crucifixion was a horrible method of execution practiced by many ancient people. It was meted out for such crimes as treason, robbery, piracy, desertion, and sedition. The form of the cross varied. There was the *crux immissa* which looks like a lower case t, the traditional cross, the type on which it is supposed Jesus died; the *crux commissa,* which was in the form of a capital letter *T;* and the *crux decussata* which was in the form of a letter *X.* Types two and three can be eliminated with a great deal of certainty since the Scriptures speak of an inscription *over* Jesus' head (Matthew 27:37). One writer claims that neither of these two was used by the Romans as an instrument of punishment.

Him. The Son of God. The Savior of mankind. He who is the Rose of Sharon, the Lily of the Valley, the Bright and Morning Star, the Fairest of Ten Thousand, the One Altogether Lovely. He who never did a wrong deed nor thought an evil thought, whose soul was as pure at death as at birth. This is He who died on Calvary.

> Probably the cross of Jesus' crucifixion was the crux immissa, since it would allow room for an inscription above His head (Matthew 27:37).

INQUIRIES AND INSIGHTS

The Torture by the Roman Soldiers . . . Matthew 27:27-30; Mark 15:16-19

1. Is the scourging mentioned in Matthew and Mark the same as that in John 19?
(See Lesson Twenty-three, page 202.)

2. What did the soldiers do to mock Him?
The soldiers used Jesus' claim to be the King of the Jews as the basis of their mockery. They put on Him a scarlet robe, and a crown of thorns, and placed a reed in His right hand to serve as His scepter. Then they bowed before Him and said: "Hail, King of the Jews!" Mark adds that they smote Him on the head with a reed, and spat on Him.

3. Is this robe, put on Him by the soldiers of Pilate (Matthew 27:28; Mark 15:17), the same as the one used by Herod's soldiers (Luke 23:11)?
Luke says that when the soldiers of Herod mocked Jesus, they put on Him a gorgeous robe (Greek,

"bright," "shining"). Although some writers have tried to prove it was white in color there is no textual evidence to substantiate it. Concerning the robe used by Pilate's soldiers, Matthew says it was scarlet, and Mark and John (19:2), purple. These words were used interchangeably by the ancients (to them any color with a mixture of red was considered purple). Although it cannot be proven, it's likely that the robe supplied by Herod was the one used by Pilate's soldiers.

The Way to Golgotha ... Matthew 27:31-34; Mark 15:20-23; Luke 23:26-33; John 19:16, 17

1. Why compel Simon to bear Jesus' cross?
No reason is given in the texts. Tradition says Jesus fell under the weight of the cross (estimated at about 150 pounds), and that Simon, being nearby, was impressed into this service. All that is known about this man is that he was from the city of Cyrene on the north coast of Africa, was the father of Alexander and Rufus (evidently leaders in the early church), and was probably a Jew (as indicated by his name).

2. Who were Alexander and Rufus?
It is assumed they were well-known leaders in the early church. Perhaps this Rufus is the one mentioned in Romans 16:13 who was a member of the church in Rome.

3. Who were the women, mentioned by Luke, who followed Jesus?
We are told they were daughters of Jerusalem (Luke 23:28). They followed Jesus weeping, thus we conclude they were His disciples.

4. To what days did Jesus refer in speaking to them?
His reference was to the time of the destruction of Jerusalem, and to the horrible suffering to be experienced then. Note that His concern, even with His own death approaching, was for others.

5. What did Jesus mean by the green tree and the dry?
It's a proverbial expression. The green tree refers to Christ, the dry tree to the Jewish nation. His question means: "If the Romans do these things (mock, scourge, crucify) to me, who am innocent, what will they do to this nation?"

6. Who were the two malefactors?
Matthew says they were thieves (27:44). In the apocryphal gospel, *The Gospel of the Infancy,*

Golgotha (Calvary)

Fortress of Antonia (Pilate's Praetorium)

Temple

"The thieves also, which were crucified with him, cast the same in his teeth" (Matthew 27:44).

they are called Titus and Dumachus. There an interesting story, obviously fictitious, is told concerning how these thieves met Joseph, Mary, and Jesus on their flight to Egypt, and how Jesus then predicted they would be crucified with Him. Another tradition gives their names as Gestas and Dysmas. Some think they were companions of Barabbas.

7. Why did Jesus refuse the drink that was offered Him?

"This mixture of sour wine mingled with gall and myrrh was intended to dull the sense of pain of those being crucified or otherwise severely punished. The custom is said to have originated with the Jews and not with the Romans. Jesus declined it because it was the Father's will that he should suffer. He would not go upon the cross in a drugged, semi-unconscious condition."—*The Fourfold Gospel*, p. 724. (Edersheim says this service was performed by an association of women in Jerusalem.)

The Death of Christ . . . Matthew 27:35-50; Mark 15:24-37; Luke 23:33-46; John 19:18-30

1. What words were placed over Christ's head?

It was a Roman custom to inscribe on a board the name of the condemned, and the nature of his crime. This was carried before the criminal, or worn about his neck, to the place of crucifixion, where it was attached to his cross. The Gospels differ as to the actual wording on Jesus' *titulus,* but the main accusation—that of being the King of the Jews—is found in all four records:

This is Jesus of Nazareth, the King of the Jews

Matthew 27:37	Mark 15:26	Luke 23:38	John 19:19
This is Jesus		This is	Jesus of Nazareth
the King of the Jews	The King of the Jews	the King of the Jews	the King of the Jews

2. Who railed on the Christ?

Three groups are cited: (1) they that passed by (Matthew and Mark); (2) the rulers, specifically the chief priests, scribes, and elders (Matthew, Mark, and Luke); (3) the thieves. Matthew and Mark speak of both the thieves as participating in the reviling of Christ; Luke mentions only one. Probably both men shared in the reviling, but after awhile the one ceased and repented of his evil. Then Jesus told him, "Today shalt thou be with me in paradise" (Luke 23:43).

April 7,	A.D. 30		8:00 a.m.	9:00	10:00	11:00	12:00	1:00 p.m.	2:00	3:00	4:00	5:00	6:00	7:00	

Friday

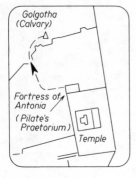

Golgotha (Calvary)

Fortress of Antonia
(Pilate's Praetorium)

Temple

3. Which disciples were present for the crucifixion?

The following ones are mentioned: Jesus' mother, Mary Magdalene, Mary the mother of James and Joses (called Mary, the wife of Cleopas, by John), the mother of Zebedee's children (Salome, in Mark), and John. Joseph of Arimathea and Nicodemus were possibly present. In addition to these named disciples there were many women who had followed Him from Galilee (Matthew 27:55). Luke says "all his acquaintance" were present (23:49). No doubt there were some disciples in the group mentioned by Luke (23:48) who came, beheld the things which were done, smote their breasts, and returned to Jerusalem.

4. Who parted Christ's garments?

The soldiers who crucified Jesus parted His garments among themselves. There were four of them (John 19:23), and each man took his part. Jesus' coat, which was without seam, woven from the top throughout, they considered too valuable to tear, so they cast lots for it (John 19:24).

5. What is the order of the seven sayings of the cross?

The probable order is:

First saying: "Father, forgive them; for they know not what they do" (Luke 23:34);

Second saying: "Verily I say unto thee, Today shalt thou be with me in paradise" (Luke 23:43);

Third saying: "Woman, behold thy son! . . . Behold thy mother!" (John 19:26, 27);

Fourth saying: "My God, my God, why hast thou forsaken me?" (Matthew 27:46; Mark 15:34);

Fifth saying: "I thirst" (John 19:28);

Sixth saying: "It is finished" (John 19:30);

Seventh saying: "Father, into thy hands I commend my spirit" (Luke 23:46).

6. How many times was Christ offered a drink?

Two times: once near the beginning of the crucifixion (Matthew 27:34; Mark 15:23; Luke 23:36), and the other time near the end of His consciousness (Matthew 27:48; Mark 15:36; John 19:29). The first drink was refused. (See the discussion under "The Way to Golgotha," in this lesson.) The second was given in response to His statement, "I thirst" (John 19:28). Some think He was offered a drink three times while on the cross: first—Matthew 27:34; Mark 15:23; second—Luke 23:36; third—Matthew 27:48; Mark 15:36; John 19:29.

				8:00 a.m.	9:00	10:00	11:00	12:00	1:00 p.m.	2:00	3:00	4:00	5:00	6:00	7:00	

April 7, A.D. 30 — Friday

7. How were the Jews ignorant of what they did?

It is difficult to understand how they were, yet Jesus so indicated in His first saying from the cross. He may have meant that they didn't understand the full import and consequence of their deed.

8. What is Paradise?

Paradise is the temporary abiding place of the spirits of the righteous dead. The place is called Abraham's bosom in Luke 16 (see the chart and fuller explanation of this question in Lesson Sixteen). The Bible teaches that when a person dies his body returns to the dust, and his spirit passes into *Hades* (see Acts 2:31 in A.S.V.). If he has received the saving grace of God, he will go to that section of Hades known as *Paradise;* otherwise he will go to *Tartarus* (2 Peter 2:4). For the Judgment, Hades will yield up its dead, the graves will give up their dead (Revelation. 20:13; see also John 5:28, 29), and all men will be judged. The righteous will then pass into Heaven and sinners into Hell.

> Paradise, or Abraham's bosom, is the abode for the spirits of the blessed.

9. Why commit Mary to John's keeping?

The last reference to Joseph in the New Testament is in Luke 2, when Jesus was twelve years old. Thus it is concluded that he must have died sometime before Jesus began His ministry. This, plus the fact that Jesus' brothers were nonbelievers (John 7:5), explains why Jesus, in His hour of death, thought about His mother and entrusted her to the care of His most loving disciple.

10. What was the purpose of the darkness?

There was darkness "over all the land" from the sixth to the ninth hour (Matthew 27:45), but we are not told its purpose. Perhaps God was concealing the last few, agonizing hours of His Son's life from the curious and insulting multitude. We can't be certain as to the extent of the darkness, whether universal or limited to Judea and the surrounding area, but probably the latter.

> Darkness covered the land from noon until 3:00 p.m.

11. In what sense did God forsake His Son?

In commenting on Jesus' words, J. W. Shepard states: "The best that we can offer in the way of explanation is that, in these distressing words, we face an inscrutable mystery beyond our human ability to understand."—*The Christ of the Gospels,* p. 602. Most writers concur. However there are two facts of which we can be sure: (1) It is certain that God approved Jesus' work. (2) It is

209

certain that He was innocent. Any explanation that invalidates either of these facts must be rejected. Albert Barnes says: "He hath redeemed us from the curse of the law, being made a curse for us (Galatians 3:13); he was made a sin-offering (2 Corinthians 5:21); he died *in our place*, on *our* account, that he might bring us near to God. It was this, doubtless, which caused his intense sufferings. It was the manifestation of God's hatred of sin, in some way which he has not explained, that he experienced in that dread hour. It was suffering endured by *him* that was due to *us*, and suffering by which, and by which alone, we can be saved from eternal death."—*Notes on the New Testament, Matthew*, pp. 312, 313.

12. Why did some people think that Jesus called for Elijah?

"Eli, Eli, . . ." (Matthew 27:46); "Eloi, Eloi, . . ." (Mark 15:34).

There are two possible answers. Perhaps because of parched lips and throat, and a swollen tongue, His enunciation wasn't clear. This, plus the noise and confusion on Calvary, could account for the misunderstanding. Another possible explanation is that those who didn't understand were non-Jewish soldiers. We can't be certain what language Jesus used in uttering this cry to God. *"Eli,"* found in Matthew is Hebrew; *"Eloi,"* in Mark is Aramaic. *"Lama,"* used by both writers is Hebrew, but *"Sabachthani,"* also used by both, is Aramaic. It's thought that Jesus usually used Aramaic in His preaching and teaching, but since He was here quoting from the Old Testament (Psalms 22:1), He quite likely used Hebrew. That some of the words appear in Aramaic in the texts is probably due to an attempt by Matthew and Mark to make this expression of Jesus clear to their Jewish readers.

13. What is the meaning of Jesus' statement, "It is finished"?

Tetélestai = "It is finished."

The Greek word *tetélestai*, which is translated correctly, "It is finished," in John 19:30, can also be translated, "It is paid." The word has been found on numerous tax receipts where the latter meaning is meant. Perhaps by this statement Jesus meant not only that His suffering was over, the bitter cup drunk, and the victory won, but also that the account was settled, the debt wiped out, the price of redemption paid.

14. In what sense did Jesus commend His spirit to God?

With His work completed, He was now ready to leave His earthly tabernacle and resume a fuller,

				8:00 a.m.	9:00	10:00	11:00	12:00	1:00 p.m.	2:00	3:00	4:00	5:00	6:00	7:00	

April 7,   A.D. 30   Friday

more intimate fellowship with God. Notice that both the first and last of the seven sayings of the cross are prayers—the first on behalf of His enemies, the last for himself.

Miracles Accompanying the Death of Christ . . . Matthew 27:51-56; Mark 15:38-41; Luke 23:45, 47-49

1. How many miracles accompanied Jesus' death?

Three different miracles are mentioned in the Synoptics as occurring at this time. The rending of the veil of the temple is cited by all three writers. Matthew further relates that there was an earthquake, and that "graves were opened; and many bodies of the saints which slept arose" (27:51, 52). Mark and Luke tell only of the veil of the temple.

2. What was the significance of the temple veil being torn?

This veil was the thick curtain, sixty feet long and thirty feet wide that separated the Holy Place from the Holy of Holies. Beyond it, into the Holy of Holies, only the high priest was permitted to pass, and that only once a year, on the Day of Atonement. The tearing of the veil from top to bottom signified that access to Heaven's throne is available to all men without the aid of earthly mediators. (See Hebrews 10:19-22.)

3. When were the dead raised?

Although the tombs were opened at the time of Jesus' death, the resurrection of the saints didn't occur until after His own resurrection (Matthew 27:52).

4. What was the meaning of the centurion's words?

The centurion, impressed by the day's happenings, especially by Jesus' conduct, said, "Truly this was the Son of God." He knew that Jesus claimed to be the Son of God, and because of the events that accompanied His death, concluded that He must surely be all He professed to be. It is doubtful he understood the full significance of his words, but he was definitely moved by the experience. In his evaluation he was joined by other soldiers (Matthew 27:54).

5. Why did the people smite their breasts?

By this act (comparable to wringing one's hands or gritting one's teeth) they showed their fear and wonderment.

> Three miracles accompanied Jesus' death: 1. The veil of the temple was torn in two; 2. An earthquake 3. Some graves were open, and saints arose.

The Burial . . . Matthew 27:57-60; Mark 15:42-46; Luke 23:50-54; John 19:31-42

> "Then came the soldiers, and brake the legs of the first, and of the other which was crucified with him. But when they came to Jesus, and saw that he was dead already, they brake not his legs" (John 19:32, 33).

1. How were the legs of the malefactors broken?

It wasn't unusual for the Romans to leave bodies on crosses until beasts and birds of prey ate them or putrification destroyed them. However, this was against the Jewish law which specified that a body should not be allowed to hang over night (Deuteronomy 21:23). Since the day following was the weekly Sabbath, the Jewish leaders were particularly insistent that the bodies be removed. The soldiers broke the legs of the two malefactors, and would have broken those of Jesus had He not been dead already. The breaking was done with clubs, and involved the pulverizing of the legs of the victims to hasten their death.

2. What was the significance of the blood and water?

To be certain Jesus was dead, a soldier pierced His side with a spear. Although we aren't told which side was pierced, it is assumed it was His left side. Probably both the membrane which surrounds the heart with a water-like substance, and the heart itself were punctured by the spear, causing the blood and water to flow. John's purpose in mentioning this no doubt was to establish that Jesus actually was dead.

• Arimathea

Bethel •
Ramah •

Jerusalem •

3. What is known about Joseph of Arimathea?

John tells us he was a secret disciple (19:38). Luke explains that he was a counsellor (member of the Sanhedrin), a good and just man who did not consent to Jesus' death, one who was waiting for the kingdom of God (23:50, 51). The location of Arimathea is commonly identified with Rama, in the territory of Benjamin, near Jerusalem.

4. What caused Pilate to marvel?

Usually the victim of crucifixion didn't expire for two or three days, sometimes for six or seven. That Jesus was so soon dead caused Pilate to marvel, and he checked with the centurion to see if it was really true (Mark 15:44).

5. How was Jesus prepared for burial?

Joseph of Arimathea requested and received the body of Jesus from Pilate. With the aid of Nicodemus, he prepared the body to be buried in his own tomb. Since there wasn't adequate time for regular embalming, they simply wrapped His body in linen cloth, between the folds of which

					8:00 a.m.	9:00	10:00	11:00	12:00	1:00 p.m.	2:00	3:00	4:00	5:00	6:00	7:00	

April 7, A.D. 30   Friday

they put myrrh and aloes. John says they used about one hundred pounds of these aromatics (19:39). The body was then placed in the tomb. Some of the women disciples prepared other spices and ointments for use on the first day of the week to further prepare His body for permanent interment (Luke 23:56).

6. In what type of tomb was Jesus buried?

It was a cave-like room cut into the rock of a mountainside. It was located in a garden near the place of crucifixion. Off of this main room were *loculi* (chambers dug into the rock) where bodies would be buried. Jesus' body was not in a loculus, but was left in the main room (John 20:12).

Garden tomb

The Watch at the Tomb . . . Matthew 27:61-66; Mark 15:47; Luke 23:55, 56

1. How would the last error be greater than the first?

If Jesus' body should be stolen from the tomb and word spread that He had been resurrected, this error or deception would be worse, in terms of seducing the masses, than His whole life had been. It would be so because the influence and impact of such a story would be greater.

2. How did they seal the tomb?

The tomb wasn't sealed as with cement to make entering it difficult. Rather, a cord was placed across the large rock which had been rolled to its door, and wax placed on the cord. On this wax a Roman insignia was imprinted. To open the tomb one would go against the authority of Rome.

WHEN AND WHERE

Jesus was crucified on Friday, Nisan 15. Although this is disputed, the evidence is overwhelming. By using the Scriptures connected with the observance of the Passover meal by Jesus (see Lesson Twenty-two), and tracing forward, it is clear that Friday was the day of His death. This same conclusion can be reached by beginning with Friday and moving forward to the first day of the week, the day of His resurrection. Luke outlines these days in his record (23:54—24:1). Notice the sequence:

Friday: The day of Jesus' death and burial

Sabbath: The women rested "according to the commandment."

First day of week: The resurrection

A suggested chronology for that Friday follows:

9:00 a.m. . . . Jesus placed on the cross (Mark 15:25)

His prayer for His enemies

His words to the penitent thief

His words to His mother and John

12:00 to
3:00 p.m. . . . Darkness over the whole land (Mark 15:33)

His cry to God at the close of this period of darkness

3:00 to
6:00 p.m. . . . His words, "I thirst"

His words, "It is finished"

His prayer to God

His death and burial

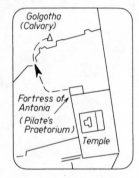

Golgotha (Calvary)

Fortress of Antonia (Pilate's Praetorium)

Temple

Calvary's location is unknown. Samuel Andrews, in a fine discussion about possible sites, lists four requirements: (1) It was outside the city walls (John 19:20; Hebrews 13:12); (2) It was near Jerusalem (John 19:20); (3) Near it was a garden with a rock-hewn sepulchre (John 19:41); (4) It was near a frequented road, for such spots were chosen by the Romans as sites for crucifixions.— *The Life of Our Lord upon the Earth,* pp. 575-588. These requirements are met by Gordon's Calvary, a hillside located a few hundred feet northeast of the Old Damascus gate. Of course there is no way to be positive that this is the actual spot.

PROJECTS AND PLANS

Get permission to conduct a mid-week service for the church. At the service, individual members of the class can read the Scriptures pertaining to Jesus' death. Pause after each main thought, and ask someone to offer a prayer of gratitude to God for that phase of the Lord's death.

To prepare for the next lesson, read the following passages: Matthew 28, Mark 16, Luke 24, and John 20 and 21. Also read the chapter, "On the Resurrection of Christ from the Dead," in *The Life and Times of Jesus the Messiah,* Vol. 2, Book 5, Ch. 16, pp. 621-629.

RESURRECTED AND SEEN

TOPICS AND TEXTS

The Resurrection of Christ . . . Matthew 28:1-8; Mark 16:1-8; Luke 24:1-8; John 20:1
The Report of the Women and the Visit of Peter and John . . . Luke 24:9-12; John 20:2-10
The Appearance to Mary . . . Mark 16:9-11; John 20:11-18
The Appearance to the Other Women . . . Matthew 28:9, 10
The Report of the Roman Guard . . . Matthew 28:11-15
The Appearance to the Two Disciples . . . Mark 16:12; Luke 24:13-32
The Report of the Two: Appearance to Peter (1 Corinthians 15:5) . . . Mark 16:13; Luke 24:33-35
Appearance to the Ten . . . Mark 16:14; Luke 24:36-43; John 20:19-25

CONTEXT AND CONTINUITY

Christ is risen! This grand truth is heralded by each of the four Gospel writers. It is indeed the supreme truth which each presents, the keystone upon which every other part of the gospel story rests, the only logical conclusion to a life which began and was continually attended with the miraculous. It is the climactic truth toward which the Old Testament moved and the foundation upon which the New Testament rests. It is the fulfillment of a dream which men from Adam to Christ shared, and the issuance of a promise upon which men from then till now have built their lives. It is all of this and more—so much more that words are inadequate.

Christ's resurrection occurred on Nisan 17, the first day of the week following the Passover. None witnessed it, so the exact procedure is unknown. After it had taken place there was an earthquake. At that time two angels descended, one of whom rolled away the stone from the tomb's entrance.

Soon a group of women (Mary Magdalene, Mary the mother of James, Salome, Joanna, and other women) arrived on the scene. They came with spices to complete the embalming of Jesus. When they saw the open tomb, they were shocked and confused. Perhaps they looked in and saw that the tomb was empty, or perhaps they surmised, since the tomb was open, that the Lord's body had been stolen. (At this time they did not see the angels nor hear their message.) Immediately Mary Magdalene left to take this news to Peter and John. (Perhaps she intended to tell all of the disciples but found only Peter and John—maybe outside the place where the group was staying.) Of course, at this stage all she could tell them was that the tomb was open and Jesus' body was gone (which, as stated above, she may have surmised). When the two men heard this they were undecided momentarily as to what to do.

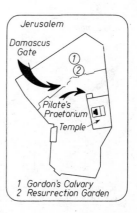

Jerusalem

Damascus Gate

Pilate's Praetorium

Temple

1 Gordon's Calvary
2 Resurrection Garden

> Angels are spiritual beings created by God to serve Him. Angel means messenger.

Perhaps they discussed whether they should share this strange news with the other disciples or first go to the tomb to verify it. While they talked, Mary ran off toward the garden, hoping to rejoin the other women.

After Mary had left the other women they looked inside the tomb (either again or for the first time). They were greeted by two angels who told them about Jesus' resurrection and commissioned them to take this news to the disciples. They were just a few minutes behind Mary Magdalene who had gone with her news of the empty tomb. Now they came with their *better* news of the resurrection, which they had learned from the angels. When Peter and John heard the fuller story, they set out running for the tomb. They arrived, looked in, failed to see the angels or Jesus, and departed for their home (John 20:10).

By this time Mary Magdalene was back in the garden, searching in vain for the women (who were a few minutes behind her on their way back to the garden). She was in a state of confusion. Unlike the other women, who had been spoken to by an angel, she was unaware of the resurrection. When she arrived at the tomb and saw that the other women were not present, she looked inside. When she did she was greeted by the angels who talked with her.

As this conversation proceeded, Jesus appeared to her and told her to go and tell His brethren that He would meet them in Galilee. Mary, therefore, went a second time to the place where the disciples were lodging. This time she shared with the group her glorious news of the resurrection of Christ.

While this was taking place, Jesus made His second appearance, this one to the other women who, by this time, had returned to the garden from their trip to share with the disciples.

Later that same day He showed himself to two disciples on their way to Emmaus, and appeared to Simon Peter (Luke 24:34; 1 Corinthians 15:5). That evening He appeared to ten of the apostles in an upper room in Jerusalem. (Mark's use of "the eleven" is simply a title for the group, and was not intended to specify the actual number of apostles present. John makes it clear that Thomas was not present on this occasion.)

Reconstructing this period of Jesus' life isn't easy. In fact, no other period of His life is as difficult to harmonize as the first few hours after sunrise on His resurrection day. The arrangement suggested above seems to agree with all of the Scriptures and therefore appears to be correct.

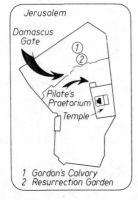

Jerusalem

Damascus Gate

Pilate's Praetorium

Temple

1 Gordon's Calvary
2 Resurrection Garden

Why so much difficulty with this period? Perhaps Alfred Edersheim says it best: "In general we ought to remember, that the Evangelists, and . . . St. Paul, are not so much concerned to narrate the whole *history* of the Resurrection as to furnish the evidence for it."—*The Life and Times of Jesus the Messiah,* p. 622. Each writer had his own viewpoint, from which he presented the phases of the resurrection that were convincing to him.

INQUIRIES AND INSIGHTS

The Resurrection of Christ . . . Matthew 28:1-8; Mark 16:1-8; Luke 24:1-8; John 20:1

1. What was the purpose of the visit of the women?
John gives no reason, Matthew states that they came to see the tomb, Mark explains that it was to anoint Jesus' body with spices, and Luke corroborates this. The preparations made by Joseph and Nicodemus (John 19:38-42) apparently were rushed and inadequate. The women came to finish the work of preparing His body for final burial in one of the loculi in Joseph's tomb.

2. Why was the stone rolled away from the tomb?
Not to allow Jesus to get out. This wasn't necessary since Jesus' body could pass through walls (see John 20:19). There was a twofold purpose: to make the keepers aware that a marvelous act of God was taking place; to allow the disciples to enter the tomb and see that Jesus' body was gone.

3. How is the angel described?
Matthew and Mark mention only one angel, but Luke and John speak of two. Evidently one was the spokesman, and Matthew and Mark saw fit to mention only him. Angels are often described, as they are here by Mark and Luke, as young men. Mark says the "young man" was clothed in a long white garment, described by Matthew as "white as snow" and by Luke as "shining." Matthew adds that his countenance was "like lightning."

4. Who saw these angels?
The keepers (members of the guard), the women, and Mary Magdalene are mentioned specifically as seeing one or two angels.

5. Why did Jesus wish to meet with His disciples in Galilee?
No reason is given. We can speculate that since Galilee was the scene of so much of His labor,

Jewish tomb—loculi

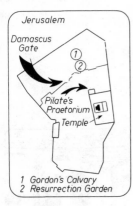

Jerusalem
Damascus Gate
Pilate's Praetorium
Temple

1 Gordon's Calvary
2 Resurrection Garden

Jesus had cast seven demons out of Mary Magdalene. (See Luke 8:2.)

and since so many of His disciples lived there, that He wished to return to confirm that He indeed had been raised. A specific place of meeting had been appointed (Matthew 28:16), but we aren't told where it was, or when it was selected. The appearance described in John 21 would indicate that the designated mountain was near the Sea of Galilee.

6. Why did the angel specifically mention Peter?
Mark states that the angel singled out Peter as one to whom the message of Christ's resurrection should be told (16:7). This was an act of mercy on behalf of the Lord who knew that Peter was in agony of soul, and needed consolation because of his denial. It were as though the angel said: "Tell Peter his repentance is accepted and he is forgiven."

7. Why does John mention only Mary Magdalene as going to the tomb?
Probably because she played a much more important part in Christ's resurrection than the other women. She was the first person to see Him alive after His resurrection. By the use of the word, "we" (20:2), John indicated that others also went to the tomb.

The Report of the Women and the Visit of Peter and John . . . Luke 24:9-12; John 20:2-10

1. Which women reported to the disciples?
Luke says the entire group of women went (24:9, 10). Matthew similarly speaks of the entire group as running to take word to the disciples (28:8-10). Mark says that the whole group, having seen the angel, was afraid and said nothing to any man (16:8), but that Mary Magdalene, after seeing the resurrected Christ, went and revealed this to the disciples (16:10). John, who speaks only of Mary Magdalene, declares that she twice carried messages to the disciples: the first to Peter and John that the tomb was empty (20:2); the second to the disciples that she had seen Jesus (20:18). This question is dealt with more thoroughly in the chart, "Suggested Chronology of Resurrection Morning," at the end of this lesson.

2. Why the unwillingness of the disciples to believe?
Although Jesus had promised He would be raised, the disciples, in their extreme grief, had forgotten His promises. With His death they were convinced that all of their dreams and aspirations had

been destroyed. When word of His resurrection was brought to them, the news was too good to believe. Later, when the apostles saw Him, they "believed not for joy" (Luke 24:41). Their reluctance to believe that Jesus had been raised adds strength to their later testimony that He was indeed resurrected.

3. Why the mention of the linen clothes and the napkin?

The linen clothes are mentioned by both Luke and John, but only John speaks of the napkin. The reference serves as further evidence against the theory that Jesus' body was stolen. Had someone taken His corpse, it is hard to believe that time would have been wasted in unswathing it and carefully folding the head napkin and placing it by itself.

> Burial customs vary from culture to culture.

4. What conclusion is drawn from the detail that John outran Peter?

No legitimate conclusion can be drawn. Many contend that this indicates that John was a younger man than Peter. Although probably true, it can't be proven from this text since some older men are faster runners than younger ones.

The Appearance to Mary . . . Mark 16:9-11; John 20:11-18

1. Why did Jesus appear first to Mary Magdalene?

We don't know. By doing so He bestowed honor on all womanhood. Mary Magdalene is mentioned only one other time in the Gospels, in Luke 8:2, where we're told that seven devils had been cast out of her. Some identify her with Mary of Bethany, others with the sinful woman of Luke 7:36-50, but with no real basis.

> Mary was from Magdala on the Sea of Galilee.

2. When did this appearance take place?

John says it was after Mary had returned to the garden from her journey to inform Peter and John of the situation at the tomb.

3. Why didn't Mary recognize Jesus?

Several factors entered into this: she didn't expect to see Him; her vision possibly was blurred with tears; the appearance of Jesus was somewhat changed.

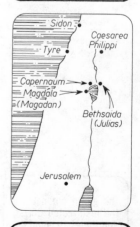

4. How did Jesus make himself known to Mary?

He spoke her name with the same tender, compassionate voice which she had heard before. This

> Mary = "bitter things"; but this was a pleasant experience.

caused her to recognize Him, and she immediately responded, "Rabboni, Master."

5. What did Jesus mean, "Touch me not"?
His prohibition wasn't against merely touching Him, but against clinging to Him and detaining Him. Much had to be done, and this was not the time for a display of her love and devotion. He commanded her to go and tell His brethren that He was to ascend to Heaven.

> "Detain me not."

The Appearance to the Other Women . . .
Matthew 28:9, 10

1. When did this appearance take place?
Matthew says it happened as the women went to "tell his disciples" (28:9). The apparent meaning is that it occurred as they went to share with the disciples the message of the angel (vv. 5-8). However, for harmony purposes, it appears that a break is needed between verses 8 and 9. It may be that the women went and told the disciples the message of the angel (v. 8), left, and later as they were returning (v. 9), were met by Jesus. Another possibility is that the women went to *some* of the disciples (v. 8) with their message about the angel (angels actually; see Luke 24:4), and while on their way to share the same news with *other* disciples (v. 9) were met by Jesus. Basic to both explanations is the belief that Matthew has condensed his account. (See the comment about this appearance in the chart which follows this lesson.)

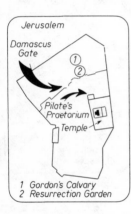

Jerusalem

Damascus Gate

①
②

Pilate's Praetorium

Temple

1 *Gordon's Calvary*
2 *Resurrection Garden*

2. Why were these women permitted to touch Him when Mary Magdalene had been forbidden to do so?
Mary had been forbidden to touch Him in the sense of detaining Him. These women would have been prohibited from that also, but were allowed to hold Him by the feet for a brief time.

The Report of the Roman Guard . . . Matthew 28:11-15

1. What things could the guard report?
The keepers had been frightened by an earthquake, the appearance of one or two angels (there were two involved, but perhaps the keepers saw only one of them), and by the rolling away of the stone by one of them. After the stone had been removed perhaps they saw that the tomb was empty. These things they reported to their superiors. They couldn't tell about the resurrection, for they hadn't witnessed it. After the story of Jesus' resurrection began to circulate, the lie that His body had been stolen was spread abroad.

> The guard did not see the resurrected Christ, and therefore could not report that He was raised.

2. Why did the chief priests and elders pay them money?

The money was a bribe to keep them from telling the true story.

3. What obvious error is there in the lie they told?

The watch was told to say that Jesus' disciples came at night and stole His body *while they slept.* If they had been asleep, how could they know what happened to the body? There is often some weakness in a lie that serves for its undoing.

The Appearance to the Two Disciples . . . Mark 16:12; Luke 24:13-32

1. Who were these men?

One of them was named Cleopas, but about him nothing more is known. Some identify him with Alpheus, the father of James (Matthew 10:3). The name of the other man isn't given. Some think he was Luke; others, Cephas, or Nathanael.

> The companion of Cleopas is unnamed. Claims have been made for Luke, Cephas, and Nathanael.

2. What were they discussing?

They had been in Jerusalem and had either seen or heard about the crucifixion. They had heard also the testimony of the women that angels had told them Jesus was alive. Consequently they could think and talk about nothing else. No doubt in their hearts was a burning hope that what they had heard was true, but the flame of that hope was kept low by a reluctance to believe that any such wonderful thing could happen.

3. What is meant by, "their eyes were holden"?

Perhaps nothing more is meant than that they didn't know who He was. More likely, however, there was a divine restraint placed upon them to keep them from recognizing Him until the appropriate moment.

4. Why did Jesus act as He did?

By asking them questions, He caused them to think seriously about the whole issue. Then by using evidence from the Old Testament He convinced them that it was proper for the Christ to suffer. He did all of this before revealing His identity. It was a marvelous teaching procedure that firmly fixed the truth of His resurrection in their minds.

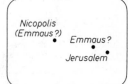

Nicopolis (Emmaus?) • Emmaus? • Jerusalem •

5. Did these men know about the two appearances Jesus had made?

They must have left Jerusalem after the women

reported about the empty tomb and prior to the report of Christ's appearances. Had they known about these, they would surely have mentioned them when relating the events of the morning. This fits well with the explanations given in answer to Question 1 in the section, "The Appearance to the Other Women," above.

6. Was this "breaking of bread" the Lord's Supper?

We have no evidence that the apostles observed this ordinance until after the beginning of the church. Alexander Campbell, as well as other writers, contends that it was the Lord's Supper.

The Report of the Two: Appearance to Peter (1 Corinthians 15:5) . . . Mark 16:13; Luke 24:33-35

1. Were there eleven or only ten gathered together?

Although both Mark (16:14) and Luke (24:33) speak of the eleven, there were evidently only ten of the apostles at this meeting. Thomas and, naturally, Judas were the ones absent. The term, "the eleven," was used to refer to the group of apostles.

2. When did Jesus appear to Simon?

This appearance isn't mentioned elsewhere in the Gospels. Paul lists it, along with other appearances, in 1 Corinthians 15. It must have taken place sometime after the two disciples departed for Emmaus, and obviously before they arrived back in Jerusalem.

Appearance to the Ten . . . Mark 16:14; Luke 24:36-43; John 20:19-25

1. How did Jesus get into the room when the doors were shut?

John implies (20:19) that the door was not only shut, but locked (*kleîs* means "key," which seems to indicate that the door was locked). Jesus wasn't hampered by that which inhibits the ordinary human body, for He was in a resurrected state. He no doubt passed through the locked door in the same way He vacated the sealed tomb—by a miracle.

2. Why were the apostles afraid?

To be confronted by the walking, talking body of one who is known to have died would frighten the fearless. Although the apostles had been informed He was alive, they were reluctant to believe it. When He suddenly appeared in their midst, in a room which they knew to be locked, they were terrified.

THE TEN
Peter
Andrew
James
John
Philip
Bartholomew
Matthew
Thaddeus
James
Simon

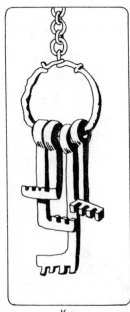

Keys

3. Why did He show them His hands and His side?

Both this action and that of eating before them were done in order to convince them that He was not an illusion. He wanted them to know that He was the same Jesus whom they had known and loved, that this was His same body, only somewhat changed.

4. How did the apostles receive the Holy Spirit at this time?

In one sense the apostles had already received the Holy Spirit. In another, He wasn't to be fully received by them until they were baptized in Him on the day of Pentecost. Although they received a special dispensation of the Spirit at this time, the act of Jesus was also symbolic, a foretelling of what was to come.

5. How could the apostles remit and retain the sins of men?

This promise is similar to the one given earlier to Peter (Matthew 16:19), and to the twelve (Matthew 18:18). As representatives of Christ, the apostles proclaimed His message. That message is one of forgiveness when accepted, and condemnation when rejected. Through this message the sins of men are remitted or retained.

6. Why was Thomas absent?

No reason is given. We would assume he had a valid reason for his absence.

7. Why was Thomas reluctant to believe?

For the same reason the other apostles at first doubted. The news was too good to believe. Barnes comments: "It is not known what was the ground of the incredulity of Thomas. It is probable, however, that it was, in part at least, the effect of deep grief, and of that despondency which fills the mind when a long-cherished hope is taken away. In such a case it requires proof of uncommon clearness and strength to overcome the despondency, and to convince us that we *may* obtain the object of our desires."—*Notes on the New Testament, John,* p. 378.

WHEN AND WHERE

Mark says that Jesus was raised from the dead early on the first day of the week (16:9). How early this was is a matter of speculation. From the terminology used to describe the time of the visit of the women it's generally conceded that they arrived about 5:00 a.m. At the time of their arrival

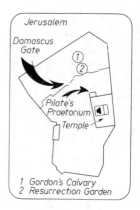

Jerusalem

Damascus Gate

Pilate's Praetorium

Temple

1 Gordon's Calvary
2 Resurrection Garden

"Verily I say unto you, Whatsoever ye shall bind on earth shall be bound in heaven; and whatsoever ye shall loose on earth shall be loosed in heaven" (Matthew 18:18).

the resurrection had already taken place, and the stone had already been rolled from the entrance of the tomb. Probably Christ's resurrection took place sometime between 3:00 and 5:00 a.m., during the fourth watch of the night (3:00—6:00 a.m.).

The location of Emmaus is unknown. There are three hints given in Luke 24:13. 1. its name (Emmaus); 2. its distance from Jerusalem (threescore furlongs); 3. its designation as a village *(komá)*. There are two places that seem to qualify equally well: Kubeibeh, which from the time of the crusades has had its advocates; Urtas, which was selected after ten years of diligent search. Kubeibeh lies northwest from Jerusalem on the road to Lydda, nearly sixty furlongs from Jerusalem. Urtas is a little eastward of the main road from Bethlehem to Hebron, and also about sixty furlongs from Jerusalem. Either place could have been known as Emmaus in the time of Christ. Locate these villages on the map which is provided.

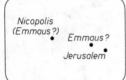

PROJECTS AND PLANS

As a lesson project endeavor to discover the exact sequence of events on the morning of Christ's resurrection. Compare it to the one suggested in this lesson.

To prepare for the next lesson memorize one or all of the following Scriptures: Matthew 28:16-20; Mark 16:15, 16; Luke 24:44-49.

SUGGESTED CHRONOLOGY OF RESURRECTION MORNING

EVENT	MATT.	MARK	LUKE	JOHN
Women start out from places of abode for the tomb.	28:1	16:1		
Before their arrival, an earthquake, tomb is opened, guard leaves.	28:2-4			
Women (including Mary Magdalene) arrive, see the open tomb (perhaps look in and see it is empty). They are uncertain as to what to do.		16:2-4	24:1, 2	20:1
Mary Magdalene leaves immediately to tell Peter and John (perhaps intend to tell other disciples, but find only the two). After sharing her news Mary leaves to rejoin women in garden.				20:2*

After Mary leaves, the women enter the tomb (perhaps for second time). They are greeted by two angels who tell about the resurrection.	28:5-7	16:5-7	24:3-8	
The women run to share their good news with the disciples. They arrive shortly after Mary Magdalene has told Peter and John about the open tomb, and tell their fuller story about the angels and their message. They leave in quest of Mary.	28:8#	16:8+	24:9-11	
Peter and John run to the tomb, look in, and return to their home.			24:12	20:3-10
Mary Magdalene who has returned to garden is confused. She is unaware of the resurrection. She looks in tomb, sees the angels and talks with them.				20:11-13
Jesus appears to Mary Magdalene and tells her to go and tell his brethren.		16:9		20:14-17
Mary Magdalene goes to the disciples with her news that she has seen the resurrected Christ.		16:10, 11		20:18
Jesus appears to the other women who, after failing to find Mary, have started back to the disciples. Perhaps they arrive while Mary Magdalene is still there.	28:9, # 10			

*Mary Magdalene's message to Peter and John, "They have taken away the Lord out of the sepulchre, and we know not where they have laid him," was perhaps a surmise, based on seeing an open tomb. Or, it may have been her conclusion, based upon looking in and seeing the empty tomb. Neither she nor any of the other women saw the angels at this time.

+Mark's statement that the women said nothing to anyone must mean that they said nothing to anyone except the ones they were told to tell, i.e., the disciples.

#It is assumed that there should be a break between verses 8 and 9 of Matthew 28, and that Matthew has condensed his material. The other women (not including Mary Magdalene) went and told the disciples their message about the angels (v. 8), and left, perhaps in quest of Mary Magdalene. Later, as they returned to the place where the disciples were, Jesus appeared to them (v. 9). Another possible explanation is that the women went to *some* of the disciples (v. 8) with their message about the angels, and while on their way to share the same news with *other* disciples (v. 9), Jesus appeared to them. (John 20:10 may imply that Peter and John went to a place other than where the disciples were staying.) If the women made only one trip to the disciples (at which time they told of seeing Jesus) as Matthew's account is often interpreted as saying, why didn't the two disciples going to Emmaus mention that the women had reported seeing Him? (See Luke 24:22, 23.)

OTHER APPEARANCES AND ASCENSION

TOPICS AND TEXTS

Appearance to the Eleven (1 Corinthians 15:5) . . . John 20:26-31
Appearance to Seven by the Sea of Galilee . . . John 21:1-23
Appearance to Five Hundred: The Great Commission (1 Corinthians 15:6) . . .
Matthew 28:16-20
Appearance in Jerusalem: Great Commission Repeated . . . Mark 16:15-18
Appearance to James (1 Corinthians 15:7)
Appearance to the Disciples, With Further Commission (Acts 1:3-8) . . . Luke
24:44-49
The Ascension (Acts 1:9-12) . . . Mark 16:19, 20; Luke 24:50-53
Epilogue . . . John 21:24, 25

CONTEXT AND CONTINUITY

We cannot be sure how many post-resurrection appearances Jesus made. This is so for two reasons: First, we can't be certain that all of His appearances were recorded by the Gospel writers. Second, in one or two instances it's difficult to determine whether the same or different appearances are being discussed by the writers. The following list is a suggested chronology of His known appearances:

I. In and Near Jerusalem
1. Appearance to Mary Magdalene—Mark 16:9-11; John 20:11-18
2. Appearance to the Other Women—Matthew 28:9, 10
3. Appearance to the Two Disciples on Way to Emmaus—Mark 16:12, 13; Luke 24:13-32
4. Appearance to Peter—Luke 24:34; 1 Corinthians 15:5
5. Appearance to the Ten—Mark 16:14; Luke 24:36-43; John 20:19-25
6. Appearance to the Eleven—John 20:26-29; 1 Corinthians 15:5

II. In Galilee
7. Appearance to the Seven by the Sea—John 21:1-23
8. Appearance to Five Hundred Brethren—Matthew 28:16-20; 1 Corinthians 15:6

III. In and Near Jerusalem After His Return From Galilee
9. Appearance to Apostles—Mark 16:15-18
10. Appearance to James—1 Corinthians 15:7 (This appearance could have been in Galilee.)
11. Appearance at Bethany—Luke 24:44-49; Acts 1:3-8

IV. Later Appearances
12. Appearance to Paul—1 Corinthians 15:8
13. Appearance to John—Revelation 1:13

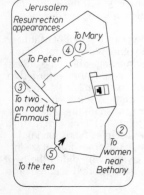

Jerusalem
Resurrection appearances
To Mary
To Peter
To two on road to Emmaus
To the ten
To women near Bethany

There are some questions about this arrangement. Whether Christ appeared first to Peter or to the two on the way to Emmaus is unknown. When the appearance to James took place is subject to question. (We know only that it occurred after the appearance to the five hundred, and before the appearance to "all the apostles," 1 Corinthians 15:6, 7.) It is possible that the appearance mentioned in Mark 16:15-18 is the same as that described in Matthew 28:16-20. Or, it could be that the Mark text is parallel to the Luke 24:44-49 account. Neither of these possibilities seems likely.

The appearances of Jesus, whatever their exact number, were sufficient to convince the doubting apostles and other disciples that their Master had indeed been raised from the dead, that He had actually conquered death. So convinced were they that they devoted their lives to the spreading of this wonderful news. Not one of the apostles who saw the resurrected Lord apostasized, and if tradition is correct, all but one of them, John, died a martyr's death. It is hoped that a thorough study of the material in this lesson will convince you of the truthfulness of Jesus' resurrection, or reconfirm you in your faith in this cardinal Christian doctrine.

"He was seen of Cephas, then of the twelve: after that, he was seen of above five hundred brethren at once; of whom the greater part remain unto this present, but some are fallen asleep. After that, he was seen of James; then of all the apostles. And last of all he was seen of me also, as of one born out of due time" (1 Corinthians 15:5-8).

INQUIRIES AND INSIGHTS

Appearance to the Eleven (1 Corinthians 15:5) . . . John 20:26-31

1. Why did the apostles remain in Jerusalem? The message of the angels was that they should depart into Galilee where they would see the resurrected Christ. Instead of immediately obeying this command, they remained in Jerusalem for at least a week before beginning their journey northward. Why they delayed is unknown. Perhaps the fact that Jesus continued to appear in and near Jerusalem throughout that first Lord's Day gave them encouragement to remain in that area.

2. On what day of the week did this appearance take place?
Christ appeared to the ten apostles on the evening of His resurrection, which was the first day of the week (John 20:19). Using that as his starting point, John says that "after eight days" He appeared to the eleven (20:26). Beginning with the Sunday of the resurrection, and including it in the count (the Jewish way of reckoning time), would make John's eighth day the first day of the next week. Although

April,   A.D. 30 ↓ | May ↓

we can't be certain, it is possible the appearance
to the seven by the Sea of Galilee was also on
Sunday. Because Jesus was resurrected on the first
day of the week (Mark 16:9), the day is called the
Lord's Day. That several of Jesus' appearances
were made on this day strengthens the position
that this day is the day Jesus intended as the day of
Christian worship.

3. Did Thomas feel the wounds of Jesus?
Certainly not! Seeing Jesus with His wounds was
sufficient to convince him. In repentance and
worship, he fell before his Master and cried out,
"My Lord and my God."

> "My Lord and my God."

4. Why the statement in verses 30, 31 at this time instead of at the close of the book?
In this statement John gives the two-fold purpose
of his book: (1) To prove that Jesus is the Messiah;
(2) To offer eternal life to all who will believe this
truth. This statement has a ring of finality about it
which implies that the end of the book has been
reached. It may be that John originally ended his
book with chapter 20, and that chapter 21 is an
appendix, added by him at a later date.

> John's Purpose:
>   1. To prove that Jesus is the Messiah;
>   2. To offer eternal life to all who believe this truth.

*Appearance to Seven by the Sea of Galilee . . .
John 21:1-23*

1. Why does John call it, "the sea of Tiberias"?
The more popular name for this body of water is
the Sea of Galilee. However, in the Bible it is also
called "the lake of Gennesaret" (Luke 5:1), "the
sea of Chinnereth" (Numbers 34:11), or "Chin-
neroth" (Joshua 12:3), and, as in our text, "the sea
of Tiberias." The latter name came from the city of
Tiberias, the capital of Herod Antipas, located on
the western shore of the lake. John chose to use
this, the Roman name, since his Gospel was to
circulate in the Roman world.

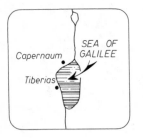

2. What is the meaning of *Didymus?*
Thomas was called *Didymus,* a word which
means, "the twin." Whether he was in fact a twin
is unknown.

3. What was Peter's motive in going fishing at this time?
Possibly he had a two-fold purpose: to pass the
time until Jesus came; and to secure food to sus-
tain him and the other apostles during their wait.
Some have accused him of forsaking his spiritual
work, and of returning to his former manner of
livelihood, but there is no suggestion of this in the
text.

4. Who were the two unnamed disciples?
Some commentators believe they were Andrew and Philip, but this is speculation.

5. How did the apostles know that it was the Lord?
Separated from Him by about one hundred yards, the apostles were unable to see clearly through the twilight the features of the one who spoke. However, by the title He used in addressing them ("children"), as well as by His knowledge as to where to cast the net for a large catch of fish, John concluded that it was Jesus.

6. Was Peter completely naked?
No, he was wearing his undergarment or tunic, but didn't have on his outer garment or coat. It seems strange that with a distance of about one hundred yards to swim, Peter would put on additional clothing, but apparently it was done out of respect to his Master.

7. What did Jesus mean, "Lovest thou me more than these?"
There are two possible interpretations. The Greek word for "these" is *toúton,* and may be in either the neuter or the masculine gender. If it is in the neuter, Jesus' meaning is, "Do you love me more than you love these things (boat, fishing, utensils, etc.)?" If it is in the masculine, the meaning is, "Do you love me more than these other apostles?" The latter seems to be the correct meaning. On the night of the betrayal, Peter had claimed to have a greater attachment to Jesus than the other apostles. Now Jesus is inquiring whether Peter still believes this. Notice that the question was asked three times, the same number of denials made by Peter.

8. Why repeat the question three times?
As indicated above, the question probably was asked three times as a reminder to Peter of his three denials. This conversation has an interesting twist in the Greek that isn't seen in the translations. Two Greek words for love are used— *agapáo* and *philéo.* Jesus twice asked Peter concerning his love with the word *agapáo,* and the third time He switched and used *philéo.* Peter, in responding, continually used the word *philéo.* In John's writings both of these verbs are used of God's love for man, of God's love for His Son, of the love of men for other men, and of the love of men for Jesus. It isn't easy to determine the purpose for the two words here. It may be that Jesus

> Present: Simon Peter, Thomas, Nathanael, James, John, and two unnamed disciples (Andrew and Philip?).

> Two Greek words used for love here:
> agapao
> phileo

229

asked, "Do you love me with the kind of love that men have toward others? Do you regard me as a friend?" Each time Peter responded, "I love you with the kind of devotion and reverence that I owe to God." The third time Jesus switched and asked, "So it is true that you love me with a high and lofty love?" "Yes, Lord, that is how I love You." Although this isn't the popular view, it seems to be the correct one.

9. What did Jesus tell Peter to do to prove his love?

After Peter's first affirmation of his love, Jesus said, "Feed my lambs." After the next two, He said, "Feed my sheep." Peter thus was commissioned to care for the disciples of the Lord, the young and the old.

10. What is the meaning of the prediction regarding Peter?

It relates to Peter's old age and manner of death. Whereas he was free and able to gird himself and go where he desired, this condition would be changed when he was old. Then someone else would gird him and take him where he didn't want to go. Tradition relates that Peter was crucified at Rome in about A. D. 67, when he was approximately 75 years old. Feeling unworthy to die in the exact manner of his Lord, he requested to be crucified with his head downward. At that time he stretched forth his hands and others bound him, and led him to his death, to which his flesh, but not his spirit, went unwillingly.

> Traditional view of Peter's death: Rome, A.D. 67, Peter about 75 years old; crucified upside down.

11. Why was Peter so concerned about John's future?

Peter and John were close companions. Since Jesus foretold Peter's future, it is understandable that Peter should be concerned about the future of his friend. What should happen to John, however, was not any of Peter's business, and Jesus told him so.

Appearance to Five Hundred: The Great Commission (1 Corinthians 15:6) . . . Matthew 28:16-20

1. In which mountain did this meeting take place?

We don't know. Probably it was one of those near the Sea of Galilee. The mountain on which Jesus taught the Sermon on the Mount has been suggested, and would have been a memorable spot. Others which have been mentioned are the one where He was transfigured, and the one near where He fed the five thousand.

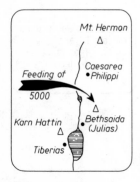

230

2. Can we be sure that the appearance in Matthew 28 is the same as the one in 1 Corinthians 15:6?

That these two accounts are of the same appearance is only an assumption. One sentence which leads to this conclusion however, is the statement of Matthew, "some doubted." It is scarcely conceivable that any of the eleven could still doubt. While it is true that Matthew 28:16 mentions "the eleven," it doesn't say *only* the eleven. If the two texts are parallel, and if at this appearance there were not only the eleven but a much larger company of disciples (500), it is quite likely that some of the larger number were still in doubt. Here lies the basis of the assumption that equates the two appearances.

3. In what sense was all power given unto Jesus?

As Creator (with the Father and Holy Spirit), Jesus had an original right over everything. Now as the resurrected Lord, the universe was put more particularly under Him, "that he might redeem his people; that he might gather a church; that he might defend his chosen; that he might subdue all their enemies, and bring them off conquerers and more than conquerors." *Notes on the New Testament, Matthew,* p. 322.

4. What commission did Jesus give His disciples?

Jesus instructed His followers to go and teach, i.e., *disciple,* all nations. This was to be accomplished by baptizing in the name of the Father, Son, and Holy Spirit all those individuals who would accept their testimony. After they had been discipled, they were to be taught to observe all the things which Jesus had commanded. Probably more was said on this occasion than is contained in Matthew's account, but he has preserved the essential message.

> Christ's Commission in the New Testament: Matthew 28:16-20; Mark 16:15, 16; Luke 24:44-49; John 20:21-23; Acts 1:6-8.

5. How were they to baptize?

The Greek word *baptídzo* means "to dip, plunge, immerse." Jesus said the disciples should go and immerse believers in the name of the Father, Son, and Holy Spirit.

6. Should a candidate be baptized once or three times?

Some insist that a candidate be baptized once in the name of the Father, again in the name of the Son, and a third time in the name of the Holy Spirit. This was not Jesus' meaning.

Appearance in Jerusalem: Great Commission Repeated . . . Mark 16:15-18

1. Was the command of Mark 16:15 given at the meeting mentioned in verse 14?
Apparently not. Mark (as well as the other three writers) greatly condenses his material concerning the appearances of Jesus. The meeting described in verse 14 seems to have taken place on the evening of the day of Christ's resurrection; that in verse 15 probably occurred several weeks following.

2. Is this meeting the same as that mentioned in Matthew 28?
We must not be dogmatic, but it seems the two are separate meetings. At each meeting with His apostles after they were convinced of His resurrection, Jesus answered the question that was foremost in their minds, "What shall we do now?" That question Jesus consistently answered with the commission to go and win others. (See also Luke 24:44-49, the record of another meeting where Jesus spoke regarding the future work of His disciples on earth.)

> "Go ye into all the world, and preach the gospel to every creature. He that believeth and is baptized shall be saved; but he that believeth not shall be damned" (Mark 16:15, 16).

3. Why don't the signs mentioned by Jesus follow those who believe today?
The apostles, as well as others in the age of primitive Christianity, had the power, and performed the miracles, promised by Jesus in this text. That not all of the early Christians possessed such power is indicated in the New Testament. We conclude that Jesus didn't mean that all Christians would be able to perform miracles. Some did, and thereby fulfilled the promise of this text. Miracles were never intended as a permanent part of Christianity (see 1 Corinthians 12 and 13). It has been said that miracles are to Christianity what the scaffolding is to a new building: after the structure is completed, the scaffolding can be removed.

The Appearance to James (1 Corinthians 15:7)

1. Which James was this?
Some identify him as the apostle James, the son of Zebedee. Most, however, contend that this was the half-brother of Jesus. (See Matthew 13:55.)

> Three disciples named James: James, the son of Zebedee; James, the son of Alpheus; and James, the son of Joseph.

2. When did this appearance take place?
We know neither when nor where it occurred. It isn't mentioned by the four Gospel writers, only by Paul, who places it between the appearance to the five hundred and the one to "all the apostles" (1 Corinthians 15:6, 7).

Appearance to the Disciples, With Further Commission (Acts 1:3-8) . . . Luke 24:44-49

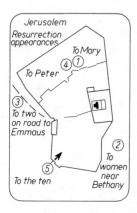

Jerusalem
Resurrection appearances

1. Is there a break between Luke 24:43 and 44?
A mere reading of Luke 24 would lead one to believe that all the appearances in this chapter took place on the day Jesus was resurrected. From other sources, we know that this wasn't true, and conclude that Luke was condensing his account. A break is needed near the end of this chapter, but we can't be positive where it should come—perhaps after verse 43; perhaps after verse 48. Verses 49-52 are parallel to the passage in Acts 1:3-12, which describes what happened forty days after His resurrection (Acts 1:3). It seems that verses 44-48, with their messsage concerning world evangelism, fit better with the end, rather than the beginning, of the post-resurrection period, and hence the placement. Edersheim thinks that Luke 24:44-48 doesn't describe a specific appearance made by Jesus but "is a condensed narrative—without distinction of time or place—of what occurred during all the forty days." *The Life and Times of Jesus the Messiah,* footnote on page 647.

2. Had all things about the Christ now been fulfilled?
No, not everything. The meaning is that every expectation of His life up until this particular time, including His death, burial, and resurrection, had been fulfilled.

3. Is this another occasion when Jesus gave the great commission?
It is either a distinct occasion or a parallel text to Mark 16:15-18. The former view is preferred.(See question 1 above.)

4. What was the promise of the Father which Jesus was to send upon the apostles?
In His farewell discourse (John 14, 15, 16), Jesus repeatedly declared that after His departure from the world, He would send the Holy Spirit to guide and comfort the apostles (John 14:16, 26; 15:26; 16:13). It is to these promises that He made reference. The power of the Holy Spirit was that power from on high with which they were to be endued (Luke 24:49; Acts 1:8). John the Baptist also had foretold the coming of the Holy Spirit (Matthew 3:11), and in the Acts 1 passage, the meaning of John's prophecy is explained by Jesus (1:5). Ten days after Jesus' ascension, while the apostles waited in Jerusalem, the Holy Spirit came, they

HOLY SPIRIT

Comforter, Eternal Spirit, Spirit of God, Good Spirit, Spirit of Life, Spirit of Wisdom.

233

were baptized in Him, and the church was inaugurated (Acts 2).

5. How did the apostles expect the kingdom of Israel to be restored?

There was widespread belief among the Jews that a Messiah was coming who would be a powerful earthly leader, similar to King David. It was held that he would expel the enemies of Israel and establish a mighty earthly kingdom. Although the apostles had been with Jesus for over three years, and had heard Him teach concerning the nature of the kingdom, they still couldn't free their minds of this worldly concept.

6. Where were the apostles to witness for Him?

In the Acts 1 passage, a parallel one to Luke 24, Jesus explained that they were to witness for Him in Jerusalem, Judea, Samaria, "and unto the uttermost part of the earth." Notice the order: they were to begin in Jerusalem where they were, work then in Judea, spread into Samaria, and ultimately go to the distant parts of the world. Some have forced Jesus' words to mean that they should stay in Jerusalem until everyone there was converted, and then go into Judea, etc. Jesus didn't say this, nor would such a practice be sensible. Rather, the meaning is that after getting the work well grounded in one place, they should move on to the next. The book of Acts indicates that this is what they did.

The Ascension (Acts 1:9-12) . . . Mark 16:19, 20; Luke 24:50-53

1. How did Jesus bless them?

We are told only that "he lifted up his hands, and blessed them" (Luke 24:50). It must have been a beautiful and touching scene, one never forgotten by the apostles.

2. How is the ascension described?

Luke says that He was carried up into Heaven (24:51); Mark, that He was received up (16:19); and the Acts passage, of which Luke was also the author, that He was taken up (1:9). The latter passage is the most complete. It explains how a cloud received Him out of the sight of the apostles. The ascension was of course miraculous.

3. What was the message of the angels?

They informed the apostles that Jesus was going to return to the earth "in like manner" as He went into Heaven (Acts 1:11).

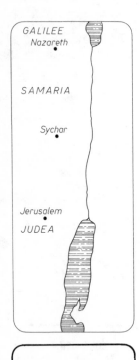

GALILEE
Nazareth •

SAMARIA

Sychar •

Jerusalem •
JUDEA

"Ye men of Galilee, why stand ye gazing up into heaven? this same Jesus, which is taken up from you into heaven, shall so come in like manner as ye have seen him go into heaven" (Acts 1:11).

4. What did the apostles do after the ascension?

Jesus had instructed them to remain in Jerusalem until they received the promise of the Father (Acts 1:4). The apostles returned from Bethany to Jerusalem, went into an upper room, and prayed (Acts 1:13, 14). This continued for ten days, until Pentecost. During this interval they selected Matthias to succeed Judas Iscariot (Acts 1:15-26). Luke sums up the ten day period by saying that the apostles were continually in the temple, praising and blessing God (Luke 24:53). Mark omits the period of waiting and tells about their evangelistic efforts after Pentecost (16:20). Neither Matthew nor John mentions the ascension.

5. Did Jesus literally sit on the right hand of God?

No, nor are we to suppose that God has hands, or that Jesus is located in a particular direction from Him. This is an anthropomorphism, a case of attributing to God the characteristics of men. Among the Jews, the place of chief honor was on the right side of a person. By this phrase Mark indicates that Jesus was exalted to the highest honor in the universe. (See Ephesians 1:20-23.)

Epilogue . . . John 21:24, 25

1. Which disciple is meant?

Although he doesn't directly identify himself as the author of the fourth Gospel, a study of the book reveals that none other could have written it than John, the son of Zebedee.

2. Why the use of the pronoun "we"?

There are two possible explanations: (1) John uses the word editorially. His use of "we" in 1 John 1, and of "I" in 1 John 2, shows that he used the words interchangeably. (2) This epilogue was added to John's Gospel by the Ephesian elders. It was to this church that John originally committed his Gospel. There he lived and served in his old age. It was from there that he was exiled to Patmos, and to it that he returned after his island imprisonment. If this theory is correct, then the statement was designed as an attestation of the truthfulness of the Gospel by men who were recognized as Christian leaders. These men knew John well and had confidence in his veracity. This seems to be the preferable view.

3. Why don't we have a record of all that Jesus did?

Such a record is unnecessary. That which has

been recorded is adequate to convince men of the sonship of Jesus. The statement that the world couldn't contain the books that could be written about Jesus is a hyperbole, a purposeful exaggeration.

WHEN AND WHERE

The appearances of Jesus took place over a period of forty days, beginning on the day of His resurrection (17th of Nisan, which in the year A. D. 30 fell on April 9th), and ending with His ascension (Thursday, May 18). The apostles returned to Jerusalem where they remained in prayer and supplication for ten days, until the coming of the Holy Spirit on the day of Pentecost. This holy day, also called the feast of Weeks and the feast of Harvest, was celebrated on the sixth of Sivan (comparable to the latter part of May and June). It marked the completion of the wheat harvest. Its name, *Pentecost,* was derived from the fact that it came fifty days after the Passover. It lasted for only one day. From Leviticus 23:15, 16 it is learned that Pentecost was observed on the first day of the week.

Luke writes that the Lord "led them out as far as to Bethany" (24:50), and ascended from there. In Acts he states: "Then returned they unto Jerusalem from the mount called Olivet, which is from Jerusalem a sabbath day's journey" (1:12). These two statements present a problem, for Bethany was farther than a Sabbath day's journey (seven-eighths of a mile) from Jerusalem. A better rendering of the verse in Luke eliminates this problem: "He led them out until they were over against Bethany" (A.S.V.). The site must be somewhere on the Mount of Olives, in the direction of Bethany, and about a Sabbath's journey from Jerusalem. Such a spot has been located by Barclay, and is described by McGarvey. It is a rounded knoll which has Bethany under its eastern slope. (See *Lands of the Bible,* pp. 210, 211.) Locate this site on the map which is provided.

"And ye shall count unto you from the morrow after the sabbath, from the day that ye brought the sheaf of the wave offering; seven sabbaths shall be complete: even unto the morrow after the seventh sabbath shall ye number fifty days; and ye shall offer a new meat offering unto the Lord" (Leviticus 23:15, 16).

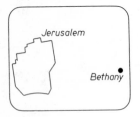

Jerusalem

Bethany

PROJECTS AND PLANS

In order to help spread the good news which you have learned in this study course, volunteer your services to the Sunday-school superintendent, offering to teach whenever and wherever you are needed.

Make plans for another course of instruction. As a class decide what you wish to study next. A number of similar texts are available. Your teacher, preacher, or superintendent will no doubt be happy to help you secure what you need.

THE HERODIAN FAMILY

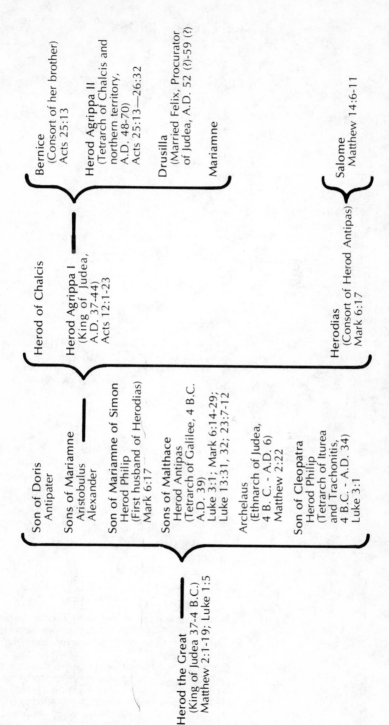

Herod the Great
(King of Judea 37-4 B.C.)
Matthew 2:1-19; Luke 1:5

Son of Doris
Antipater

Sons of Mariamne
Aristobulus
Alexander

Son of Mariamne of Simon
Herod Philip
(First husband of Herodias)
Mark 6:17

Sons of Malthace
Herod Antipas
(Tetrarch of Galilee, 4 B.C. -
A.D. 39)
Luke 3:1; Mark 6:14-29;
Luke 13:31, 32; 23:7-12

Archelaus
(Ethnarch of Judea,
4 B. C. - A.D. 6)
Matthew 2:22

Son of Cleopatra
Herod Philip
(Tetrarch of Iturea
and Trachonitis,
4 B.C. - A.D. 34)
Luke 3:1

Herod of Chalcis

Herod Agrippa I
(King of Judea,
A.D. 37-44)
Acts 12:1-23

Herodias
(Consort of Herod Antipas)
Mark 6:17

Bernice
(Consort of her brother)
Acts 25:13

Herod Agrippa II
(Tetrarch of Chalcis and
northern territory,
A.D. 48-70)
Acts 25:13—26:32

Drusilla
(Married Felix, Procurator
of Judea, A.D. 52 (?)-59 (?)

Mariamne

Salome
Matthew 14:6-11

REFERENCE INDEX

REFERENCE INDEX

Bibliography

Andrews, Samuel J. *The Life of Our Lord Upon the Earth*. Grand Rapids: Zondervan Publishing House. 1954.

Barclay, William. *Daily Study Bible (Matthew, Mark, Luke, John)*. Edinburgh: The Saint Andrew Press. 1961.

Barnes, Albert. *Notes on the New Testament*. Grand Rapids: Baker Book House. 1949.

Dean, B.S. *An Outline of Bible History*. Cincinnati: The Standard Publishing Co.

Edersheim, Alfred. *The Life and Times of Jesus the Messiah*. Grand Rapids: Wm. B. Eerdmans Publishing Co. 1945.

Foster, R.C. *An Introduction to the Life of Christ*. Cincinnati: The Standard Publishing Co. 1938.

Foster, R.C. *Gospels Syllabus*. The Cincinnati Bible Seminary.

The International Standard Bible Encyclopedia. Grand Rapids: Wm. B. Eerdmans Publishing Co. 1955.

Johnson, B.W. *The New Testament Commentary, John*. Des Moines: Eugene S. Smith.

Lamar, J.S. *The New Testament Commentary, Vol. 2, Luke*. Des Moines: Eugene S. Smith.

McGarvey, J.W., Pendleton, P.Y. *The Fourfold Gospel*. Cincinnati: The Standard Publishing Co.

McGarvey, J.W. *Lands of the Bible*. Cincinnati: The Standard Publishing Co.

McGarvey, J.W. *Sermons*. Cincinnati: The Standard Publishing Co.

Shepard, J.W. *The Christ of the Gospels*. Grand Rapids: Wm. B. Eerdmans. 1939.

Tenney, Merrill C. *New Testament Survey*. Grand Rapids: Wm. B. Eerdmans Publishing Co. 1962.

Tenney, Merrill C. *Pictorial Bible Dictionary*. Grand Rapids: Zondervan Publishing House. 1963.

Trench, R.C. *Notes on the Parables*. Grand Rapids: Baker Book House. 1950.